W9-BZE-751

FACE TO FACE

FACE TO FACE

Toward a

Sociological Theory of

Interpersonal Behavior

JONATHAN H. TURNER

STANFORD UNIVERSITY PRESS

Stanford, California

EMERSON COLLEGE LIBRARY

HM
1106
.T87
2002

Stanford University Press
Stanford, California

© 2002 by the Board of Trustees of the
Leland Stanford Junior University

Printed in the United States of America
on acid-free, archival-qualiy paper

Library of Congress Cataloging-in-Publication Data

Turner, Jonathan H.
  Face to face : toward a sociological theory of interpersonal behavior /
Jonathan H. Turner.
      p.   cm.
Includes bibliographical references and index.
ISBN 0-8047-4416-5 (alk. paper) — ISBN 0-8047-4417-3 (pbk. : alk. paper)
  1. Interpersonal relations.   I. Title.
HM1106 .T87   2002
302—dc21   2001049793

Original printing 2002

Last figure below indicates year of this printing:
11   10   09   08   07   06   05   04   03   02

Designed by Janet Wood
Typeset by James P. Brommer in 11/14 Garamond

To Tamotsu Shibutani,

who first aroused my interest in microsocial processes.

CONTENTS

ACKNOWLEDGMENTS

I am grateful to the Academic Senate at the University of California at Riverside, which supported the research for this book. I thank also my typist of thirty-two years, Clara Dean, who makes my life easier by catching errors I make when writing.

FACE TO FACE

Theoretical Foundations

Despite modern technologies that mediate communication among individuals, face-to-face interaction is still primal and primary. True, we can communicate in instrumental tasks without seeing others, and we can even interact on a more personal level through nonvisual technologies. But, when we fail to see others, we imagine what they look like and what visual cues they give. The more emotions are aroused in an interaction, the more we try to visualize the facial expressions and body movements of others. The auditory channel alone simply does not communicate sufficiently the emotional side of interaction. Even when visual media, such as video-conferencing, provide us a picture of others, these images are often too crude for fine-grained reading of emotions; we can see the person, but our visual senses still cannot detect all the information that we naturally perceive when interacting in real face-to-face situations. Just how far technologies will advance in producing sharper images of others is hard to predict, but the very need to develop more refined technologies tells us something about what humans seek. We prefer visual contact with copresent others, especially with those in whom we have emotional investments; therefore, a theory of microsocial processes must begin with conceptualizations of the dynamics of face-to-face interaction.

Much recent social theory has postulated a dramatic change in the nature of human relationships stemming from what is seen as a "postmodern condition." Let me list some of the forces of postmodernity: the expansion of high-speed, high-volume, high-velocity global markets that can extract the symbols of local groups and distribute them as commodities for consumption by others; the influence of imaging technologies on social relations; the extension of visual advertising to marketing symbols and lifestyles over utilitarian commodities; the compression of time and space to the point of disrupting the rhythms of local groups that once formed people's identities; the cognitive overload generated by too much information and sensory input; the hyperdifferentiation making a self marginal to all groups and organizations; the ability to use an emotionally neutral medium like money to buy into groups; the ability to purchase in markets symbols of multiple selves for different occasions and stages of life; and the hyperreflexivity of self-analysis to the point of making the self unstable and unviable beyond the hard reality of the body. These and many other forces are hypothesized by various commentators to have changed the fundamental nature of social reality, including one's sense of self, commitments to local groups, emotional attachments, and forms of interpersonal behavior.[1] Rarely are these outcomes of market dynamics, commodification of symbols, time-space compression, hyperdifferentiation, imaging technologies, reflexivity, and other forces of the postmodern world examined empirically. There can, of course, be little doubt that markets, advertising, commodification, imaging technologies, time-space compression, and differentiation have changed over the last few decades, but we can cast a skeptical eye to the hypothesized but rarely tested outcomes of these conditions. Has human interaction become less emotional? Have humans abandoned their emotional attachments to local groups? Have people lost their sense of a core self (Dunn 1998)? Has culture become incapable of providing emotionally charged symbols for group attachments in local time and place? Have individuals become incapable of meaningful interpersonal relationships? I think that even a cursory sense of the empirical world would answer these questions in the negative (Allan and Turner 2000). There are some good reasons for this conclusion.

First of all, like early modernist theory during the classical period in soci-

[1] For works making these points about the postmodern condition, see Anderson 1998; Baudrillard [1981] 1994, [1976] 1993, 1989, 1983, [1972] 1981, [1973] 1975; Bauman 1992; Bertens 1995; Brown 1993, 1990, 1987; Cahoone 1996; Denzin 1991, 1986; Dunn 1998; Gergen 1991; Gottdiener 1993, 1990; Harvey 1989; Jameson 1998, 1991, 1984; Lash and Urry 1994, 1987; Lemert 1995, 1992, 1990; Lyotard [1979] 1984. For a useful overview of postmodern theory, see Ritzer 1997. See also Allan 1998; and Allan and Turner 2000.

ology (that is, 1800–1920), present-day postmodern theorists compare contemporary trends against the backdrop of a rather romanticized view of community in preindustrial societies. Against this naive and romantic portrayal, early theorists saw modernity as generating pathologies, such as anomie, alienation, egoism, and marginality; and postmodernity implicitly engages in much the same futile exercise, comparing late-twentieth-century capitalism to a past reality that never really existed.

Secondly, postmodernists make the same unsubstantiated assumptions about human nature as modernist theorists, assuming that humans are naturally highly social and that, therefore, forces that reduce sociality and solidarity among individuals are pathological. Although humans are social, to a degree, they have never been emotional junkies who seek deep, personal contact with all others in all social relations. In fact, as I will argue, human needs for sociality are not nearly as powerful as most sociologists postulate. People must work at face-to-face contact to keep it on track, as can be seen in the constant use of rituals and in the animation of vocalizations, facial expressions, and body gestures. Indeed, taciturn individuals are hard to "read," and we often find ourselves trying to carry both sides of the interaction when others do not seem responsive. Closely synchronized face-to-face interaction is not as natural as we often think; rather, it is a process that requires considerable effort in most instances. Why should this be so if humans are naturally so social?

An answer to this question forces an examination of human evolution, as I briefly explore in Chapter 3, but more fundamentally, we should begin our inquiry into face-to-face interaction by suspending old biases that have come down to us from old and tired philosophies and from unexamined assumptions about human nature. Let us question these assumptions about human needs for sociality and solidarity with others, and simply ask: What occurs when individuals engage in face-to-face interaction? What are the processes and mechanisms involved in interpersonal behavior, and how are these constrained by human biology, social structure, and culture? These are the questions I will address in the chapters to follow, but before moving on to them, we need to specify the domain of inquiry.

In approaching the study of interpersonal processes with a more open mind, freed from unquestioned past assumptions and untested contemporary assertions, we will see that the nature of human interaction always reveals certain fundamental properties and processes. These are invariant in the sense that they always exist when humans interact, whether in the past,

in early capitalism, in late capitalism, or in any historical stage of human social organization. The goal of theory is to seek out what is universal about
human organization, and one place to begin is to ask: What always occurs
when people interact face to face? We can begin to answer this question by
examining the elementary principles of interaction from those who made
some of the early theoretical breakthroughs.

First Principles of Interaction

The theory that I will develop in these pages is, in reality, a synthesis of ideas
presented by others. I offer few blazing new insights, but rather a repackag-
ing and extension of a wide range of theoretical ideas developed by others.
At the core of this synthesis are a number of scholars whom I see as providing the first principles of face-to-face interaction; I will build on the conceptual base laid down by George Herbert Mead, Sigmund Freud, Alfred
Schutz, Émile Durkheim, and Erving Goffman. These scholars provided
key breakthroughs to get theorizing started in the right direction, but each
of their theories is limited and flawed. Thus, we should not be intellectual
slaves, viewing their works as sacred texts and seeing rejection of bad ideas
as blasphemy. Instead, we should view their works as a starting point for further theorizing. I do not wish to summarize in detail their theories here, but
let me review briefly the "first principles" that I consider most important in
their works.

GEORGE HERBERT MEAD'S FIRST PRINCIPLES

We can rightly see George Herbert Mead (1938, 1934) as the thinker who
first exposed the fundamental dynamics of interaction. At its most basic
level, social interaction involves the mutual sending, receiving, reading, and
interpreting of significant symbols, both verbal and nonverbal. On the basis
of reading gestures, individuals can role take or place themselves in the position or role of the other, see themselves as objects, anticipate the responses
of others, and adjust their conduct in ways that both confirm self and facilitate cooperation with others. The ability to *role take* depends on cognitive
capacities of the brain for what Mead termed "mind" and "self"—behavioral capacities that Mead thought only humans to possess. *Mind* is the ability to covertly see alternative lines of action, to imagine the likely outcome

of each, and to select that alternative that facilitates cooperation. *Self* is the ability to see oneself as an object in a situation by reading the gestures of others and to bring to a situation a more stable set of attitudes toward oneself as an object. Mead was clearly wrong in his belief that only humans possess these abilities, since those primates closest to humans can see themselves as objects, role take, use language, and adjust responses accordingly (see Savage-Rumbaugh, Rumbaugh, and McDonald 1985). Thus, the discontinuity that Mead perceived between humans and animals is a matter of degree. Indeed, humans' nearest relatives, chimpanzees, reveal many behavioral capacities that Mead saw as uniquely human.

Rather amazingly, Mead did not provide us with a conceptualization of emotions, despite the fact that he cited Darwin's account of emotions in animals and used Darwinian metaphors to conceptualize interaction as a process of adaptation. Even Mead's (1938) theory of *the act* leaves the discussion of emotions implicit. *Impulses* or *states of disequilibrium* with the environment arouse perceptual awareness of objects that might consummate the impulse; and as *perception* is heightened, covert and overt *manipulations* occur in an effort to *consummate* the impulse; and if such manipulations are successful, the impulse is indeed consummated. At any given time, individuals have many impulses at different phases of the act influencing their perceptions, minded deliberations (covert manipulation), and behaviors (overt manipulations). Impulses that go unconsummated build in intensity and come to occupy ever more of the perceptual attention as well as both covert and overt manipulations of individuals. Mead never pushed this insight into a theory of emotional dynamics; however, he did offer a theory of the motivational processes of individuals, conceptualizing them as revolving around efforts to eliminate sources of disequilibrium with the environment through perception and manipulation.

Mead also understood that role taking occurs within more inclusive social structures, or what he termed "society." For Mead, any individual human is born and raised in existing patterns of organization; thus, there is no chicken-and-egg argument in Mead's work: interaction occurs within existing institutional patterns. Mead never conceptualized these in precise ways, but his notion of the "generalized other" captures the more cultural dimension of these institutional patterns. As individuals role take, they assume the perspective of broader "communities of attitudes." Although his discussion of these processes is brief, he apparently conceived of various levels of generalized others, some locally produced in the interaction, others attached to more immediate

Mead's First Principles

I. Human action is motivated by individuals' impulses to eliminate states of disequilibrium with their environment, especially the environment composed of others engaged in cooperative behavior.

   A. The greater is the disequilibrium with the environment, the more individuals' perceptual field is devoted to discovering objects and options that can eliminate the impulse.

   B. The greater is the disequilibrium with the environment, and the more perceptual fields are activated, the greater will be the level of covert and overt manipulation of objects and options that can eliminate the impulse.

   C. The more successful is the manipulation of objects and options, the more likely will the impulse be consummated. Conversely, the less successful the manipulations, the more the impulse will increase in intensity.

   D. The likelihood of consummation of impulses through perception and manipulation of objects and options is an additive function of the behavioral capacities for

      1. using significant gestures;
      2. role taking with others and generalized others;
      3. engaging in minded deliberations over alternatives; and
      4. seeing self as an object in relation to others and generalized others.

II. Humans' behavioral capacities for using and interpreting significant gestures, for minded deliberations, and for self are a positive function of the extent to which they have been socialized in, and now must participate in, organized social contexts.

   A. The ability to read significant gestures is a positive and additive function of

      1. biological maturation; and
      2. rates of interaction with others.

   B. The ability to role take and assume the position of others and generalized others is a positive, multiplicative function of

      1. biological maturation;
      2. rates of interaction with others in ever more diverse social structures;
      3. capacities for minded deliberations; and
      4. capacities to see self as an object.

       c. The ability to see self as an object in a situation is a positive, multiplicative function of

         1. biological maturation;
         2. capacities for role taking; and
         3. capacities for minded deliberations.

       D. The ability to engage in minded deliberations is a positive, multiplicative function of

         1. biological maturation;
         2. rates of interaction with others in diverse social structures; and
         3. capacities to use significant symbols.

III. The viability of social structures is a positive function of the behavioral capacities for cooperative behaviors by individuals, with these being a positive and additive function of

       A. The ability of individuals to consummate impulses and engage in cooperation with others which, in turn, is a positive, multiplicative function of

         1. capacities to role take with others and assume their perspective;
         2. capacities to role take with ever more inclusive generalized others;
         3. capacities to see self as an object and to evaluate self from the perspective of others and generalized others; and
         4. capacities to engage in minded deliberations and, thereby, to choose that alternative course of action that meets the expectations of others, generalized others, and more stable conceptions of self as an object.

group structures, and still others of larger-scale structures (for an analysis, see J. Turner 1982, 1981). Thus, interaction for Mead involves a simultaneity of several processes: reading conventional gestures that mean the same thing to sending and receiving parties, interpretation of gestures so as to see oneself as an object and to place oneself in the position of others, the assumption of the perspective of various communities of others at various levels of social struc-

ture, the evaluation of self from the perspective of others and different generalized others, and the imaginative rehearsal of alternatives in order to cooper-
ate with others while sustaining a more enduring self-conception.

In sum, Mead's theory sees interaction as driven by impulses that shape
perceptions of self and relevant generalized others, while constraining minded
deliberations. As these manipulations reveal relevant objects including self
and generalized others, individuals engage in overt manipulations through
signaling to others; reciprocally, the gestures of others are interpreted through
the capacities for mind, with these minded deliberations being constrained by
self-conceptions, generalized others, and perceptions driven by impulses. If
the signals of others confirm self, conform to expectations by generalized others, and are perceived to consummate impulses, then the configuration of impulses driving interaction is altered. The failure to have self confirmed or to
conform to the expectations of generalized others generates new impulses that
bias perception, self-awareness, minded deliberations, perceptions of generalized others, signaling, and interpreting. What emerges, then, is a cybernetic
view of human action and interaction (Shibutani 1968). Any theory of face-
to-face behavior, then, must begin with these core ideas since they are the
most fundamental properties of interaction. The following outline summarizes these ideas as a series of first principles from the argument developed in
Mind, Self, and Society and early sections of *The Philosophy of the Act*. As is evident, Mead's principles have a somewhat circular quality, but this is the nature of mind, self, and society—at least in Mead's eyes. The behavioral capacities for using conventional gestures, for role taking, for mind, and for self
are acquired by virtue of interaction in society, whereas the persistence of society is only possible because of these behavioral abilities.

Mead's scheme provides us with the basic conceptual core for developing
a theory of interaction. It emphasizes that, ultimately, interaction is a face-
to-face process of mutually sending and receiving conventional gestures,
both verbal and nonverbal, that carry common meanings to the sending and
receiving parties and that allow each individual to see the situation from the
perspective of the other. Mead's theory emphasizes that the sending and receiving of gestures is motivated by needs to eliminate impulses and that interaction involves selective perception of relevant objects in the environment, including self, others, and generalized others. The theory thus stresses
that thinking always involves an adjudication among (a) need states or impulses, (b) expectations from generalized others or sets of cultural expectations, (c) enduring self-conceptions of oneself as a particular type of object

as well as more situational images of oneself in a situation, and (d) the expectations, need states, and self-conceptions of others. Just how signaling and interpreting proceed will reflect this adjudication. Although this theory provides a core, it is far from complete. We will need to develop a much more robust conception of the structural and cultural contexts of interaction, a new conception of the biology of humans as they interact, a more refined approach to need states and motives, an entirely new conception of emotions, a less vague view of self, and a more fine-grained conception of the dimensions along which signaling and interpreting run. Mead presented us with a beginning; my goal is to see how this core can be elaborated into a more complete theory of interpersonal behavior.

ALFRED SCHUTZ'S FIRST PRINCIPLES OF PHENOMENOLOGY

Two years before the posthumous publication of Mead's lectures in *Mind, Self, and Society*, Alfred Schutz published his *The Phenomenology of the Social World* ([1932] 1967). Although the book begins with a critique of Max Weber's conceptualization of action, this critique is merely a foil to convert Edmund Husserl's phenomenological project into a sociological analysis of social interaction. In so doing, Schutz added important refinements to Mead's pragmatist approach, although in many respects their schemes are similar (J. Turner 1988: 79–84). Schutz attempted to anchor an analysis of consciousness and experience in the exchange of significant signs or gestures. The key problem for him was to understand the processes by which individuals achieve *intersubjectivity*, or the sense that they experience the world in similar ways, or, if there are perceived differences, that they can be understood. Mead conceptualized this process as role taking, and there is not much difference between Mead and Schutz on the basic process. What separates their respective approaches is that Schutz was much more concerned with the properties of consciousness, per se, and on the details of how individuals plug themselves into each other's flow of consciousness.

Schutz had only the most vague theory of motivation, arguing that *interests*, which can seemingly be goals, needs, or any state of affairs, push actors to interrupt their normal flow of consciousness. When this occurs, individuals have generated an *act of attention* or what he often termed "acts" or "activity." An *act* thus calls attention to some aspect of the stream of consciousness and makes an experience discrete, opening it up to potential inspection. This conceptualization is, of course, similar to Mead's views on impulses, perception, and covert manipulation. *Pure ego*, a vague concept that parallels Mead's views on self, can circumscribe acts of attention since, as individuals interrupt the normal flow of consciousness, they become self-aware, with individuals' sense of who they are circumscribing what they perceive as they make experiences discrete. *Behavior* is the process of interpreting experiences in consciousness by virtue of an act; *action* is a type of behavior where meaning is created by visualizing the projected act in the future (a view that parallels Mead's conception of mind).

These conceptual distinctions are, however, less interesting than Schutz's views on how consciousness reveals a structure and how this structure influences signaling and intersubjectivity. Schutz uses the term "unity of experience" to denote the fact that acts of attention build up and synthesize meanings over time; and once synthesized, this unity of experience shapes what individuals perceive when they interrupt the flow of consciousness with acts of attention. Experiences become ordered and are sensed by individuals to be a unified whole; for, just as the external world is perceived to have an order, so the internal universe of consciousness presents itself to the person as ordered, constituting one's *stocks of knowledge at hand*. These stocks cannot generally be articulated with full clarity, but a person has a sense that they are ordered and available for use in interaction.

Interaction is the process of mutual awareness of *signitive-symbolic* signs —words, body and face movements, artifacts, and virtually anything that symbolizes meaning. These signs constitute a "field of expression" of an individual; and as they are mutually read, individuals begin the process of constructing a sense of intersubjectivity. A person sees another's signs, and at the same time, experiences his or her own stream of consciousness. As a result, through their acts of attention on their own flow of consciousness and through their interpretation of the signs of others, individuals simultaneously see each other as well as their own respective streams of consciousness. This perception of the other's stream of consciousness is, however, limited by a person's stocks of knowledge at hand that guide the interpretation of meanings communicated by signs.

There are, in Schutz's view, two levels or types of intersubjective understanding. One is the interpretation of signs (through the processes outlined above) that are not intended by others as deliberate communication. The other is what Schutz saw as "genuine intersubjectivity" that comes when the emission of signs is intended as communication. The first level of intersubjectivity involves (a) seeing the signs of others as they behave, (b) calling attention to these signs by putting oneself in the place of the other and interpreting this other's lived experiences through the filter of one's own stocks of knowledge, and then (c) imputing *in order to* motives to the other's behavior by placing these signs into a "meaning context" that allows the person to see these signs as part of an ongoing project. The second and deeper level of intersubjectivity builds on this first and is initiated when signs are emitted with the explicit intent of communicating a particular meaning context. Such signs are employed under the presumption that both parties understand the signs and have attached similar experiences to them. As this process of communication unfolds, individuals put themselves in each others' place, imagining that they themselves are selecting the signs being emitted by others. In so doing, individuals are able to impute *because of* motives, seeing actions as the result of certain lived experiences contained in others' stocks of knowledge. Yet, the more this process proceeds, the more individuals come to recognize, at least implicitly, that their respective experiences as ordered in their stocks of knowledge are not common and, thereby, preclude full and deep understanding of the other. But, despite this recognition, individuals do not seek to break the bubble of intersubjectivity, or the sense that they have experienced the current situation in the same way because of their common stocks of knowledge. Indeed, Schutz implies that a great deal of interaction seeks to avoid challenging the implicit presumption of intersubjectivity since to do so would disrupt the flow of the interaction. Thus, although interaction seeks to achieve intersubjectivity at some level, individuals avoid destroying the illusion that they experience the current situation in similar ways or, even if perceived differences of experience are recognized, that they can understand these differences in terms of their respective stocks of knowledge. To break the illusion of intersubjectivity removes the footing necessary to sustain the flow of interaction; because of this fact, individuals try not to question their presumption of intersubjectivity.

As social interaction proceeds, individuals not only work to achieve some level of intersubjectivity, but also they plug themselves into other "realms" and "worlds" that exist beyond the face-to-face situation. There is a "universe of contemporaries," Schutz argued, who are not actually present but toward whom individuals can become oriented. This world of contemporaries exists at many levels: people whom one has encountered in the past, those who were encountered by the other, those whom one plans to meet in the future, those individuals who are not present or known but whose function is recognized, those collectivities whose functions (but not its members) are known, those anonymous collectivities (for example, state, nation) with whom a direct relationship is not possible, those configurations of meaning (for example, rules of grammar, legal codes) that are perceived but live an anonymous life, and those artifacts that carry meanings now and in the past. These contemporaries represent a kind of "they-orientation" and constitute Schutz's conception of what Mead labeled "the generalized other." Much like in Mead's views, they only hint at, but do not theorize in any fine-grained manner, the ways that broader social structures and cultural symbols influence the ongoing process of interaction.

The existence of a world of contemporaries leads Schutz into one of his most interesting concepts, interaction with *ideal types*. The signs of others do not necessarily lead to efforts to penetrate and interpret the consciousness of others directly. Others can be reacted to as instances of a social category; and when this occurs, the other is not seen as a concrete individual but rather as a type or as an abstraction whose general qualities are known. As such, the ideal type is responded to in terms of the information in a person's stocks of knowledge. "In order to" and "because of" motives are imputed to these ideal-typical others, but the information for making this imputation comes from an individual's own stocks of knowledge rather than from sympathetic penetration into another's stocks of knowledge. If an individual continues to interact with another categorized as an ideal type in a face-to-face situation, however, the direct reading of the other's gestures may initiate efforts at more direct intersubjectivity.

In the outline below, Schutz's first principles of interaction are summarized. Let me briefly highlight what he added to Mead's conceptualization. Interaction revolves around the mutual reading of gestures or signals whose meaning is indexical or context-dependent and is defined by reference to the ordered experiences in each person's stocks of knowledge. Once stocks of knowledge are used to interpret another's and one's own signals, the process of generating intersubjectivity is initiated. Interaction operates at different levels of intersubjectivity, moving from categorizations of others as ideal types to various levels of "in order to" and "because of" motives. Intersubjectivity depends on individuals' ability to not only interpret significant gestures that mean the same thing to the sending and receiving parties, but also to use these signs to assess and understand the flow of consciousness and stocks of knowledge of others. Stocks of knowledge are ordered experiences that, over time, have become synthesized into an implicit body of information that is

Schutz's First Principles

I. The viability of interaction is a positive function of the degree to which individuals can use gestures to achieve implicit agreement on the appropriate level of intersubjectivity for a situation.

II. The level of intersubjectivity is a positive and additive function of

  A. The degree to which each individual's respective interests and self can be accommodated by others.

  B. The degree to which individuals' stocks of knowledge carry the relevant information for reading and interpreting the gestures of others in terms of common meanings.

  C. The degree to which stocks of knowledge allow individuals to place others into social categories to which motives can be attributed with respect to

   1. the larger project guiding the behaviors of persons in the social category; and

   2. the experiences pushing persons in the social category to behave in certain ways.

  D. The degree to which stocks of knowledge can be used to interpret the gestures of others with respect to the flow of another's consciousness, while at the same time, to denote with acts of attention one's own flow of consciousness.

  E. The degree to which stocks of knowledge can be used to interpret intended communications from others and to interpret others as well as one's own flow of consciousness with respect to

   1. the larger project guiding the behaviors of self and others in the current situation; and

   2. the lived experiences ordered by stocks of knowledge pushing self and others to behave in certain ways in the current situation.

  F. The degree to which individuals can mutually orient themselves to others and collectivities of others not present in the situation and use these mutual orientations as a common frame of reference.

  G. The degree to which individuals can perceive that they are experiencing the situation with common stocks of knowledge, or, if there are perceived differences, that these differences can be understood by reference to their respective stocks of knowledge.

sensed to have a kind of unity by individuals; and this body of information is drawn upon at all levels of intersubjectivity. Much interaction is devoted to an ever-increased sense of intersubjectivity, but at the same time individuals try to avoid fully recognizing and acknowledging that they do not experience a situation in a common way and that they do not share stocks of knowledge. Interaction is also guided not only by interpretations of gestures but also by orientations to differentiated and varied worlds of contemporaries whom individuals use as a frame of reference in interpreting their own acts of attention and their interpretation of others' behaviors and actions. This theoretical argument is summarized above as a series of elementary principles.

What can we take from Schutz's analysis in building a more robust theory of interpersonal behavior? First, the concept of stocks of knowledge is important. Although it glosses over only what is ordered, it is important to recognize that individuals have vast stores of information that they can draw on in face-to-face interaction. We will need to be more explicit as to the most critical dimensions along which this information is ordered, but Schutz's scheme at least forces us to recognize that the flow and structure of consciousness cannot be considered a black box. Second, individuals role take, to use Mead's term, at many different levels, from seeing each other as categories to deep sympathetic penetration of each other's consciousness. The insight that much interaction involves seeing others as categories is, itself, important, but it also suggests that we need to recognize that categorization is a more general process in which self, others, and situation are all categorized in ways that shape the flow of interaction. Third, individuals' need to sense that they share common stocks of knowledge or, if not common, that their differences can be understood. Schutz gives us an important idea here, because he implied that without this sense of a shared experience, interaction becomes problematic. Moreover, individuals implicitly recognize that to break the illusion of shared experiences disrupts the interaction, and so, they try to avoid questioning this presumption, if they can. Thus, like Mead, Schutz gives us many leads for a more general theory of face-to-face interaction.

SIGMUND FREUD'S FIRST PRINCIPLES OF INTERACTION

We do not normally consider Sigmund Freud to be a sociological theorist of interaction or interpersonal processes, but a moment's reflection tells us that his entire psychoanalytic approach explores emotionally charged interactions that have become pathological as a result of (a) the negative responses from others and (b) the activation of defense mechanisms. It is not necessary, of course, to accept Freud's (1900) entire psychosocial model to find useful leads for sociological theorizing. Let us start with Freud's famous trilogy—id, ego, and superego—which are not so much entities or structures but processes and phases. Libido or sexual drives in the inclusive sense of needs for sex, love, affection, and approval, coupled with more organic drives, are channeled through *id* processes that mobilize individuals by generating need states requiring fulfillment or *cathexis* or, in Mead's terms, "consummation." As these needs increase in intensity, they activate ego processes generating perceptions of relevant ways to consummate impulses, while at the same time they force ego to reconcile id impulses with the realities of the physical, cultural, and social environments. Superego processes bring to bear on ego the general values, ethical standards, and norms of social structures. Freud saw these processes as revolving around two subprocesses: (1) the internalization of group expectations and evaluative cultural standards creating a *conscience*; and (2) the internalization of group goals and standards as *ego ideal*. Mead's "generalized other" and Schutz's "world of contemporaries" only touch on these dynamics, probably because their works underemphasize the extent to which internalization of stocks of knowledge (to use Schutz's vocabulary) is loaded with emotions. Conscience and ego ideal, the cornerstones of superego processes, influence the flow of interaction because they activate emotional responses that produce either pleasure or pain. *Ego* processes also create, confirm, and sustain a sexual identity, which Freud saw as much more than a narrow definition of one's sex, although he probably did not have in mind a conception as broad as Mead's notion of self.

Thus, if we can make Freud more sociological, his theory emphasizes that signaling and interpreting between ego and alter revolve around efforts by individuals to integrate impulses (id) with internalized standards of groups and culture (superego) and with self-definitions (sexual identity). When interaction is nonproblematic, ego interprets the gestures of alters as communicating positive sentiments that, in turn, increase the likelihood that id impulses will be consummated, that identity will be reinforced, and that commitments to group expectations, goals, and ideals as well as cultural standards have been demonstrated. A lifetime during which interaction has followed this cycle will produce emotionally healthy and socially adjusted individuals.

What makes Freud's contribution so important to a theory of interaction, however, is the recognition that these efforts by ego often lead to negative

Freud's First Principles of Interaction

I. The viability of an interaction for individuals is a multiplicative function of the extent to which ego processes can

  A. orchestrate gestures in ways producing positive responses from others;

  B. consummate impulses or meet need states;

  C. confirm identity; and

  D. affirm commitments to group expectations and goals/ideals as well as cultural values and beliefs.

II. The ability to orchestrate gestures in ways producing positive responses from others is a negative function of the degree to which ego activates defense mechanisms and a positive, multiplicative function of ego's capacity to

  A. channel efforts to consummate impulses and to meet need states in a direction that follows group expectations, affirms group ideals/goals, and affirms cultural values and beliefs; and

  B. present identities that personify cultural values and beliefs, conform to group expectations, and affirm group goals/ideals.

III. The ability to consummate impulses and meet need states is a negative function of the degree to which ego activates defense mechanisms and a positive, multiplicative function of ego's capacity to

  A. orchestrate gestures in ways producing positive responses from others; and

  B. present identities that personify cultural values and beliefs, conform to group expectations, and affirm group goals/ideals.

IV. The ability to confirm identity is a negative function of the degree to which ego activates defense mechanisms and a positive, multiplicative function of ego's capacity to

  A. orchestrate gestures in ways producing positive responses from others; and

  B. confirm commitments to group goals/ideals and affirm cultural values and beliefs.

V. The ability to confirm commitments to group expectations and goals/ideals as well as affirm cultural values and beliefs is a positive, multiplicative function of ego's capacity to

A. present identities that personify cultural values and beliefs, conform to group expectations, and affirm group goals/ideals; and

B. control and channel efforts to consummate impulses and meet need states without activating defense mechanisms.

emotional responses from others, thereby setting off new sociodynamic cycles that potentially can cause pathology and maladjustment. When individuals interpret others' signals as not accepting their behaviors as appropriate or competent, ego activates *defense mechanisms* that are used to manage the negative emotions—fear, anger, guilt, shame—that come with perceptions of having failed to behave properly in the eyes of others. Freud emphasized *repression* in which the painful emotions experienced are pushed by ego below the level of consciousness, but he also recognized as significant other defense mechanisms, such as *displacement* and *projection*. If defense mechanisms are habitually activated, ego builds a defensive regime to preserve identity and evaluate self positively from the perspective of group expectations/ideals and more general cultural standards. Activation of defense mechanisms thus initiates a series of cycles that alter the individual's perceptions of others and situation in an effort to sustain self; in so doing, these mechanisms change the emotional valences and, hence, the flow of the interaction (J. Turner 1999a; Turner and Boyns 2002).

If ego's interpretations of the responses of others generate negative emotions—for example, shame, fear, guilt, anxiety—indicating that ego has failed to meet expectations and performed inadequately, incompetently, or immorally, then ego will activate defense mechanisms in an effort to block negative evaluations of identity. Moreover, since the negative responses of others are likely to have prevented ego from meeting needs, the activation of defense mechanisms only serves to block id impulses further and, as a result, causes these need states to increase in power at the same time that they are being blocked. Over time, these multiple sources of blockage begin to place enormous pressure on ego processes to reconcile (a) unconsummated id impulses growing in intensity, (b) guilt associated with unacknowledged failures to meet group standards and morality, and (c) self-doubts about who one is. As these pressures grow, they distort signaling and interpreting in ways that typically force ego to sustain a defensive regime or, indeed, to intensify this regime. Others, in turn, are more likely to respond in ways that, once again, fail to reinforce the efforts of ego; and in the end, severe emotional and behavioral pathology can result. We do not need to go as far as Freud, who after all was studying pathological biographies of maladapted persons, to recognize that these dynamics operate in all interactions and that the emotions expressed and experienced are, to some degree, shaped by ego's use of defense mechanisms.

The following outline summarizes Freud's principles in a more sociological guise. As can be seen, the principles all cycle back on each other because this is the way that Freud conceptualized psychodynamic processes. I have made his model more sociodynamic, but the propositions give us a sense for how the flow of interaction is influenced by several interconnected forces. For Freud, first and foremost, interaction is an emotional process; signaling and interpreting always involve the activation and communication of emotions that significantly determine the flow of face-to-face behavior. The most critical variables are the emotions received from others, whether positive or negative, and the degree to which defense mechanisms are activated. Emotions become convoluted with the activation of defense mechanisms, potentially pushing individuals into cycles of emotional pathology that distort signaling and interpreting. Whether these emotional dynamics become chronic and long term or only momentarily breach the interaction, they tend to operate along three dimensions: blocking individuals' ability to meet their needs; blocking individuals' capacity to manage negative feelings; and blocking individuals' ability to sustain a stable identity. As I will argue, these dynamics must be incorporated into a sociological theory of interpersonal behavior.

ÉMILE DURKHEIM'S FIRST PRINCIPLES

Émile Durkheim's major works appear before those by Alfred Schutz, but since Durkheim exerted the most influence on Erving Goffman, I have delayed addressing Durkheim's contribution to the theory of face-to-face interaction until I was ready to examine Goffman (see next section). Durkheim's ([1893] 1984) early work stressed the relationship between social morphology or structure (nature, number, and mode of relationship among parts) and culture or the *collective conscience*. The collective conscious—also termed *common conscience* and *collective representations*—consists of those "beliefs and sentiments common to the average citizen . . . [forming] a determinate system which has its own life" (Durkheim [1893] 1984: 79–80). The collective conscience varies along a number of dimensions: the extent to which values, beliefs, and rules of conduct are shared by members of a society, the intensity or regulative power over thought and action of cultural symbols, the clarity of cultural symbols, and the degree of religious versus secular content in symbol systems. By the early decades of the twentieth century, Durkheim had begun to relax his extreme sociologistic position (for example, Durkheim [1895] 1938) and was willing to become more social psychological in examining the interpersonal dynamics that create and sustain the collective conscience and that, as a consequence, maintain sociocultural arrangements in society. During this period from around 1903 to his death, Durkheim's sociology developed some important ideas that have been used to study face-to-face interaction. These are tied together in Durkheim's last great work on *The Elementary Forms of the Religious Life* ([1912] 1946). In this work, Durkheim saw the source of religion as residing in society itself, arguing that religion is simply the worship of society. More interesting than this provocative thesis, however, is his analysis of the mechanisms by which religion is created. He portrays Australian aborigines incorrectly as the simplest societal type, stripped of the complexities that normally obscure the analysis of the functions of religion, but his argument generates an important insight nonetheless. He portrays aboriginals as gathering at particular times and places, with such gatherings accelerating rates of interaction. Under these conditions, crowd stimulation heightens emotions, leading to a kind of collective contagion. This contagion creates an "effervescence" that gives individuals common sentiments perceived as external and constraining. The power of these sentiments needs to be represented by individuals, since humans innately seek group solidarity; as a result, the power of these sentiments is represented as "mana" or as a sacred force above and beyond individuals. Mana is then symbolized by totems imbued with a sacredness that provides a sense of solidarity and that leads individuals to engage in ritual activities directed at totems. Hence, religion is nothing more than the worship of the relationships among individuals. There is a number of questionable assumptions in Durkheim's analysis, such as the view that individuals have psychological needs to represent mana with material objects and that they have innate needs for high levels of solidarity in social structures ("clans" in the case of Australian aboriginals).

These and many other flaws do not, however, detract from the insight that Erving Goffman was to seize. Interaction occurs in a structural and cul-

---

Durkheim's Principles of Interaction Rituals

I. The viability of social structural arrangements and the cultural symbols legitimating and regulating these arrangements is a positive function of the level of ritual activity among individuals in face-to-face contact in a social setting.

II. The likelihood of ritual activity among individuals in face-to-face contact in a setting is a positive and additive function of

   A. the degree to which social structures concentrate individuals in space;

   B. the degree to which individuals share common cognitive categories of time, space, relations, cause-effect, and sacred-profane;

   C. the degree to which previous interactions have aroused emotionally charged symbols among individuals; and

   D. the degree to which emotionally charged symbols have become "objectified" and "reified" so that they appear outside, above, or external to an individual, with objectification being an additive function of

      1. the conditions under II-A, II-B, and II-C;

      2. the extent to which symbols are embodied in physical objects marking group memberships; and

      3. the extent to which the symbols, themselves, become totems in the form of special utterances marking of group membership.

---

tural context, and at the same time, generates symbols to which individuals develop emotional attachments and that they use to guide their affairs. The key mechanism is rituals, or stereotyped sequences of behavior that have the capacity to arouse emotions and reinforce existing symbols and, hence, social structures; or, if symbols and structure do not exist or are vague, rituals are employed to generate new symbols and structures. Thus, the flow of interaction and its relationship to culture and social structure are, in Durkheim's model, determined by the emotional feelings that develop among individuals, their ability to represent these sentiments in objects, and their capacity to enact rituals that arouse the emotions associated with these sentiments. Durkheim saw this process as the origin of religion; more modern theorists have recognized that it is the backbone of face-to-face interaction in all social contexts. In the outline above, Durkheim's argument is presented as a series of principles.

Durkheim's theory of ritual, although not explicitly intended as a theory of interaction, provides a number of useful leads. First, Durkheim recognized that interactions are constrained by social structure and, most particularly, by the systems of rules, beliefs, and values associated with social structure. Interaction rarely occurs outside of sociocultural systems and has consequences for the viability of these systems. In all social settings, therefore, value premises, beliefs, and rules guide the flow of interaction; in those interactions that produced solidarity, these cultural systems become, themselves, objects onto themselves that are seen as a force above and beyond individuals. Second, the key mechanism by which individuals are plugged into social structure and culture is ritual, and the more that ritual enactments can be directed toward the symbolization of a group's culture and social structure as a totem, the greater will be the emotional arousal and solidarity among individuals. Third, emotions are an important part of those interactions that sustain social structures and cultural symbols. High rates of interaction, per se, generate emotions that become the totems toward which rituals are enacted, but rituals sustain the flow of emotional energy. Emotions are thus the glue holding social structures together and sustaining the cultural systems legitimating these structures. Many theorists (for example, Goffman 1967, 1959; Collins 1981, 1975; J. Turner 1988) have pursued these insights; and they will all need to be a part of the theory of interpersonal processes. But, it was Erving Goffman who made the key breakthrough in translating Durkheim's theory on the origins of religion (and solidarity) into a theory of interaction processes.

ERVING GOFFMAN'S FIRST PRINCIPLES OF ENCOUNTERS

Mead, Schutz, Durkheim, and Freud formulated their respective scheme in the early decades of the twentieth century, and it would be surprising, of course, if they told a complete story on the dynamics of interaction. In the second half of the twentieth century, considerable progress was made in conceptualizing interaction processes, and, as will become evident, key ideas from contemporary theorists will be used in developing the theory presented in Chapters 4–10. Despite the creative efforts by a substantial number of scholars, one figure stands out: Erving Goffman. His conceptualization of encounters will guide much of my analysis of face-to-face interaction, although I will not adopt all elements of his scheme.

Goffman (1983, 1961) was correct, I believe, in the view that the most elemental unit of sociological analysis is *the encounter*. Moreover, as a Durkheimian, Goffman recognized that encounters are embedded in social structures and systems of cultural meanings, but he did not pursue the nature of this embedding very far. The most immediate level of embedding is the *gathering* that assembles people in copresence; in turn, gatherings are part of a more inclusive unit, the *social occasion*, composed of fixed equipment, distinctive ethos and emotional structure, program and agenda, rules of proper and improper conduct, and preestablished sequences of activities. Even though Goffman never explored the properties of these more inclusive structures, he recognized their importance. A more general sociological theory of interpersonal behavior will, therefore, need to add more conceptual refinement to this aspect of Goffman's analysis. Moreover, encounters are always embedded in systems of rules that shape how individuals will define situations, what roles they will play, how they will talk, what emotions they will display, what rituals they will use, and what selves will be offered to others. Thus, embedding is both structural and cultural.

Two types of encounters form the basis of social structure at the microlevel of analysis, *focused* and *unfocused* encounters. For Goffman (1961), a *focused* encounter "occurs when people effectively agree to sustain for a time a single focus of cognitive and visual attention." In so doing, they exhibit a mutual and preferential openness to verbal communication; a heightened attention to relevance acts; an eye-to-eye ecological huddle; a maximization of mutual perception and monitoring; an emergent "we" feeling of solidarity and flow of feeling; a ritual and ceremonial punctuation of openings, closings, entrances and exits; and a set of procedures for corrective compensation for deviant acts. Although interaction in focused encounters is generally strategic, it is always regulated by norms (Goffman 1967). As noted above and bears repeating, rules determine how individuals define or frame a situation as to what it should include and exclude; rules direct the forms of talk; rules define the expectations for roles; rules constrain the selves that are to be presented or accepted by others; and rules establish the appropriate rituals with which to open, structure, close, and repair an episode of interaction. With the demise of functional theorizing and the misperception by critics that such theories overemphasize the power of rules, it has often been con-

venient to reconstruct Goffman as a Chicago School symbolic interactionist, but in fact, Goffman was a Durkheimian. As a Durkheimian, he emphasized the normative dimensions of interaction.

In Figure 1.1, the basic elements of Goffman's analysis of interaction are
delineated. Any focused encounter (and indeed most unfocused encounters
as well) occurs within social structures and the cultural systems associated
with these structures. On the basis of their location in a sociocultural system,
individuals make strategic assessments, deliberate on situational expectations,
and decide how to present self. The presentation of self occurs along several
fundamental dimensions. First, individuals always employ rituals to open
and close the interaction as well as to regulate the flow of mutual signaling
and interpreting as the interaction proceeds. These rituals consist of stereotyped sequences of gestures that, when emitted, carry meanings to which
others respond. Cultural scripts dictate when and just what rituals to emit.
Second, individuals always define situations or, in Goffman's later terminology, "frame" situations as to what is to be included and excluded from the interaction. Creating, changing, and breaking frames are generally guided by
strategic use of rituals and particular forms of talk, shifting frames is always
guided by the rules of the situation, although individuals can manipulate
frames for purely strategic and often manipulative purposes. Third, as individuals define and frame situations, they also categorize them with respect to
the relative amounts of work-practical (instrumental), social, and ceremonial
content required (Goffman 1967). On the basis of this categorization, they
impose frames, rituals, forms of talk, emotions, and roles. Fourth, individuals stage an interaction, bringing with them physical objects that carry meaning, using existing props provided by the structure of the setting, and moving their bodies in juxtaposition to these props to communicate meaning.
The ways in which props are used help to frame a situation, and the staging
of an interaction is almost always guided by rituals and forms of talk. Just
how one uses props to communicate meanings is, again, determined by the
cultural context in which the interaction occurs. Fifth, individuals always
seek to establish the role that they are playing, with *role* being defined as "a
bundle of activities visibly performed before a set of others and visibly
meshed into the activities of these others" (Goffman 1961: 96). Individuals
read the cultural scripts and structure of a situation to see what roles are
available and appropriate, and then they seek to assume a role that is consistent with the self that they are presenting in the situation and that, at the
same time, fits into the roles others are trying to make for themselves. Sixth,

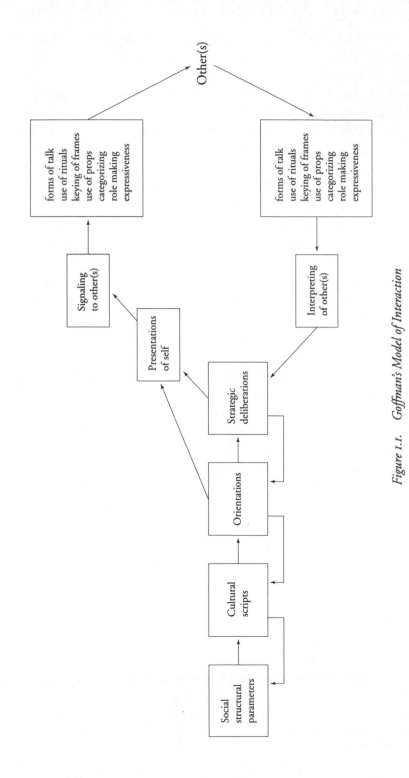

Figure 1.1. Goffman's Model of Interaction

as mentioned above, individuals use "talk" to focus and sustain attention over time; the forms of talk employed are dictated by the cultural rules and structure of the situation. Talk operates at many levels and includes not just the pattern and form of words spoken, but also the use of verbal fillers, pauses, and other features of conversations that structure the flow of interaction. Rituals are generally expressed through talk; frames are established, changed, and manipulated through talk; roles are at least partially established through talk; and staging often involves a back channel of talk. Seventh, individuals always engage in expressive control of their faces and bodies as they use rituals, impose frames, establish roles, set the stage, and engage in talk. Interaction is an expressive and emotional activity, with the result that individuals seek to control emotional outputs in an encounter. Just what emotions are seen as appropriate, how they are to be expressed, and when they are to be shown are all regulated by cultural scripts.

In any encounter, then, individuals are engaged in mutual signaling and interpreting of each other's presentations of self along at least six dimensions: rituals, frames, talk, staging, roles, and emotions. Encounters are formed and sustained by individuals' ability to (a) take cognizance of the structure and cultural script of a situation, (b) categorize the situation in terms of the relative amounts of work-practical, social, and ceremonial content, (c) deliberate over how to present self, and (d) strategically engage in emitting rituals, making frames, using particular forms of talk, manipulating stage props, creating roles, and controlling emotions. These dimensions along which self-presentations occur are, in Goffman's view, interrelated; each one influences the others, although Goffman did not disentangle their dynamic relations in great detail. In the outline below, the essential principles in Goffman's theory are summarized in ways that emphasize these mutual effects among forces, but these propositions do not sort out the causal processes among talk, categories, frames, rituals, roles, staging, and emotions. To the extent that these elements of Goffman's theory are retained, we will need to be more precise about their causal connections.

Let me conclude this brief review of Goffman's approach with a note on his analysis of unfocused interaction. Goffman's (1971, 1963) examination of unfocused interaction is less well studied, but it is equally important. Although the focus of this book is on focused encounters, much of the theory that I develop applies to unfocused interaction as well. In Goffman's words, an unfocused interaction consists of "interpersonal communications that result solely by virtue of persons being in one another's presence, as when two

Goffman's Principles on Focused Encounters

I. The likelihood of an encounter is a positive, additive function of

    A. the existence of social occasions that put individuals in a physical proximity and that provide fixed equipment, staging areas, program and agenda, distinctive ethos, emotion culture, and rules of conduct; and

    B. the formation of a gathering that assembles individuals in sufficiently closed physical space so that they perceive copresence.

II. The viability of a focused encounter is a positive function of each individuals' ability to use the resources of a social occasion (see I-A above) to present an acceptable self to each other and, at the same time, abide by the rules of the gathering.

III. The ability to present an acceptable self to others is a positive and multiplicative function of individuals' ability to

    A. use appropriate forms of talk to focus attention and to sustain this focus of attention during the flow of interaction;

    B. emit appropriate rituals to open, close, form, and repair the flow of interaction;

    C. frame and reframe the situation so as to develop common definitions of the situation;

    D. establish roles that are consistent with self and, at the same time, integrate the behaviors of self with the behaviors of others; and

    E. control expressions of emotions so as to communicate affect towards self and roles, while avoiding breaches to the flow of interaction.

IV. The ability of individuals to abide by the rules of the gathering is an additive function of

    A. the clarity of rules, emotion culture, ethos, and staging areas of the larger social occasion in which a gathering is embedded; and

    B. the ability of individuals to use appropriate rituals, forms of talk, frames, roles, and emotions to create or reinforce rules, emotion culture, ethos, and staging areas.

strangers across the room from each other check up on each other's clothing, posture, and general manner, while each modifies his own demeanor alike because he himself is under observation" (1961: 7). Unfocused interactions are, in many ways, like focused encounters because they call for a performance, include presentations of self, follow rules, employ rituals, and depend on etiquette and tact. They are unlike focused encounters in the relative amounts of inattention communicated by parties as they position their bodies in space, move about, fix their visual attention, and present themselves. I will not develop models and principles for this form of interaction (see J. Turner 1998: 406, for a list of principles on unfocused interaction), because my concern in this book is primarily on focused interactions.

Preview

In the chapters that follow, my goal is to build on the basic insights of the theorists briefly reviewed. As the theory unfolds, it will be necessary to bring in more recent theories to fine-tune the analysis. Still, there is a core of ideas in Mead, Schutz, Freud, Durkheim, and Goffman that provides the starting point and framework for further theorizing.

I will first address in the next chapter the issue of embeddedness of interaction in sociocultural systems. None of the theorists examined above adequately conceptualized the structures and cultural systems in which encounters are embedded. Their frameworks are all vague on this score, and as we will see, more recent theorists have not done much better in theorizing about the dynamics of embeddedness. Encounters are rarely isolated from mesostructures and institutional systems, and thus, a theory of microprocesses must take account of this fact. The number of people copresent, the characteristics of these individuals, the density of their copresence, the positions they hold and the relations among these positions, the roles they play, the rules governing their actions, and the emotions experienced and expressed are all constrained by mesostructures and the broader institutional systems in which these mesostructures are embedded. A theory of interpersonal behavior must theorize about these interconnections, as they influence the flow of face-to-face interaction in encounters. Obviously, I cannot develop a general theory of meso- and macrodynamics here, because such a theory involves many concepts, models, and principles that do not make reference to microdynamics (J. Turner 1995). Yet, it is necessary to develop models and principles that explain how the processes of encounters are influenced by mesodynamics and macrodynamics (J. Turner 2001, 2000b; Turner and Boyns 2002). In the next chapter, I will elaborate on the simple framework presented in Figure 1.1. In so doing, the dynamics of embeddedness can be pursued as we explore the various forces driving encounters.

In Chapter 3, I briefly explore the biology of humans as this relates to processes of face-to-face interaction. Humans are a primate—really just an evolved ape—and this fact has important implications for how humans act and interact (J. Turner 2000a, 1999b). Interaction does not transcend biology; it is embedded in biology. Of the early theorists, only Freud even suggests the biological embeddedness of interaction, and here his contribution is limited. Thus, one of the great weaknesses of early and contemporary theory on interpersonal processes is the absence of biological considerations. A robust theory of human interaction must bring biology back into a more central place.

This initial group of three chapters sets the stage from the analysis of microdynamics proper. Chapter 4 shifts to emotional dynamics in an encounter. The culture and structure of the macro- and mesounits within which encounters are embedded provide a broad set of feeling rules. Freud and Goffman recognized that interaction is an emotional process, and Durkheim saw rituals as the key to developing emotional attachments to the collective conscience. Yet, for the first two-thirds of the twentieth century, the sociology of emotions hardly existed, but over the last three decades, an enormous amount of creative work on emotions has emerged, and we will have to incorporate this work into a conception of interaction as an emotional process.

Chapter 5 examines motivational dynamics or those processes that energize interaction (J. Turner 2000b, 1989, 1987). The early theorists had implicit theories of motivation, but none of these is well developed. We should move beyond vague pronouncements of impulses and needs; in their place, a more specific conceptualization of the impulses and needs driving interaction must be developed. I conceptualize motivation in terms of *transactional needs*, or states of being that all individuals in all encounters must realize if they are to avoid feeling deprived, anxious, fearful, or potentially angry. These transactional needs drive the flow of interaction in certain universal directions, despite the widely varying contexts of encounters. The degree to which these transactional needs are met or fulfilled dramatically influences the flow of the interaction and the viability of the encounter.

Chapter 6 turns to the culture of an encounter, particularly the texts, technologies, values, beliefs, and norms that regulate how individuals define situations, categorize each other, talk, present self, use rituals, establish roles, and perform other key behaviors. Early theorists saw the importance of these cultural forces; our task will be to add detail to their conceptualizations.

Chapter 7 examines role processes. Individuals carry in their stocks of knowledge conceptions of configurations of gestures that mark particular types of roles that others seek to play. Conversely, they also orchestrate, both consciously and unconsciously, configurations of gestures to make a role for themselves, thereby providing the material for role taking by others. Although roles are tied to status, culture, and self, they have distinctive dynamics and, hence, need to be understood as a separate force in interaction.

Chapter 8 examines the dynamics of status positions in an encounter. The positions that individuals occupy, the connectedness of these positions to each other, and the relative amounts of power, authority, prestige, and other resources attached to positions all shape the flow of face-to-face interaction. Theorizing on status has been highly cumulative over the last few decades; and we will need to take advantage of this theoretical progress.

Chapter 9 explores demographic and ecological dynamics. We often see demography as the study of larger population characteristics, movements, and trends, but we can just as well study these at a more microlevel. The number of people present, their characteristics, their movements, their density of ties, and other features of the people and their arrangement in space and use of props are important to understanding the dynamics of encounters. Only Goffman hinted at these demographic forces; we will need to bring in the ideas of others and develop some new lines of thought on the demography of interaction.

In Chapter 10, I will try to pull all of the tentative generalizations in the preceding chapters together into a relatively small set of principles on the dynamics of face-to-face interaction. These principles will, of course, be provisional, but my goal is to develop a robust theory of interaction that is parsimonious and amenable to empirical assessment. The subtitle of this book only claims to move "toward a sociological theory of interpersonal processes." I make no claims that the theory is complete.

TWO

Sociocultural Embeddedness

If we casually observe the social universe, we see people moving about in various modes of transport, people sitting in private and public places, and people forming small huddles of mutual talk in various settings. There is a fluidity to social life, and by cursory observation alone, the only structure appears to be the patterns of relations among individuals dictated by buildings, modes of conveyance, and arrangement of public and private places. But, we know better, recognizing that the patterns of relations among individuals follow cultural scripts attached to social structures. In a sense, the study of social life by sociologists imposes analytical constructs about culture and social structure on the flow of social life, but these constructs are deemed by most sociologists to denote the key properties of the social universe. Yet, some argue that the only "real reality" is what we observe by watching people; all else imposes analytical categories and, hence, amounts to the reification of analytical thinking. This charge is particularly likely to be leveled against analysis of macrolevel structures such as institutional systems that are, for some, simply reifications of organizational systems and, for others, hypostatizations of people engaged in face-to-face interaction. If this kind of extreme reductionism in sociology were actually followed in practice, we would know a great deal about people and almost nothing about the actual operation of the social universe.

I take the rather extreme position that visualizing levels of social reality is more than an analytical convenience; the levels *are* reality. The social world actually unfolds, I argue, along macro-, meso-, and microlevels (J. Turner

2001, 2000b). These levels are not just analytical; they denote a reality that is always present when humans organize. Many would see this position as gross reification, but I would contend just the opposite. Let me elaborate.

To survive, humans need to organize collectively, and once the collective organization of a population becomes the unit to be studied, it is no longer possible to understand fully social organization by reference to interpersonal behavior alone, particularly as the population gets larger. The original social units in human evolution—families in small bands of hunter-gatherers within a larger regional population carrying a common culture—were sustained mostly by interpersonal behaviors among their members. But, if we look more carefully, we can see in embryonic form the elements of more macrolevel structures that became ever more pronounced as the size of populations to be organized increased. For example, the shared culture—language, values, beliefs, traditions, lore, and the like—transcended any local band of hunter-gatherers, and, as such, it reveals more macrolevel properties. In the basic axes of activity—political leadership (although highly muted in most bands), kinship, religion (in some cases), and economy—are the seeds that develop into larger-scale structures as populations grow and become settled. It would be hard to conceptualize these activities as simple interpersonal behaviors because they are guided by more macrolevel cultural scripts and by fundamental pressures of survival that transcend local encounters among individuals. To say that the only reality among hunter-gatherers is evident in the daily routines is to miss what is sociologically interesting about this most simple mode of organization. And what is true of hunter-gatherers becomes ever more the case as the scale of organization increases. To consider the only reality the strings of encounters among individuals is, indeed, to miss the forest for the trees.

I visualize social reality as unfolding along the micro-, meso-, and macro-levels. There is nothing new in this view, since sociologists have implicitly developed their analytical categories along these lines. For example, Max Weber's ([1922] 1968) distinctions among action, organization, and patterns of domination (stratification), and institutional orders follow this tripart division. Randall Collins (1975), for all his claims about chains of interaction rituals as the basis of macrostructure, divides the universe into state, economy, religion, education at the macrolevel, organizations and strata at the mesolevel, and interaction rituals at the microlevel. Many others do the same thing, and they have done so for good reason: this is how social reality unfolds.

The focus of this book is the encounter, but to understand the dynamics of encounters, we must recognize the nature of their embeddedness in meso- and macrolevel structures as well as the culture associated with these structures. Indeed, Goffman (1983) saw encounters as embedded in "gatherings" and "social occasions" dictated by more meso- and macrostructures, although he never pursued this matter further. Similarly, without much detail, early microtheorists, to varying degrees, recognized embeddedness. Mead conceptualized the macro and meso as "society" and the culture of society as constituting "generalized others." Durkheim emphasized that religious rituals worshipped society and the "collective conscience." Schutz's "stocks of knowledge" and "world of contemporaries" acknowledged the embeddedness of interaction in cultural and structural systems. Freud's concepts of "superego" and "ego ideal," coupled with the "reality principle" in ego processes reconciling id impulses to society and civilization, also acknowledged the power of broader sociocultural forces.

But all these early approaches, and most contemporary ones as well, are vague in the details. It is one thing to recognize, or even to assert, embeddedness; it is another matter to conceptualize the dynamics of embeddedness. Most arguments become metaphorical and imprecise; my goal is to be less metaphorical and more precise in documenting how meso- and macrostructures and culture constrain the forces driving an encounter.[1]

Macrolevel Reality

INSTITUTIONAL SYSTEMS AND DOMAINS

Institutions are the most macrolevel reality of societies and systems of societies (J. Turner 1997a). Ultimately, a society is composed of institutional domains, and intersocietal relations are connections among the institutions of different societies. For example, a political alliance or a war is a relation between political institutions of two or more societies (and indirectly, their respective economies producing the tools of war and their families reproducing soldiers); similarly the global economy is a network of relations among the respective economies of societies (and other institutions, such as educa-

---

[1] For various commentaries on macro-micro linkages, see Alexander et al. 1986; Ritzer 1990, 1988; Ritzer and Gindoff 1994; J. Turner 2001, 1984; Turner and Boyns 2002.

tion, law, and polity that shape the dynamics of an economy). The number, level of differentiation, modes of interdependence, scale, and other variables that can describe institutional domains obviously vary depending on the selection pressures confronting a population. For example, the size of a population generates selection pressures for, at a minimum, expansion of the economic domain and for development of new forms of political regulation.[2] Or, alterations in the technology of the cultural storehouse of a society will change the economy, which, in turn, generates selection pressures for transformation of other institutional domains, particularly the polity and education. Or, the emergence of new institutional domains, such as science and medicine, activates new selection pressures on other domains such as the economy, polity, religion, education, and family. Thus, a general theory of institutions would explore the selection pressures generated by environments, both the external environments of the biophysical world and other societies as well as the internal environments that a population has generated by the expansion and differentiation of institutional domains themselves

[2] The notion of "selection" is undertheorized in the social sciences. Social scientists, to the extent that they address the issue at all, have a Darwinian view: natural selection increases with changes in the environment or with increases in the number of individuals within a species or between species relative to the environmental capacity to support species. In this sense, selection is "blind" because it sorts out "the fit" from the "less fit." But there is also what I (J. Turner 2001, 1995) term *Spencerian selection* or *functional selection* in which there is an absence of structures to deal with new problematic conditions in the environment and in which the actors have the capacity for intentional behavior. Much change in human societies is driven by both Darwinian and Spencerian selection together. For example, a change in the economy creates a new environment for other institutional systems, forcing actors into competition to find new niches (Darwinian selection) and forcing goal-oriented actors to make plans and consciously forge solutions to new problems posed by changes in the economy. Much functional analysis contained a hidden view of selection, in which problems of survival-generated selection pressures on actors to come up with new ways to deal with these problems. A theory of macrolevel reality needs the concept of selection in its explanatory schema, although few theories in sociology appear to recognize this fact. For my purposes, "selection pressure" occurs when either or both the external or internal environments of actors change and, as a consequence, pose problems of adaptation that must be addressed if actors are to remain viable in their environment.

(J. Turner 1997a, 1995). For our purposes, we need not develop this theory, but only recognize that virtually all encounters are lodged within an institutional domain whose structure and culture circumscribe the flow of interaction among individuals.

Mesolevel Reality

Institutional systems must be built from something, and this something is the structures of the mesolevel. Institutions cannot be reduced to mesolevel structures because these institutional domains are composed of *the relations among* mesostructures as well as the use of the broader cultural symbols of a society (more on culture shortly). As such, institutions are an emergent property revealing dynamics that are different than those operating on mesostructures. Moreover, mesostructures are constrained by the institutional domains and associated culture in which they are located. For example, a business enterprise is different than a school or family because the former is constrained by the structure and culture of the economy, whereas the latter are circumscribed, respectively, by the blueprints of the educational and kinship systems of a society. What, then, are the basic kinds of structures of the mesolevel of reality. Following Amos Hawley's (1986) analysis, the two basic structures of mesoreality are (1) corporate units and (2) categoric units.[3]

CORPORATE UNITS

Corporate units reveal a division of labor among actors, whether individuals or subgroups, for organizing activity in pursuit of goals of varying degrees of clarity. Corporate units vary in terms of several fundamental properties. First is the size of the corporate unit, which can range from a small group of individuals pursuing a goal to a larger multinational corporation or governmental bureaucracy. Second is the integrity of the external boundaries differentiating a corporate unit from other corporate units as well as the partitions marking off subunits within these boundaries. The larger the size

---

[3] Most theories of society make these distinctions, at least implicitly. Organizations and stratification are often highlighted, and these are, respectively, corporate and categoric units. My goal is to make this conception more abstract and, hence, universal; and Hawley (1986) provides the useful labels.

of a corporate unit, the more visible are its external boundaries (for example, physical barriers) and its internal partitions into subsets of corporate units (divisions, offices, subgroups, cliques, and so on). In contrast, a small corporate unit generally reveals less pronounced boundaries, less explicit division of labor, and less pronounced internal partitions. Third is the formality of structures, which can range from unstated informal positions, roles, and norms (for example, a family or informal group) to codified rules defining duties for incumbents in explicitly titled positions (such as a bureaucracy). Fourth is the explicitness and scope of the horizontal division of labor, which can range from few distinctions (a group of friends) to vast differences in the duties that individuals and offices are supposed to perform. Fifth is the vertical division of labor, which can be muted to two levels (parents and children, for example) to vast formal hierarchies of offices and positions (a governmental bureaucracy or the Roman Catholic Church).

If a corporate unit is described along these five dimensions, then its basic structure is revealed. For our purposes, variations in the configurations of corporate units along these five properties will be important in understanding the dynamics of embedded encounters. What transpires in an encounter is very much constrained by the nature of the corporate units in which it is lodged, and as we will see in later chapters, propositions describing these dynamics will need to take account of how these properties of corporate units constrain the forces operating in the encounter.

CATEGORIC UNITS

Categoric units are subpopulations of individuals who are defined as possessing distinctive characteristics and who, as a result, are treated by others in a distinctive manner (social class, ethnicity, gender, sexual preference, age cohorts).[4] Unlike corporate units, then, categoric units do not reveal a division

---

[4] This idea overlaps with Peter Blau's (1994, 1977) conception of "parameters." Categoric distinctions can be nominal (for example, race, gender) or graduated (for instance, income, years of education), and they mark distinctions that affect rates of interaction. Both nominal and graduated parameters can become categoric units because they mark difference and, on the basis of this difference, actors respond to each other in varying ways. Even seemingly graduated parameters become, in most cases, more like nominal ones because humans "chunk" and "draw lines" at various points in a graduated parameter. For example, wealth and

of labor or pursue explicit goals, although some members of categoric units can become transformed into a corporate unit when they organize to push the interests of those in a categoric unit. Like corporate units, categoric units can be seen to possess five fundamental properties. First is the relative homogeneity or heterogeneity of members in a categoric unit. When a categoric unit is homogeneous, its members are marked by one point of distinction (lesbian, for example) whereas a categoric unit is more heterogeneous when the distinction placing individuals in the units (such as skin color) encompasses other distinctions (men, women, children). Second is the discreteness or clarity of the features defining individuals as members of a categoric unit. Some distinctions are relatively discrete (male, female), while others are more continuous (amount of pigmentation in skin or level of income, for example). A third feature of categoric units is the extent to which distinctions that define individuals as members of a unit are differentially valued and rank-ordered (wealthy-poor). Fourth is the correlation among, or superimposition of, categoric distinctions. When membership in one categoric unit overlaps significantly with membership in other categoric units (poverty and minority status), the dynamics of categoric units are altered, especially if the rank-order of membership in the categoric units is highly correlated. And fifth is the correlation of categoric membership with the structure and division of labor in corporate units (wealthy-corporate head, poor-laborer).

Nesting of Encounters in Corporate and Categoric Units

Virtually all encounters are nested within either a corporate or categoric unit, and often in both. Even unfocused encounters are lodged in one or both of these basic types of mesostructures, as when individuals pass each other on the street in a city (a corporate unit) and take cognizance of each others' gen-

---

income are generally converted nominal parameters: rich, poor, middle class, and the like. Similarly, authority in a corporate unit is generally converted into a nominal parameter: boss-worker. Education is also converted this way, as when various degrees mark individuals as having achieved a certain level of education: for example, high school, college, graduate degrees. Miller McPherson's and J. Ranger-Moore's (1991) conception of a "Blau Space" captures some of what I am trying to communicate by categoric units, but my emphasis is on these *as structures* rather than resources in an environment of competing organizations.

der, age, and ethnicity (all categoric units). The respective configurations among properties of corporate and categoric units thus become crucial in shaping the flow of interaction. Although I will develop more specific propositions later, let me offer a few illustrative generalizations to emphasize this point. Turning to categoric units, an encounter among members of the same category (men, for example) will have very different dynamics than one where heterogeneity exists (men, women); and generally, the greater is the heterogeneity, the more individuals will have to work at sustaining the focus and flow of the encounter. The clarity of categories is also critical; categories that fade into each other often pose challenges for individuals as they work to "place" the individual, whereas discrete categories (male-female, and so on) provide clear guidelines as to who others are (even if extra interpersonal work will be required to sustain the focus and flow of the interaction when the respective categories of parties are extremely different). Rank among categories changes the dynamics of an encounter dramatically; the greater the differences in rank of categories, the more strained will be the interaction and the more individuals, especially low-ranking ones, will try to limit interaction with those in superordinate categories or, if possible, leave the encounter altogether. The correlation of membership in varying categories also alters the flow of interaction; when memberships are superimposed (white, male, rich, for example), this correlation magnifies the salience of the categoric distinctions. Categoric units are often associated with incumbency in corporate units; when categories reflect positions in corporate units (managerial, manual laborer), the effects of corporate structures on other properties are magnified.

As I noted earlier, size of the corporate unit influences many of the other properties of a corporate unit. With greater size, external boundaries and internal partitions are more visible; with size, formality of structure increases, as does both the horizontal and vertical divisions of labor. In general, when the boundaries of a unit are discrete, when the structure is formal, when the division of labor is explicit and hierarchical, positions and categoric distinctions within the corporate unit influence the flow of interaction more than categoric distinctions coming from outside the corporate unit. These generalizations are, however, only approximate, because an encounter has its own distinctive dynamics that shape just how and in what manner corporate and categoric mesostructures exert their influence. As we will see, the dynamics of iterated encounters can potentially change the structure of mesostructures and, ultimately, institutional systems.

Thus, the distinctions among macro-, meso-, and microlevels of reality are more than analytical; they *are* reality. The social world is inevitably structured in this way because as a population grows, it requires *systems* of corporate and categoric units forming the institutional domains necessary for sustaining the viability of the population in its environments. Although institutional systems are structured from mesostructures, they cannot be reduced to them. No one organizational or categoric unit can be said to define an institution or explain its operation, because it is in *the interactions among corporate and categoric units* as they are formed to address specific problems of maintaining a population in its environment that the reality of an institutional domain resides.

Similarly, corporate and categoric units reveal their own dynamics. The structure and operation of corporate and categoric units are, of course, constrained by the institutional domain in which they reside, but these mesostructures cannot be completely explained by this domain. Both corporate and categoric units have autonomy of structure and process unique to this level of reality. Corporate and categoric units are constructed of iterated encounters, but like institutions, mesostructures cannot be explained by their constituent parts because they constitute an emergent system revealing its own dynamics. Even the smallest corporate unit—a group—cannot be explained by one encounter; a group is often composed of several encounters operating simultaneously, and a group persists by iterated encounters. Despite the close fit between an informal group and an encounter, a group reveals dynamics above and beyond those of the encounter. And the larger the corporate unit and the more complex its division of labor, the more obvious this difference becomes. Similarly, categoric units cannot be explained by any one encounter or set of encounters; rather, distinctions are reproduced by repeated encounters in many contexts, creating an emergent phenomenon and making the dynamics of categoric units different from those of an encounter.

Microlevel Reality

Encounters are episodes of face-to-face interaction. Almost all encounters are constrained by the mesostructures and associated culture of corporate and categoric units and, by extension, the institutional domain in which they occur. Yet, encounters cannot be fully explained by these more inclusive structures. As we will see, the flow of interaction shifts depending on the nature of the mesostructures in which the encounter is lodged, but still, the dynamic properties of encounters are distinctive to the microlevel of reality.

Table 2.1. Dynamic Properties of Interactions

EMOTIONAL PROPERTIES	The level and type of emotion experienced by self and displayed toward others, and the reactions of others and self to emotions
TRANSACTIONAL PROPERTIES	The needs of individuals with respect to (a) confirming self, (b) receiving positive exchange payoffs, (c) trusting others, (d) sustaining a sense of group inclusion, and (e) sensing facticity
SYMBOLIC PROPERTIES	The texts, technologies, values, beliefs/ideologies, and norms guiding (a) the categorization of persons and situations, (b) the frames delimiting what materials are to be included and excluded, (c) the modes of communication to be employed, (d) the types of rituals to be emitted, and (e) the nature, intensity, and timing of emotions to be displayed
ROLE PROPERTIES	The mutual emission and interpretation of configurations and syndromes of gestures signaling the likely courses of behavior of individuals toward (a) each other, (b) others, and (c) broader cultural and social contexts
STATUS PROPERTIES	The placement of individuals in positions, revealing different characteristics, power, and prestige, as well as varying patterns of network relations
DEMOGRAPHIC/ECOLOGICAL PROPERTIES	The number of individuals copresent, the distinctions among them, the distribution of individuals in space, the use of stages and props, and the movement of individuals

Indeed, the goal of this book is to outline a theory of these dynamic properties. There are, I believe, six basic properties of encounters that explain their operation; these are briefly defined in Table 2.1.

One force in an encounter is emotions. All interaction is valenced with emotions. Individuals experience feelings about self, others, and situations; and both consciously and unconsciously, they emit gestures to others containing varying levels and types of affect. A second property of encounters is transactional forces, which are need states that individuals always seek to fulfill; and when these needs cannot be met in an encounter, people experience negative emotions. Individuals' perceptions of how these need states can be fulfilled varies with the nature of the mesostructure in which the encounter is embedded, but this contextual feature of transactional needs should not obscure the invariant nature of needs for (a) self-confirmation, (b) positive exchange outcomes, (c) a sense of group inclusion, (d) trust of others, and (e) perceptions of facticity. These needs always exist among participants in an encounter, and they drive the flow of interaction. A third force is symbolic. All interactions are directed by cultural scripts imposed by the meso- and macrostructures in which an encounter is embedded, but once particular sets of norms, beliefs, and values are present, they set into motion symbolic processes that can either reinforce or change culture as individuals normatize the encounter in terms of modes of communication, frames, rituals, categories, and feelings or emotions. Moreover, when the cultural directives from mesostructures are unclear, weak, or conflictual, participants to the encounter will set about creating new symbols that they can use to sustain the focus and flow of the interaction. A fourth property of an interaction is role. When individuals interact, they use cultural scripts and status positions of meso- and macrostructures to signal and interpret each others' gestures. These gestures are implicitly presumed by each party to an interaction to constitute a syndrome of consistent responses and thereby to mark an underlying role that enables each person to predict the likely courses of action of the other. Although the dynamics of this process are constrained by other properties of an interaction, they exert an independent force and, hence, can influence the dynamics of other properties and the flow of interaction in an encounter. A fifth force is status. Corporate and categoric units generally shape the (a) distribution of status, (b) diffuse status characteristics, and (c) relations among positions, but status forces reveal their own dynamics once put into play. Status is the way that social structure impinges on individuals in an encounter, and thus, concern is with the number of positions and their modes of relations as well as with the differences in power and authority, prestige, and honor as these shape the flow of interaction. A final set of forces is demography/ecology. The number of people copresent, the distinctions among them, and the movements of individuals in and out of an encounter very much determine what will transpire. The spatial distribution of individuals, the use of staging areas, and the use of props will similarly shape the flow of interaction. The demographic and ecological profile of any encounter is often highly circumscribed by corporate and categoric units, but this profile only sets into motion the operation of demographic/ecological dynamics at the microlevel of reality.

These six properties are, I believe, what structure the flow of interaction in encounters embedded in meso- and macrostructures. Embedding constrains, circumscribes, and loads the values of these properties, but the dynamics of the encounter are to be explained by the actual operation of these properties. Thus, the theory that I propose is one that seeks to explain the operation of each property, the relation of the properties to each other, and the reciprocal effects between these properties and the embedding of encounters in mesostructures.

The Unfolding of Social Reality

If we conducted a thought experiment on how populations of highly intelligent animals would organize themselves, what would they do? First, they might use their intelligence to generate symbols that they could use to provide instructions and blueprints for becoming organized. Second, as the population proved to be fit and grew, its members would have to build several kinds of distinctive structures: one kind to order face-to-face interaction, and another to mark distinctions and coordinate activities. But to use face-to-face interaction to facilitate fitness, the members of a population would have to add structures that dealt with the basic problems of surviving in the environment. In order to maintain a population in an environment, episodes of interaction have to be coordinated and directed. How best to do this? My answer is etched in the story of human evolution: encounters would need to be structured by corporate and categoric units that would, in turn, coordinate and focus behavior and interaction on problems of adaptation to the environment. As the population grew and as the number as well as diversity of corporate and categoric units increased, many of the environmental problems would revolve as much around sustaining viable relations within and between social structures as dealing with the external biophysical environment.

The above is just a thought experiment, but it is confirmed by reality itself. Humans organize themselves at these three levels; this organization is built into the very nature of the species as it had to cope with problems of survival in the environment, including the social environment of its own creation. The distinctions of macro-, meso-, and microreality are, of course, analytical, but these categories denote the actual way that social reality unfolds as populations get larger. In some primordial sense, first came the categoric distinctions between males and females, which, to produce children, led to the encounter that was iterated to generate the first groups and bands that began to coordinate activities focused on basic problems of survival (production and reproduction). Later, the very success of this simple society caused it to grow, leading to the proliferation of categoric and corporate structures focused on varying problems of survival, including those posed by the structure of society itself. It is certainly debatable whether God created Adam and Eve, but it is clear what their descendants produced: a social reality operating at three distinct levels.

Culture

Culture can be defined as systems of symbols that humans create and store in their "stocks of knowledge at hand" and that they use to organize behavior, interaction, and organization. Figure 2.1 delineates a simple model of culture, and the following outline defines the terms in the figure. Culture is ultimately stores of symbols organized into languages that unfold along the basic dimensions delineated in the figure. We could distinguish many such languages, but in Figure 2.1 those that influence macro-, meso-, and micro-level structures are highlighted. Texts are systems of symbols that are organized to provide meaning to individuals, and as is obvious, these can vary from the traditions and lore of a people to modes of artistic expression and computer algorithms. Technologies are stores of knowledge about how to manipulate both social and biophysical environments. Values are symbols that specify what is good or bad, appropriate or inappropriate. These languages are obviously interrelated as is the case, for example, when advances in technology change the content, nature, and distribution of texts as well as the value premises of a population. Similarly, values, technologies, and texts circumscribe beliefs or ideologies and various types of norms. Conversely, as ideologies and norms change, so do values, texts, and technologies.

Culture provides the information needed to organize institutional systems, corporate and categoric units, and episodes of interpersonal behavior; thus, culture exists at all levels of reality. An encounter is, therefore, not only embedded in a social structure but also the cultural symbols providing the information necessary to organize this structure. A theory of face-to-face interaction needs to include this dimension of reality, and although my conceptualization is simple, it is sufficient for the theoretical purposes of this book. Indeed, as simple as this conceptualization is, most microtheories have virtually no concept on culture, offering vague pronouncements about "definitions of the situation," "frames," "cultural capital," "stocks of knowledge,"

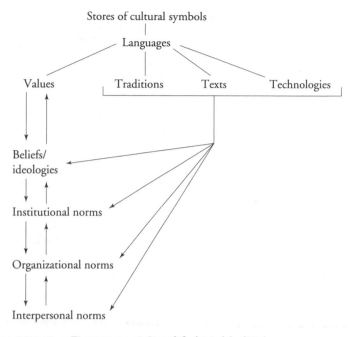

Figure 2.1. A Simplified Model of Culture

"life world," and the like. We need to unpack these glosses, as I will make evident in later chapters, but for my purposes, we do not need to develop a theory culture, as worthy as such an exercise is.

In Figure 2.2, I have highlighted the chain of constraint emanating from value premises down to ideologies/beliefs, institutional norms, organizational norms, and interpersonal norms. Values provide highly abstract and broad information of what is appropriate and inappropriate; when values are relatively clear and shared by members of a society, they provide the blueprints for beliefs or ideologies, which translate value premises to specific moral imperatives within an institutional domain. In turn, ideologies circumscribe general expectations, or institutional norms, for how individuals and collective actors are to behave within a specific institutional domain. These institutional norms, as they embody value premises and ideologies, delimit the organizational norms of various corporate and categoric units, with these organizational norms constraining the symbolic dynamics of the encounter.

This simple model obviously owes some debt to Talcott Parsons's action scheme, particularly the cybernetic hierarchy that he proposed (Parsons

Elements of Culture

Languages: Stores of organized cultural symbols.

Texts: Systems of symbols that provide meaning and interpretations of present, past, and future conditions.

Technologies: Systems of symbols that provide knowledge about how to manipulate the environment.

Values: Systems of symbols that specify right and wrong, good and bad, appropriate and inappropriate.

Beliefs/Ideologies: Systems of symbols that translate the evaluative standards of values to specific institutional domains.

Institutional norms: Systems of expectations embodying beliefs/ideologies (and by extension, value premises) into general expectations for actors within specific institutional domains.

Organizational norms: Systems of expectations applying institutional norms (and by extension, ideologies and values) to particular corporate and categoric units.

Interpersonal norms: Systems of expectations applying organizational norms (and by extension, values, ideologies, and institutional norms) to specific episodes of face-to-face interaction.

Normatizing: Systems of expectations that provide guidelines for:

Categorizing: Expectations about the nature of the situation and the individuals in the situation.

Framing: Expectations for what materials are to be included in, and excluded from, the situation.

Communicating: Expectations for the forms of talk and body-language to be employed in the situation.

Ritualizing: Expectations for the use of stereotyped sequences of gesturing to open, close, order, and repair the flow of interaction in a situation.

Feeling: Expectations for what kinds of emotions, and how much emotion, can be expressed in a situation.

1966). Although much of Parsonian functionalism has been rejected, we should avoid throwing out what is useful in functionalism. The notion that symbols form a hierarchy beginning with highly generalized values that circumscribe the culture of different levels of reality is still a useful way to conceptualize culture, especially when addressing the question of how encounters are embedded in systems of symbols. The notion of a hierarchy of symbols allows us to make several conceptual refinements. First, the culture at any level of social structure is nested in the more general symbols of a higher level. Second, symbols at the higher level contain ever more moral content of what should, ought, and must occur, whereas those at the lower provide more specific information and instruction about how actors are to behave. Third, the rate of change in culture will be greatest when initiated at higher levels, with change in the culture of institutional systems having more effects on the culture of a society than, successively, changes in meso- and micro-units. As will become evident, these simple, although perhaps controversial, conclusions about the hierarchical structure of symbols will facilitate theorizing about embedded encounters.

But the notion of hierarchy is insufficient to explain the symbolic dynamics of an encounter. We need additional ways to conceptualize how symbols constrain encounters. As I will examine in more detail in Chapter 6, I view the constraints of culture on the microlevel of reality as *normatizing* the encounter. Normatizing is a process whereby actors develop sets of expectations about how they are to behave in various contexts. Some of these expectations emerge from the flow of interaction; some come from the symbols associated with the structure in which the encounter is embedded. The relative proportions of extant and emergent norms vary with conditions that will need to be spelled out in the theory. For the present, let me just state both what normatizing is and the dimensions along which it operates at the microinterpersonal level of reality.

One axis of normatizing is the categories that individuals impose on a situation. Categorization creates normative expectations based on (1) the nature of the situation and (2) the nature of individuals in the situation. Once individuals categorize the situation and its participants, these categories impose constraints on the other axes of normatizing. One of these axes is framing in which expectations develop over what is to be included and excluded during interaction; categories help "frame the frames," but framing exerts independent effects on the expectation structure of the encounter, above and beyond categorization. Moreover, as frames shift, so must categories because individ-

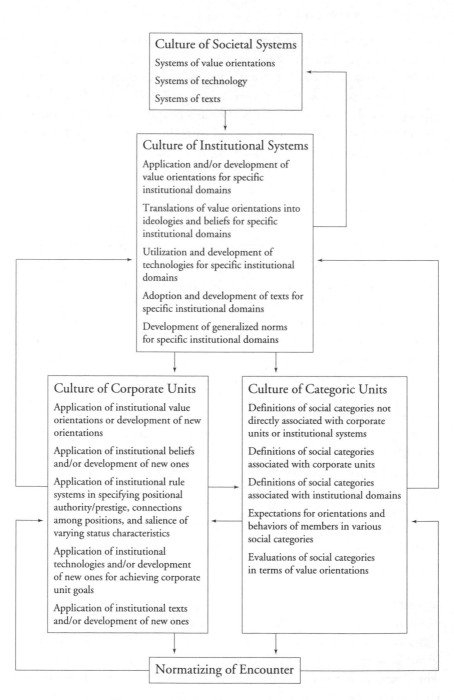

Figure 2.2. Cultural Constraints on Encounters

uals seek to sustain compatibility between categories and frames. Once expectations for categories and frames are evident, modes of communication are more readily normatized, because how individuals talk and use body language needs to be understood by all parties if the encounter is to flow smoothly. As categories, frames, and modes of communication are established, expectations for rituals are more readily agreed on by individuals. Rituals are stereotyped sequences of talk and body language, which structure the openings, closings, ordering, and repair of interaction; until normative expectations for stereotyped sequences are established, the focus and flow of the interaction will be problematic. The final axis of normatizing is feeling rules, which indicate the appropriate type, intensity, and time for emotional display. Categories, frames, modes of communication, and rituals all circumscribe the range of expectations for the expression and experience of emotion. Without rules about emotions that correspond to the nature of persons and situations, to the agreements about what is to be included and excluded, to the way talk and body presentations are to proceed, and to the use of stereotypical sequences of talk, feelings pose an ever-present threat to breach the flow of interaction. But, as feeling rules emerge, this threat is reduced.

Thus, to normatize an encounter is to develop expectations over categories, frames, communication, rituals, and feelings. Normatizing is, therefore, the point at which cultural systems impose constraint on the symbolic dynamics of the encounter. Without guidelines from the culture associated with the meso- and macrolevel structures in which the encounter is embedded, agreeing on expectations is highly problematic, requiring a considerable amount of interpersonal effort and posing the constant threat of breaches to the interaction.

Conclusions

We are close to being able to examine the dynamics of face-to-face interaction, per se. Yet, the embedding of interaction in sociocultural systems of meso- and macrostructures must be qualified by another direction of embedding: the evolved biological systems of humans. Before proceeding, therefore, this biological embedding should be examined, even if such matters make most sociologists uncomfortable. Our focus is on the encounter, or episodes of face-to-face contact, although many of the generalizations will also be applicable to unfocused interaction. In emphasizing the embedding of encounters in sociocultural systems and in human biology, I am trying to overcome the gloss that exists in much microtheory. For example, Goffman's (1983) distinction among encounters as part of *gatherings* that, in turn, are elements of more inclusive *social occasions* is a fairly typical gloss over the precise relationships between the dynamics of the encounter, on the one side, and the sociocultural properties of the structures in which the encounter is embedded, on the other. Moreover, virtually nothing is said about the biology of humans and how this biology influences what transpires in the encounter.[5] Humans are an animal; yet, remarkably, few sociologists consider the implications of this fact in studying the microdynamics of interaction where individuals, as biological organisms, meet.

[5] Indeed, it is difficult to talk about biological forces in sociology because of a stubborn refusal to recognize that not everything about humans is socially constructed. Humans are an animal, and it is remarkable that sociologists will not consider this obvious fact. But there is an unfortunate taboo about discussing biology for two reasons: one is the fear of biological reductionism, which is completely unfounded; another is the tyranny of political correctness that pervades sociology. To the extent that sociologists run away from biological forces, we look foolish in the scientific world, but more fundamentally, we will never fully understand sociocultural processes without recognizing some of the biological characteristics of our species.

THREE

Biological Embeddedness

In sociology, it is easy to forget that humans are animals. As an animal, we have been subject to evolution as it shaped our ancestors' anatomy, neuroanatomy, and behavioral propensities. *Homo sapiens sapiens* did not just arrive as fully social beings who naturally form encounters and engage in face-to-face interaction. Just *how* humans interact is still very much influenced by the evolutionary changes that occurred to our ancestors during the last sixty million years. We need, therefore, some perspective on how humans as an animal evolved.

I have told versions of this evolutionary story before (J. Turner 2000a, 1999a, 1998, 1997b, 1996a, 1996b) or helped tell it (Maryanski and Turner 1992), but it is a story worth telling again, although in a more abbreviated form. The reason my story needs to be told is that sociologists still tend to see human biology as having relatively little influence on behaviors and patterns of social organization. Yet, try as we might to assume that humans are only social creations, forged from socialization and experience in social structures, we cannot escape the fact that we are still an animal with an evolutionary history that, at each and every moment that people interact, constrains what occurs in encounters.

We do not need to become reductionists in making this point; I am certainly not arguing that human behavior and organization can be ultimately explained by our biology. Rather, interaction is embedded in our biological makeup as it has evolved. This makeup both facilitates and constrains how humans interact, but it does not determine in any precise way the dynamics of encounters. For many, this recognition is an excuse to ignore biology, but we make a large mistake in doing so, as I hope to demonstrate.

Humans Are Primates

Humans are an ape, and we are among the last of a long evolutionary line that has been in decline for millions of years. Historically, humans have been put into their own family (Hominidae) with one genus (*Homo*) containing one species (*Homo sapiens sapiens*), but it has been obvious for some time that, since humans share well over 98 percent of their genes with chimpanzees, we should not be alone in this family or genus. Indeed, some recent classifications put chimpanzees and, in some cases, other great apes such as gorillas, in Hominidae or even *Homo*. The details of classification are less important than what they assert: humans are apes at their genetic core, and in light of this fact, we should know more about them. As an ape, we possess distinctive anatomical and neuroanatomical features, as well as certain behavioral propensities, that influence interaction. Just what these are, and how they operate, is best understood in the context of primate evolution.

THE EVOLUTION OF PRIMATES IN THE ARBOREAL HABITAT

Evolution and changes in the sense modalities

Early protoprimates began to climb trees of dense forests around sixty million years ago, and as they adapted to the arboreal habitat of these forests, the primates as a distinct order began to emerge (Fleagle 1988; Campbell 1985; Gingerich and Uhen 1994; Conroy 1990). Faced with adaptation in three-dimensional space, where a misstep could spell a death by gravity, natural selection worked to change the nature of the small mammals that would evolve into primates. One important selection pressure was for better vision. Most mammals are olfactory dominant, but selection was operating to shift sensory dominance to vision, and over time this involved (a) moving the eyes forward to create stereoscopic sight in order to see depth and (b) changing visual receptors to perceive color as a means for making fine-grained distinctions. With full stereoscopic and color vision, especially when accompanied by other anatomical adaptations such as five-digit as well as sensitive hands and feet, it became easier to move rapidly and with confidence about the branches of trees. We can appreciate the power of these selection forces by considering what would happen to animals in the arboreal habitat that would remain olfactory dominant. Smelling one's way about the trees is obviously less adaptive than seeing the size and strength of as well as distance among branches. A primate that cannot see well would move slowly, clinging to branches, afraid to leap from branch to branch.

Shifting from olfactory to visual dominance is, however, a complicated process. The brain must be rewired to subordinate sensory modalities—haptic or touch, olfaction or smell, and auditory or sound—under visual dominance. Information first comes to the brain by the sensory modalities and, then, is sent to the subcortical thalamus that, subsequently, sends the impulse to the relevant lobe of the neocortex—parietal for touch, occipital for vision, and temporal for sound (the olfactory bulb remains subcortical). We can see evolution at work in expanding the association cortices among these lobes, areas such as the inferior parietal lobe (see Figure 3.1) that do the work of assuring that vision is the dominant sense modality. Thus, when sounds are heard, touch sensations are experienced, and smells are recognized, they are integrated into vision. Primates turn to look as they experience other senses, and the brain integrates them all under vision so that visual, haptic, auditory, and olfactory experiences do not contradict each other.

This shift to visual dominance is key to understanding interaction processes because humans, like any primate, subordinate other sense experiences to the visual. When others talk, touch, or even smell, it is our visual sense modality that is dominating our experience. We are neurologically wired to see more than anything else, and so face-to-face interaction is visual, with the auditory, haptic, and olfactory aspects of interaction being integrated into vision. Even when modern technologies exclude the visual, as is the case with a telephone conversation, humans imagine what others look like as they talk; and if the talk has emotional overtones, our image of another's appearance takes on greater acuity. Thus, the transformation of those mammals that would become primates to visual creatures is probably the most fundamental anatomical and neuroanatomical change for understanding face-to-face interaction. Although sociologists tend to overemphasize the auditory modality and, hence, talk and conversation, the real action in face-to-face interaction occurs along the visual modality.

Not only is olfaction subordinated to vision in primates, but also it is not a very powerful sense modality. The olfactory bulb of primates, and particularly humans, is relatively small compared to most mammals (think of the difference, for example, between the nose of a horse and humans). Prosimi-

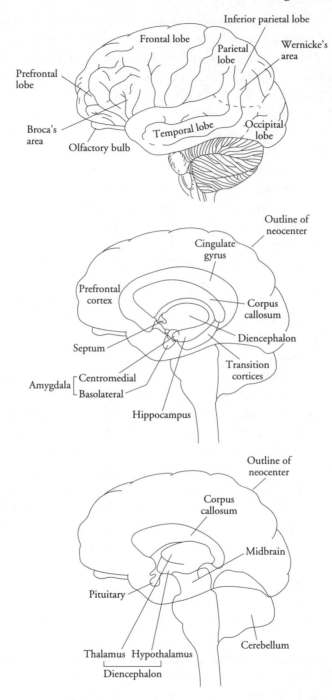

Figure 3.1.   The Human Brain and Emotions

ans (pre-monkeys) retain a well-developed sense of smell (Radinsky 1977, 1975, 1974; Rose and Fleagle 1987; Beard, Krishtalka, and Stucky 1991), but higher primates have dramatically reduced olfactory bulbs. Why should natural selection work this way? One possible answer is that since the olfactory bulb projects directly into ancient areas of the limbic systems, such as the amygdala and septum (see Figure 3.1) responsible for the production of emotions, reduction of this area was necessary to avoid emotional overload to the visual system. Smells can immediately activate emotions since they do not have to move through the neocortex, and so, a large olfactory bulb could work against integration of the sense modalities under vision. Even among humans, the olfactory bulb remains somewhat outside of direct control by the neocortex, since it is located in subcortical areas of the brain; rather than engage in extensive rewiring (although some has occurred since the neocortex has indirect control over olfaction), evolution took the conservative route and simply decreased the size of the olfactory bulb in higher primates, including humans. This reduction in the olfactory bulb helped pave the way for visual dominance. As noted above, this shift is the key evolutionary development for understanding face-to-face interaction.

Selection also worked to enhance primates' sense of touch (Kaas and Pons 1988; Maryanski 1997). If movement through the arboreal habitat was to be rapid, a heightened sense of touch would be highly adaptive. Vision alone cannot sense texture, weight, and strength of branches; touch adds critical information, allowing for a dramatic increase in the speed of movement across branches. Without this enhanced sense of touch, integrated and subordinated under vision, most of the fine-grained feats that humans can perform would not be possible (imagine making a tool with claws or hoofs, for example). And yet, touch is rather underutilized in interaction processes. It is used strategically or emotionally—as when we shake hands, pat people on the back, or give a person a hug—but in light of the sensitivity of human touch, it remains underused in most human interactions. Instead, we rely on the auditory and visual, using haptic senses to punctuate some aspect of an interaction. Before language evolved, however, vision and touch may well have been far more critical to interaction among our ancestors than it is today among humans, but the very sensitivity of touch makes it a powerful force in human interaction, *when it is activated.*

Thus, adaptations of successive generations of primates to the arboreal habitat changed the relative power of the senses. Vision became dominant, touch became more sensitive, and olfaction became attenuated. Auditory senses also increased as primates developed and used call systems, and of course, the auditory sense became even more powerful once language emerged among hominids (that is, the ancestors near or directly on the evolutionary line to humans). These changes occurred during a sixty-million-year period, but every act of face-to-face interaction among humans today is dictated by the selection forces changing the basic mammalian structure into a primate capable of surviving in the trees.

Evolution and changes in postcranial structures

Accompanying changes in sensory processes and the structure of the brain were alterations in primates' postcranial (below the skull) anatomy. Selection worked to retain the generalized skeleton, particularly five digits on hands and feet as well as a well-developed clavicle. Sensitive and flexible hands, feet, fingers, and wrists made movement among branches much easier, and the adaptive advantages of these anatomical features would push selection to improve upon them (Napier and Napier 1985; Tattersall, Delson, and van Couvering 1988; Conroy 1990). Moreover, the advantages of flexible hands, feet, fingers, and wrists drove selection for increased haptic sensitivity, and vice versa, in a spiraling process leading to humans' highly developed sense of touch.

These changes in postcranial anatomy are still significant in understanding interaction among humans, especially when accompanied by visual dominance. Watching face-to-face interaction makes us immediately aware of how much hands, feet, fingers, and wrists are used to gesture. Indeed, trying to stop movement of these flexible joints is almost impossible, or if possible, needs to be coached and placed under conscious reflection and heavy neocortical control. Without primate evolution in the trees, this facility would not exist. Movements of hands, fingers, feet, and wrists communicate important meanings and, hence, are not ancillary to interaction. They are essential to the flow of meaning and emotion in face-to-face interaction.

Aside from changes in the joints of the body's extremities, the generalized skeleton of primates allows them, if they choose, to stand up. There was no direct selection for this in the arboreal niche, or if any, comparatively little, but this ability represented a preadaptation on which selection could work to produce an upright animal, once there was a selective advantage to upright stance as primates moved from the trees to the open-country ranges of the African savanna. But, the ability to expose full bodies to each other is an important dimension of interaction. Although face is perhaps the most important set of cues for individuals during interaction, body countenance and movement are also significant, supplementing the use of flexible joints in the hands, wrists, fingers, and legs. There is, with full bodies exposed, much more to read and interpret; without this capacity *to stand* face-to-face, the nature of human interaction would be very different.

Evolution and changes in the brain

Long before the hominid brain began to move toward human proportions, many of the important changes had occurred in the arboreal habitat. Most primates have larger brains, controlling for body size correlated with brain size, than other mammals. Much of this increase in the brain size of primates is in their neocortex, evolving on top of and around the older subcortical areas of the brain, such as the brain stem, midbrain, and limbic systems (see Figure 3.1). The initial selection for a more intelligent mammal occurred in the trees because a smarter animal can remember distance, texture, strength of branches, and routes of movement; as a result, this animal can make better decisions as it moves about the three-dimensional environment of the forest canopy.

This more intelligent brain would eventually become a target of further selection, but without this preadaptation toward a larger neocortex, intelligence in the human measure could not easily have evolved. Thus, all that we associate with language and culture probably would not have evolved without earlier adaptations to the arboreal habitat. This move to more intelligence was constrained by selection working to make primates visually dominant; and so, the dominance of vision as the brain was increasing in size is critical in understanding the dynamics of face-to-face interaction.

The differentiation of monkeys and apes

These basic features of primate anatomy and neuroanatomy are the result of natural selection working on the basic mammalian body form, changing this design in ways that facilitated adaptation to the arboreal habitat. Selection produced a visually dominant mammal, with more intelligence, reduced olfaction, and increased haptic sensitivity. About thirty-four million years ago during the Oligocene epoch, early anthropoids, or animals like monkeys and apes, began to evolve alongside prosimians. These anthropoids were the ultimate ancestors of all contemporary monkeys, apes, and humans (Móya-Sóya and Köhler 1996; Ankel-Simons, Fleagle, and Chatrath 1998). By the Miocene epoch, beginning around twenty-three million years ago, these stem ancestors began to differentiate into distinguishable species of apes and monkeys, with apes being the more prevalent (Conroy 1990: 248). These apes still had many monkeylike features, but they were clearly unique. During the middle Miocene about sixteen million years ago, monkeys began to increase in prevalence. As the Miocene continued, monkeys radiated, and the species of apes that had radiated earlier began to decline. Monkeys were clearly becoming the more dominant order, and many species of African apes went extinct (Conroy 1990; Ungar 1996; Andrews 1992). How did this occur? Why was the initial adaptive radiation of the first apes reversed? The answer probably resides in the fact that apes and monkeys competed for food, with monkeys gaining the upper hand through dietary specializations for increased tolerance of unripe vegetation and other anatomical specializations, such as storage pouches for food and distinctive dental patterns (still evident in Old World monkeys today). The result is that most species of apes went extinct, with the remaining ones forced to seek food at the terminal niches of the arboreal habitat—at the very tops of trees, at the farthest extremes of branches, and on the undersides of branches. Early apes and monkeys both had run along the tops of branches to feed, and monkeys still retain this pattern of locomotion, but apes were forced to change their modes of movement and, as a consequence, their anatomy and patterns of social organization as well.

What were these changes? In contrast to monkeys that are quadrupedal with immobile shoulder joints, narrow rib cage, tail, small collar bone, and limbs of near equal length, apes and humans have (a) short and wide trunks with mobile shoulder joints allowing them to brachiate or swing arm over arm, (b) no tail, (c) flexible and strong feet, hip, hand, and wrist joints, and (d) legs much longer than arms. The changes toward more flexible and strong arms, fingers, wrists, and feet in apes reflect the work of natural selection giving apes the capacity to feed on the undersides and extremities of branches by climbing, suspending, arm swinging, and reaching with stronger and more flexible arms, fingers, and wrists. Moreover, apes have a more developed haptic sense than monkeys, particularly on the fingertips, and they reveal raised ridges or fingerprints to enhance grip on smooth surfaces. All of these changes were the outcome of the inability of apes to compete head on with monkeys, but they moved primate evolution in a new direction—one that would provide the structures for natural selection to work to produce the hominid, or human, line.

Apes are also smarter than monkeys because they had to survive in a more hazardous environment. Having to find food in the more precarious zones of the arboreal habitat would favor increased abilities to control cortically motor movements, to calculate precise distances, and to learn and remember information about distance, texture, and depth cues of branches. Thus, the inability to compete with more fit monkeys initiated a trend toward a smarter primate that would provide for natural selection the structures on which to work to produce an even smarter ape, culminating in the human line.

As dramatic as the anatomical and neuroanatomical changes in apes were, the behavioral and social structural changes in their organization were even more dramatic. Alexandra Maryanski's (1997, 1992) analysis of ape and monkey social structures reveals some striking differences, understandable in light of the different niches where apes and monkeys foraged for food. Monkeys are organized by female matrilines of several generations and hierarchies of male dominance. This pattern is sustained by females staying in their local group as part of a matriline, thereby assuring intergenerational continuity of the group, and by males transferring out of the group at puberty and migrating to other groups and competing for a place in the dominance hierarchy (Fedigan 1982; Jolly 1985; Napier and Napier 1985; Cheney, Seyfarth, and Smuts 1986; Wrangham 1980; Smuts et al. 1987). In contrast, apes reveal almost the exact opposite pattern: females leave the group at puberty, thereby destroying the continuity of group structure across generations, and in most cases, males also leave. Some male dominance exists among apes, but it is relaxed when compared to that among monkeys. Local group structures are small and fluid with individuals moving in and out of groups within a larger regional population. The end result is for apes to have relatively few strong ties beyond bonds between mother and infants and for local groups to be highly fluid, with considerable individual autonomy and freedom to move from group to group within a larger regional population of many square miles. The reasons for these changes can be found in the arboreal niches where apes had to survive; apes could not maintain larger groups in marginal niches that could not support many individuals. In contrast, monkeys could develop larger and more stable groups because they controlled the verdant portions of the arboreal habitat.

The details of Maryanski's analysis and my use of these data (see J. Turner 2000a, 1996b) need not occupy us here. The critical point is this: because humans are apes, it is likely that they exhibit behavioral propensities for weak ties, loose and fluid social structures, personal autonomy, and individual freedom. For millions of years, this is the direction that natural selection pushed apes, and it would be amazing if these basic behavioral propensities were "selected out" of the hominid line, especially since the cousin with whom we share 98 percent of our genes reveals these behavioral propensities. True, this conclusion flies in the face of arguments about the innate sociality of humans and their needs for group solidarity, but if we take seriously the fact of biological embeddedness, we need to examine and perhaps question some of the old assumptions that are widespread in sociology and philosophy. We need not assume that humans are asocial or even excessively selfish, for there were millions of years of selection on apes in more terrestrial habitats to modify these propensities of apes for autonomy, individualism, weak ties, and loose social structures. But we should be cautious in assuming that twenty million years of evolution was reversed back to a monkeylike pattern. Face-to-face interaction among humans, then, is probably very much influenced by the ape side of our ancestry that drives humans toward individuality and weak ties; and if this is the case, we may have to look at the interpersonal and biological mechanisms by which this ape ancestry is overcome to form stronger ties producing higher levels of interpersonal solidarity among humans.

EVOLUTION OF PRIMATES IN AFRICAN WOODLAND HABITATS

In the late Miocene, the tropical forest began to recede, especially in Africa. During this process, many new niches were created for hominoids (that is, apes and monkeys), with some remaining arboreal, others moving to mixes of primary and secondary forests, still others such as the ancestors of contemporary chimpanzees adapting to forests on the edges of the grasslands, and various species moving into primary and secondary forests at different altitudes, as is the case with present-day gorillas (Isbell and Young 1996; Hill 1998; Andrews 1989). There is some debate as to just how far the rainforests receded and how dominant the savanna grasslands became in the late Miocene (Kingston, Marino, and Hill 1994; McKee 1996), but there can be no doubt that many species of primates were forced to become terrestrial in dryer climatic conditions, or die (Malone 1987; Cerling et al. 1997; Agusti et al. 1998). Many species of apes and monkeys had to make this transition to a more terrestrial habitat, and among those species of apes that moved to the savanna were the ancestors of humans. Selection would thus work on what apes brought with them to this new habitat.

What, then, did apes carry to this new zone? And how did selection work on the characteristics that apes had acquired in the arboreal habitat? Apes brought, first of all, visual dominance that would allow them to see prey and predators, but these exceptional visual abilities were not accompanied by a keen sense of smell, the most prominent sense modality of terrestrial mammals and one that serves them well in open-country conditions. Those apes that would become hominids were thus unlikely to smell predators or prey; they would have to rely on vision. But to see, they would have to stand up; and selection probably began to take the already-in-place abilities of apes to walk on their hind legs to full bipedalism. Indeed, as the fossil record clearly underscores, hominids were fully bipedal long before their brains had moved much beyond the size of present-day apes, indicating that there were intense selection pressures to transform apes' generalized skeleton in this direction.

Even if the advantages of being able to see above the grasses were not responsible for this movement to bipedalism, the freeing of the hands for tool and weapon making was, no doubt, also driving selection toward making apes on the savanna bipedal (Hunt 1991; Swartz 1989). Apes' heightened haptic sensitivity would serve them well only in conjunction with strong and flexible hands, wrists, and shoulder joints to make tools and weapons; and since contemporary apes can make tools and, occasionally, weapons, selection clearly had this ability to work on. This would, indeed, be a critical adaptation for an animal that could not smell well, and for one that was not built for speed in its bipedal or even quadrupedal stance. A slow animal without an acute sense of smell to sense predators hiding in the bush was obviously vulnerable, even with refined eyesight; so there must have been rapid movement to bipedalism freeing the hands for tool use and weaponry. Moreover, and perhaps initially more important than tools and weapons, is the fact that when the hands are free, scavenging for already dead animals and foraging for fruits and vegetables are easier because food can be carried distances. Still, the fact that most apes perished tells us that even these kinds of changes did not assure survival. Some apes became very large, such as the robust Australopithecines and perhaps others remained small and comparatively fast, but still most died out, despite changes to their anatomy.

Apes also brought to the savanna auditory capacities still very much wired to more ancient subcortical emotion centers of the brain. We can see this today in contemporary apes (and monkeys as well) whereby emotion-arousing stimuli will set off auditory bursts only partially under control of the neocortex. Apes are thus potentially extremely noisy when emotionally aroused, and this feature of their neuroanatomy would not be advantageous in an open-country, terrestrial habitat. A noisy primate would scare off prey and attract predators, which would be a particularly dangerous behavioral propensity for a slow animal that could not smell predators. Thus, it is likely that selection began rewiring of the brain so that apes could gain neocortical control of emotions since a noisy primate on the savanna would soon be a dead one. Such control would not necessarily involve enlarging the neocortex, but rather a rewiring of the connections between subcortical emotional centers to neocortical centers for voluntary control. The olfactory bulb was not rewired, but this was less essential because it was so small compared to other mammals and not likely to evoke the same emotions as visual, tactile, or auditory perceptions. By gaining some cortical control of emotional responses, apes would be less noisy and, hence, more likely to avoid attracting predators or scaring away prey.

Perhaps the biggest roadblock to adaptation to open-country conditions, where predators abound and where prey can be difficult to catch, was the lack of tight-knit group structures among apes. Such structures would have selective advantages because they could be used to coordinate both food foraging and predatory defense; for this reason monkeys probably had an easier time than apes making the transition to the woodland and grassland habitats of the late Miocene and early Pliocene. Indeed, except for humans, no ape lives in the open country whereas a number of species of monkeys do. But, in contrast to monkeys, apes lack strong tendencies for male dominance, no tendency for female matrilines to hold the group together across generations, no strong ties beyond mother and infant/young-offspring bonds (which were broken at puberty with transfer of the young out of the natal group). Matrilines and dominance are the bases of monkey organization, and they give monkey troops on the savanna the advantages of larger numbers of males, females, and young marching across the open country in quasi-military formation with males at the front, rear, and flanks and with females (that are smaller than males) and young in the center. But apes brought to the savanna clear behavioral propensities for weak and fluid ties, individualism, autonomy, and mobility.

How, then, was such an animal to survive under conditions where social structure and strong ties were more adaptive? The answer is that most did not, and we can see the result today: there are only five genera of apes left in the world from the many hundreds that once existed; and the only apes that survived are completely arboreal (gibbon/siamang), or are both arboreal and terrestrial (orangutans, gorillas, and chimpanzees). A slow animal with a poorly developed sense of smell and that also possessed few propensities both to build strong social ties to sustain group continuity over time and to form cohesive group structures was thus at a great disadvantage on the savanna. How did natural selection overcome this major obstacle?

Natural selection under punctuated conditions could not convert apes to monkeys that use female matrilines and male dominance to sustain cohesive group structures; too much selection against these characteristics had occurred for too long in the arboreal habitat. Natural selection could, however, work on the moderate propensities for male dominance evident in African apes of today (since, unlike tendencies for matrilines, there was an in-place propensity to select on), but without the corresponding matrilines, this would be an evolutionary dead end. Dominant males seeking to horde males and females without propensities for the latter to stay in the group or to form intergenerational matrilines would exhaust themselves running around trying to hold the group together. Natural selection may nonetheless have taken this route for most apes, thereby dooming them to extinction.

Natural selection did have some anatomical and neuroanatomical struc tures on which to work, however. If selection had already allowed some apes to gain cortical control of their emotional outbursts, this trait could be subject to further selection. It is my hypothesis developed in other works (see J. Turner 2000a, 1998, 1997a, 1997b, 1996b) that this is just what occurred. I will not elaborate here on the neurological details, but my argument is that natural selection changed subcortical areas of the brain to make hominids, and eventually humans, more emotional animals who could use an expanded emotional repertoire to forge social bonds. In this manner, apes' propensities for autonomy, mobility, individualism, and weak-tie formation could be, to some degree, overcome. This rewiring, I argue, occurred before dramatic increases in the size of the hominid neocortex, perhaps as far back as ten million years ago; and it was made possible by the preadaptation for cortical control of emotions. We can see the evolutionary imprint of the changes involved when we compare the human brain with that of present-day great apes (chimpanzee, gorilla, and orangutan). Not only is the human neocortex dramatically larger, but so are various subcortical areas responsible for the production of emotions. These emotion centers have also increased in size, although not to the extent of the neocortex, indicating that selection was working on hominid emotion systems. Before selection made hominids smarter with the expanded neocortex, it made them emotional.

Natural selection grabbed these subcortical areas and changed them in ways to produce associative emotional propensities (see J. Turner 2000a, 2000b, for the neurological details), integrated these enhanced emotional abilities with the capacity of hominids to exercise some voluntary control of emotions. I would go so far as to argue that long before auditory language appears in hominids, emotional languages existed and were used to forge bonds; and these emotional languages relied on the dominant sense modality of all primates—vision. If natural selection were working rapidly, it would select on what it was given; and so, if selection were generating enhanced emotional abilities to overcome ape tendencies for weak ties and low solidarity, it would do so initially through the visual modality. The first languages were, I believe, visual but they were much more than the "hand signals" systems that have been postulated to be the first language (for example, Hewes 1973); rather, they were not instrumental systems of communication but systems for generating solidarity through the more subtle use of face and body to signal affect (J. Turner 2000a).

If I am correct in this conclusion—which, granted, is speculative—then face-to-face interaction is at its core a visual process. Language was, I believe, built on "body language" rather than the other way around. That is, spoken (and later written) language is a supplement to a more primal language that organizes face and body gestures to communicate emotional states. During interaction, then, people do not read body language to supplement spoken language; they do just the opposite: they read body language and use the auditory channel for talk as a source of supplemental information. Obviously, in highly instrumental communication, spoken language is heavily used; but even here, humans are constantly reading body languages, and we can ask: Why? My answer is that humans are neurologically programmed to read emotions first through their dominant sense modality: vision. If this conclusion is correct, then the overemphasis on spoken language by those studying interaction processes is misplaced; instead, we should be devoting much more effort to study emotional languages that use visual cues more than auditory signals to generate meanings. Although this line of argument may seem like wide-eyed speculation, I have tried to document these conclusions in more detail (J. Turner 2000a) so that those who are skeptical can see the data I bring to bear. Scholars have studied nonverbal communication (see Knapp and Hall 1992, for a review), but my point is that nonverbal communication is mostly about emotions; and emotions are the more primal language system in face-to-face interaction.

The Biology of Human Interaction

My arguments about biological embeddedness may seem far-fetched, especially to those sociologists who remain unwilling to consider the implications of the fact that humans are animals. Nonetheless, even to the most critical eye, I trust that the relevance of this chapter will become evident as we proceed in developing the theory. For the present, let me briefly summarize and, in cases, expand on the main points and their implications for the study of face-to-face interaction among humans.

The neuroanatomical changes to the hominid brain are perhaps the most significant biological factors in understanding human interaction. In rewiring the brain for visual dominance, the association cortices standing between the occipital, parietal, and temporal lobes have been hypothesized as the cortical structures most responsible for language production (see Figure 3.1). Norman Geschwind (1970, 1965a, 1965b), and later with Antonio Damasio (1984), argued that the ability to generate language, given selection that would favor language use, is made possible by the association cortices that integrate the sense modalities under visual dominance. The fact that present-day apes can learn language at the level of a three-year-old child indicates that this capacity is not unique to humans (Savage-Rumbaugh, Rumbaugh, and McDonald 1985; Savage-Rumbaugh et al. 1993). For language to have emerged in the first place, there had to be structures on which to select; and Geschwind and Damasio hypothesize that the inferior parietal lobe and other association cortices in this area are the likely candidates. These structures did not evolve under selection pressures for language and, hence, are preadaptations for language that emerged as a by-product of making primates visually dominant animals. One implication of this hypothesis is that these association cortices "waited" millions of years for the selection pressures that made hominids capable of auditory language, but I would argue that the neurological capacities for language were subject to selection much earlier as hominids created emotional languages for forging social bonds in the face of their ape propensities for low sociality and weak ties (see J. Turner 2000a, for the details of this argument). Cortical control of emotions in order to inhibit noisy outbursts came first as apes sought to survive in more open country, away from the protection of the trees; once the neurology for this control existed, it became yet another preadaptation for emotional languages. Thus, as a result of selection forces that first made primates visually dominant and later as a consequence of selection favoring cortical control over noisy affective outbursts, emotional language using signs and syntax existed long before spoken language. Much later, natural selection used these emotional language capacities and the neurological structures enabling such languages to operate as the structures on which to select for auditory language that would indeed increase the adaptation of animals that possessed the ability to speak through the auditory channel. At this point, probably around three million years ago, the neocortex begins to expand since a spoken language allows for culture to be created and transmitted. But this ability for spoken language is a later evolutionary "add on" to extant neurological structures for emotional languages.

This conclusion has, I believe, important implications for how we study face-to-face interaction. The primal and primary language is the syntax of gestures signaling emotional valences; the auditory channel rides along the neurology of this emotional language and supplements the meanings communicated by emotionally laden gestures. Thus, face-to-face interaction almost always revolves around trying to establish emotional overtones, moods, and meanings, even as the auditory channel carries more instrumental content. Of course, the auditory channel itself is used to communicate emotions, because it is piggybacked onto older neural substrates for generating emotional syntax. We can see this, by the way, when people are emotional; as they talk, they have great difficulty controlling facial expressions and body movements for the simple reason that these are the primal language. A theory of interaction must, therefore, be centered around the signaling of emotions, produced primarily by vision and supplemented by spoken words.

As selection reworked neuroanatomy of primates, it also made significant changes to the basic mammalian anatomy. One change, perhaps so obvious that it is rarely discussed, is that humans and their closest relatives expose much more facial skin than do other terrestrial mammals. Without extensive fur, it is possible to see emotions with much greater acuity. Humans can see blood flow through the skin; we can see striated muscle contractions; and we can see the effects of neurotransmitter and neuroactive peptides on body responses. Also, once hominids became upright and bipedal, perhaps as far back as six to ten million years ago, the ability to expose full bodies to others made the reading of body language that much more robust. Moreover, with upright stance, full face is continuously exposed and ready for fine-grained inspection. Flexible hands, feet, wrists, arms, and shoulders provide further body cues for the reading of emotional overtones to interaction supplementing face and body positioning as continuously open channels of communication. In fact, without these multiple channels of body language, interaction is strained because the verbal syntax alone can rarely carry an interaction for long, especially interactions that involve affect. Thus, humans' primate anatomy that evolved for reasons having relatively little to do with interaction have provided *Homo sapiens sapiens* with bodies capable of communicating along many channels. And because olfaction as an effective means of communication is dramatically reduced in primates, including humans, we need this anatomical system to sustain complex and subtle patterns of interaction that make encounters viable and, ultimately, patterns of social organization possible.

As an ape, humans reveal ape propensities for weak ties, relatively low sociality, individual autonomy, and preferences for movement in and out of fluid patterns of social organization. These propensities have typically been seen as pathologies in early modernist theory and, more recently, in postmodern theory. But, as Alexandra Maryanski and I (1992) have argued, these are seen as pathologies only against the backdrop of rather idealistic visions of "community" in agrarian societies; but in fact, it may be that modern societies are far more in tune with humans' biological propensities as apes than most social theorists, and particularly critical social theorists, recognize. Humans are not, I believe, solidarity-seeking emotional junkies; rather, humans clearly prefer individual autonomy, punctuated with close relationships. Thus, our ape propensities were modified through, I believe, the development of enhanced emotional capacities and the use of emotional syntax to be more social than our ape cousins in the present and in the past. But selection did not wipe out older, ape propensities; rather, enhanced abilities at sociality were laced around older propensities for individualism, mobility, and weak ties. Humans are, in a way, of two minds: on the one hand, we crave social solidarity and emotional attachments; on the other, we resent too much constraint and control in closed social circles. This two-sidedness may not be the result of ideologies and social structures, but in fact, it is part of our biology. Natural selection had to work rapidly to overcome weak-tie propensities if our ancestors were to form the groups that would enable them to survive on the savanna; thus, it rewired our subcortical emotion systems and their connections to the neocortex in ways enhancing emotional engagements. But these were added to already-in-place ape tendencies for weak ties and low sociality.

This conclusion has enormous implications for face-to-face interaction in encounters. As I will argue, humans must work hard to maintain focus in an encounter, and the mechanisms for doing so revolve around rituals that arouse emotions and structure the openings, closings, and rhythm of interaction. Humans do not naturally jump into emotional solidarities, but rather, must engage in a range of emotion-arousing behaviors in order to sustain the focus of attention and the rhythm of an interaction in an encounter. Focused encounters run against some of our behavioral propensities, while unfocused encounters are more readily sustained because they fit better with our ape ancestry. To focus an encounter requires engagement and emotional fine-tuning that pulls us into higher-solidarity interactions; to sustain an unfocused encounter simply requires that we revert to the weak-tie propensities of our ape ancestors.

Focused encounters thus involve considerably more effort for most individuals than do unfocused encounters, and the reason for this has much to do with our biology as an evolved ape. If such speculation is true, we need to reconceptualize the processes and mechanism of focused encounters; too often we assume that these are "normal" and that unfocused encounters are more pathological manifestations of modern societies. I think that just the opposite is the case, and therefore, we need to pay particular attention to how humans create and sustain focused encounters. Our hominid ancestors had to find ways to create and sustain focused encounters in order to survive, and they had to overcome older, more primal propensities for weak ties. Today, in each and every encounter, this evolutionary dilemma is played out when individuals engage in face-to-face interaction. Rather than begin with the old assumption of the innate sociality of humans, we should begin with the opposite assumption and ask how humans overcome their ape ancestry. Emotions are the key, but it takes work to arouse and sustain solidarity-producing emotions. Moreover, once aroused, emotions can exhaust us and make us less willing to sustain an interaction.

Many will find this chapter disturbing, partly because it is highly speculative and mostly because sociologists tend to have an overly social conception of humans. *Homo sapiens sapiens* are animals; we evolved in particular kinds of habitats that shaped our ancestors' neuroanatomy, anatomy, and behaviors. These products of natural selection did not suddenly go away when humans emerged on the hominid line, but sometimes sociologists act as if they did. They are with us at every moment, and they shape the flow of interaction. All encounters are embedded in our biology; and we would be wise to recognize this fact and let it enter our theorizing about social interaction. This recognition does not require that we lapse into biological determinism or reductionism, only that we always pay attention to the biological embeddedness of encounters in formulating a theory of face-to-face interaction.

Emotional Forces

Humans' emotional capacities are as distinctive as their ability to use language. The hominid brain was rewired to gain neocortical control over the auditory channel and, using this control as a base for further selection, to expand humans' emotional repertoire into emotional languages that were used to overcome the behavioral propensity of apes toward individualism, autonomy, and mobility (J. Turner 2000a). This biological embeddedness cannot, I believe, be ignored in theorizing about human interaction and organization because it is the capacity to use emotional languages that binds humans together. Encounters could not flow without the use of emotional syntax; and humans' willingness to take cognizance of, and develop attachments to, other people as well as meso- and macrostructures would not be possible without emotions. Thus, one of the most critical forces driving face-to-face interaction and its embeddedness is the arousal and use of emotions. Although "talk" can keep the instrumental aspects of an interaction on track, it is emotions that attune and bind individuals to each other.

Early sociological theory is surprisingly silent on emotions. Neither George Herbert Mead (1934) nor Alfred Schutz ([1932] 1967) had much to say on the topic, and while Durkheim's ([1912] 1946) analysis of rituals and solidarity implied positive emotional arousal, few details were offered. Charles Horton Cooley (1916, 1902) was perhaps the first sociologist to directly incorporate emotions, particularly pride, into an interactionist theory. Of course, Sigmund Freud's (1900) analysis of behavior emphasized emotions, and for this reason his work needs to be considered in a more sociological light. Even

Erving Goffman (1967), who is often considered to have been the first modern sociologist to incorporate emotions into a microlevel theory, was narrow in focus, exploring only a few emotions such as embarrassment. In this conceptual vacuum, theories emphasized auditory language, as was the case with Mead who saw thinking as an "internal conversation" or, later, Harold Garfinkel (1967) who extended Schutz's phenomenological program into ethnomethodology and "conversation analysis." Thus, sociology has a "verbal bias," and until the late 1970s, this bias kept emotions out of most sociological theory and research. In this chapter, I continue the effort, begun in the late 1970s by scholars such as Hochschild (1979), Kemper (1987, 1978), and Heise (1979) to build a microtheory of human interaction around emotional forces.

Primary Emotions

There are various lists of primary emotions, but all researchers agree on at least these four: (1) assertion-anger; (2) aversion-fear; (3) satisfaction-happiness; and (4) disappointment-sadness.[1] Other emotions such as surprise and disgust are frequently added to lists of primary emotions, but if we look at other mammals and the neurology of emotional responses (J. Turner 2000a, 1999b), we are on sure ground if we stick with these four. Mammals' most basic emotion is aversion-fear, because an animal that does not experience fear in the face of danger and predators is soon selected out. Fear is generated in a subcortical structure termed the *amygdala* (see Figure 3.1 in Chapter 3). Assertion-anger is similarly generated in the amygdala, although on separate regions of this primal center of emotions. Like fear, aggression is probably ancient because mammals often become defensively aggressive when fearful and trapped. Satisfaction-happiness is a more elusive emotion, because it is spread around both cortical and subcortical areas of the brain. One area where happiness is generated is the cingulate gyrus, composed of distinctive neocortical tissues regulating mammalian behaviors for mother-infant bonding

[1] See J. Turner 2000a, for a review. See also Johnson-Laird and Oatley 1992; Emde 1980; Panksepp 1982; Sroufe 1979; J. Turner 1996b; Trevarthen 1984; Osgood 1966; Izard 1992; Ekman 1984; Epstein 1984; Frommel and O'Brien 1982; Arieti 1970; Plutchik 1980; Fehr and Russell 1984; Gray 1982; Kemper 1987; Malatesta and Haviland 1982.

and playfulness; another area generating happiness is the amygdala, which at first glance may seem surprising, because this is also the subcortical area for fear and anger. Compared to apes, the amygdala in humans appears to have added new areas for pleasure around those generating fear and anger. Similarly, when compared to apes, the septum—the ancient subcortical center for sexual impulses—has centers for pleasure added on (Stephan 1983; Stephan and Andy 1977, 1969; Stephan, Baron, and Frahm 1988). Thus, a critical feature of humans' neuroanatomy is the jury-rigging of new centers for pleasure on top of more ancient areas of the mammalian brain.

This rewiring is understandable in light of several considerations. First, selection was working rapidly on humans' hominid ancestors to make individualistic apes more social; selection failed all other terrestrial apes, but appears to have hit on a solution with the expansion of the emotion centers of hominids. Since selection had to have something to work on, it simply usurped existing emotional centers. Second, if enhanced bonds of solidarity promoted fitness, and if emotions were being used to generate these bonds of solidarity, then positive emotions would be critical. An animal without strong instincts to herd and form troops must achieve these outcomes through emissions of positive emotions and use of positive sanctions. Anger and fear alone cannot hold individuals together, and negative sanctions invite counteranger, fearful retreat, or perhaps even sadness; and none of these emotional states is conducive to bonds of solidarity when emotions must do the work that innate instincts perform for the grouping and herding propensities of most other terrestrial mammals. Third, if fear and anger are the most primal emotions in mammals and if they are disruptive to bonds of solidarity in the absence of other bioprogrammers for group formation, their power had to be mitigated because raw negative sanctions alone cannot bind individuals together. Selection appears to have taken two routes to control fear and anger. One route involved attaching centers for pleasure and happiness onto ancient areas for fear and anger; another revolved around elaborating sadness.

There is no clear, discrete center for sadness, although the posterior portions of the cingulate gyrus may be involved. Sadness is an emotion aroused primarily (a) through the failure to generate necessary neurotransmitters or, alternately, through the acceleration of their reuptake and (b) through changes in the flow of neuroactive peptides as well as the production of hormones in the more general endocrine system. Several centers of the brain are responsible for the emission of neurotransmitters and neuroactive peptides,

Table 4.1.   Relative Size of Ape and Human Brains

BRAIN COMPONENT	APES (PONGIDS)	HUMANS (HOMO)
Neocortex	61.88	196.41
Diencephalon thalamus hypothalamus	8.57	14.76
Amygdala	1.85	4.48
centromedial	1.06	2.52
basolateral	2.45	6.02
Septum	2.16	5.45
Hippocampus	2.99	4.87
Transition cortices	2.38	4.43

SOURCES: Data from Stephan 1983, Stephan and Andy 1969, 1977, and Eccles 1989.

NOTE: Calculations use *Tenrecinae* as a base of 1 and control for body size. Numbers represent how many times larger each area of ape and human brain is compared to its counterpart in *Tenrecinae*.

the hypothalamus and pituitary gland for neuroactive peptides and the midbrain and perhaps the thalamus for neurotransmitters (although more recent data indicate that additional centers may generate some neurotransmitters). These are all ancient areas of the brain, and so, selection could work to generate sadness as a consequence of negative sanctions; as I will argue shortly, sadness is critical to mitigating fear and anger and, in the process, generating important emotions such as shame and guilt.

The neurological details need not be outlined here, but the pattern is clear: subcortical areas of the brain are all being usurped to generate new kinds of emotional states that can increase social bonding among animals that, at their genetic core, are low-sociality apes.[2] We can see, in gross terms, how this occurred by comparing the brains of present-day apes and humans, as is done in Table 4.1. These data report the relative size of human and ape brains using a primitive mammal, *Tenrecinae*, as a base of one. The numbers

[2] See J. Turner 2000a, 1999b, for a sociologically oriented review of the neurological details.

Table 4.2. *Variants of Primary Emotions*

	LOW INTENSITY	MODERATE INTENSITY	HIGH INTENSITY
SATISFACTION-HAPPINESS	content sanguine serenity gratified	cheerful buoyant friendly amiable enjoyment	joy bliss rapture jubilant gaiety elation delight thrilled exhilarated
AVERSION-FEAR	concern hesitant reluctance shyness	misgivings trepidation anxiety scared alarmed unnerved panic	terror horror high anxiety
ASSERTION-ANGER	annoyed agitated irritated vexed perturbed nettled rankled piqued	displeased frustrated belligerent contentious hostility ire animosity offended consternation	dislike loathing disgust hate despise detest hatred seething wrath furious inflamed incensed outrage
DISAPPOINTMENT-SADNESS	discouraged downcast dispirited	dismayed disheartened glum resigned gloomy woeful pained dejected	sorrow heartsick despondent anguished crestfallen

SOURCE: Data from Turner 1999a, 1999b.

in the table report how many times larger than *Tenrecinae* various areas of the ape and human brain are, controlling for body size (which correlates with brain size). The neocortical differences are the most dramatic, but other subcortical areas of the brain show significant increases in size compared to apes that, in a rough sense, can be seen as what our ape ancestors were like before selection started the hominid line. Why would these emotion centers become larger, approximately two times larger in humans than in apes (again, controlling for body size)? The answer must be, I believe, to expand the emotional capacities of hominids; and I would argue that this increase in the size of subcortical areas of the brain occurred before the larger increases in the neocortex began some three million years ago.

One outcome of the rewiring of the brain was to expand the varieties of primary emotions that hominids could use and interpret. Table 4.2 offers one listing of variations from low through moderate to high-intensity states. These variants of primary emotions greatly expand the emotional repertoire of a mammal, and although higher mammals can certainly generate some of these states, only humans rely on all of them. With more emotions to work with, it is possible to form subtle and complex social relations from more fine-grained attunement of interpersonal responses.

First-Order Emotions

Variants of primary emotions are only one way to increase the emotional repertoire. Another is to "mix" primary emotions, although the notion of "mixing" is only a metaphor. More accurately, the body systems responsible for the production of emotions—that is, the autonomic nervous system (ANS), the neurotransmitter system, the endocrine system, and the muscu-loskeletal system—are simultaneously activated and perhaps interact in ways not fully understood to generate what, following Kemper (1987), I will term the *first-order combinations* or *elaborations*. Such elaborations involve the si-multaneous (and in some cases, sequential) activation of two primary emo-tions, with one of these being the more dominant. Table 4.3 offers my views on some of the most important of these first-order elaborations.

These elaborations dramatically expand not only the number of emo-tions but also their power. Moreover, mixing varying levels of satisfaction or sadness with fear and anger reduces the latter pair's disassociative effects.

Table 4.3. First-order Elaborations of Primary Emotions

SATISFACTION-HAPPINESS

Satisfaction-happiness + *aversion-fear*	*produces* →	wonder, hopeful, relief, gratitude, pride, reverence
Satisfaction-happiness + *assertion-anger*	*produces* →	vengeance, appeased, calmed, soothed, relish, triumphant, bemused
Satisfaction-happiness + *disappointment-sadness*	*produces* →	nostalgia, yearning, hope

AVERSION-FEAR

Aversion-fear + *satisfaction-happiness*	*produces* →	awe, reverence, veneration
Aversion-fear + *assertion-anger*	*produces* →	revulsed, repulsed, antagonism, dislike, envy
Aversion-fear + *disappointment-sadness*	*produces* →	dread, wariness

ASSERTION-ANGER

Assertion-anger + *satisfaction-happiness*	*produces* →	condescension, mollified, rudeness, placated, righteousness
Assertion-anger + *aversion-fear*	*produces* →	abhorrence, jealousy, suspiciousness
Assertion-anger + *disappointment-sadness*	*produces* →	bitterness, depression, betrayed

DISAPPOINTMENT-SADNESS

Disappointment-sadness + *satisfaction-happiness*	*produces* →	acceptance, moroseness, solace, melancholy
Disappointment-sadness + *aversion-fear*	*produces* →	regret, forlornness, remorseful, misery
Disappointment-sadness + *assertion-anger*	*produces* →	aggrieved, dicontent, dissatisfied, unfulfilled, boredom, grief, envy, sullenness

For example, if fear is combined with lesser levels of happiness, emotions like awe, reverence, and veneration are produced; in this way, fear is transformed into an emotion that can be used for associative purposes such as reverence for moral codes and veneration of others or ancestors. Similarly, fear combined with smaller amounts of sadness produces emotions like dread and wariness that, while not highly associative, are not likely to produce counteranger. In fact, when individuals are wary and dreading an interaction, they are still oriented to others and the situation and still willing to participate in the encounter rather than running away or being overly assertive and disruptive. Anger combined with happiness generates emotions such as righteousness, which can be a powerful sanctioning tool with respect to norms and values, while taking the edge off aggression in ways that can potentially promote commitment to cultural codes. Other emotions produced by this combination, such as condescension and rudeness, are not associative, per se, but they can be used as negative sanctions that take much of the edge off pure aggression and, as a result, work to bring individuals back into alignment without inviting either extreme fear or counteranger. When anger is combined with sadness, emotions like bitterness, depression, and sense of betrayal can emerge; although these are not associative emotions, they do mitigate the power of raw anger alone. Thus, one outcome of first-order combinations is to reduce the power of anger or fear alone, and in some cases, to channel these emotions toward potentially more associative uses. If a low-sociality animal were to forge bonds through emotions, the negative power of fear and anger had to be mitigated and rechanneled. In fact, I would speculate that humans are most attuned to elements of fear and anger in others because these are the most primal emotions of mammals. This attention, often implicit and subconscious, to anger and its variants and elaborations makes individuals alert to negative sanctions, while sensitivity to fear and its variants like anxiety and its elaborations can move people to engage in acts reducing anxiety, thereby facilitating enhanced sociality.

In addition to reducing the disassociative effects of fear and anger, first-order combinations have even more positive outcomes when happiness or sadness is the dominant emotion, combined with lesser amounts of fear and anger. For example, when happiness is activated along with a lower level of fear, emotions like wonder, hopeful, relief, gratitude, and pride are generated. All of these can be used to reinforce cultural codes or to promote associative relations. Pride is perhaps the most important of these emotions because it makes self highly salient, as I will explore in Chapter 5. People experience pride when they are able to meet expectations, or exceed them, despite some fear that they might not be able to do so. When people experience pride, they display happiness, and they are likely to sanction positively those involved in the situation who, in turn, may experience pride. Thus, pride pulls self into the flow of emotions that can potentially set off a chain of positive affect flowing through members of an encounter. In so doing, it pushes individuals to define self and self-worth in terms of the norms, values, and beliefs of not only the encounter but also of the more inclusive structures in which the encounter is embedded. Thus, we can speculate that selection worked to transform the individualism of hominids into the ability to experience pride for engaging in appropriate and proper conduct vis-à-vis others in a situation; out of the experience of pride, the emotional tones of the situation turn positive and, hence, facilitate sociality and bond formation.

Dominant levels of happiness combined with anger generate emotions that can be associative: appeased, calmed, and soothed can be used to accept apologies for transgressions; bemused sustains a sense of quiet attachment to a situation. Vengeance, however, is not likely to generate associative relations, and for an intelligent animal that can remember negative outcomes of past interactions, this can be a highly disruptive emotion. Similarly, if triumphant is the outcome of succeeding over others, this too can be a negative emotion in an encounter because it is likely to arouse emotions such as anger or, when the anger is mixed with fear, emotions such as jealousy and suspiciousness. If the anger is combined with sadness, emotions such as bitterness, depression, and betrayed can emerge. All of these can breach the flow of interaction; as a result, humans are highly attuned to anger alone or anger mixed with happiness because of their potential to disrupt interaction.

High levels of happiness tinged with traces of sadness produce emotions like nostalgia, yearning, and hopefulness, all of which can be used to promote solidarity. Nostalgia is oriented to positive relations of the past, and although it can be used to evaluate the present in negative terms, it nonetheless orients individuals to social bonds and groups. Yearning and hopefulness can have much the same outcome, as individuals orient themselves to positive social relations that they seek to have.

When sadness is the dominant emotion, activation of lesser levels of happiness, fear, and anger can produce many emotions that can potentially promote social solidarity or, at the least, bring breached relations back into focus and put interaction back on track. Moreover, sadness alerts others that a person is unhappy and disengaged, perhaps moving them to sanction positively this person. For example, when sadness is tinged with smaller amounts of happiness, emotions like moroseness and melancholy provide a low-key way to alert others in a situation to problems; and an emotion like acceptance channels disappointment into quiet commitments to the situation. When greater amounts of sadness are activated with lesser levels of fear, forlornness and misery alert others to problems, whereas emotions like regret and remorseful can signal apologies to others for transgressions. Disappointment with smaller amounts of anger produces an array of emotions that signal to others dissatisfaction and unhappiness without inviting counteranger or fear; indeed, emotions such as aggrieved, discontent, dissatisfied, unfulfilled, bored, sullenness, and grief can operate as low-key negative sanctions that avoid counteranger or fear, or they can signal to others that attention needs to be paid to the individual. Envy is perhaps the most disassociative emotion to arise out of sadness tinged with anger, but even here a person remains oriented to the group or other persons.

Thus, first-order elaborations move the emotional spectrum to more positive valences, which can promote social bonding. They also channel anger and fear into emotions that (1) signal a person's need to receive attention or positive sanctions, (2) mark lower-key negative sanctions that do not promote counteranger or excessive fear, and (3) promote cognizance of as well as commitments to moral codes. Selection thus took the expanded stock of primary emotions and created the neurological capacity to generate first-order combinations or elaborations that mitigated the negative effects of anger, fear, and sadness, while allowing these emotions to be converted into affective states that could promote social bonding among low-sociality animals. Without an understanding of humans' ape ancestry and the biological embeddedness that this implies, we might not appreciate why and how our ancestors' neurology was reworked to expand human emotional capacities. Indeed, sociologists rarely ask: Why are humans so emotional? It is simply assumed, but when we bring biology into the picture, we can begin to answer this question. Humans are emotional because this was the only way that hominids could become more social, and it was and still is the principal mechanism by which individuals become willing to sustain the focus and flow of encounters, while developing commitments to the culture and structure of corporate and categoric units and the macrolevel institutional systems built from these mesolevel structures.

Second-Order Emotions

Although speculative, I believe that selection went a step further and combined the three negatively valenced emotions—anger, fear, and sadness—into emotions that would actively promote social solidarity. Two critical emotions—shame and guilt—are essential to viable social structures. Some have argued that guilt is simply more extreme shame, but I disagree because the affect aroused in these two emotions is very different to an individual, and to those responding to this individual (Scheff 1990; Lewis 1971). Shame is an emotion that individuals experience when they have behaved incompetently in the eyes of others or in reference to normative expectations. Guilt is an experience of having violated moral codes. These are two of the most powerful emotions that humans can experience, and they operate to promote social bonding. When individuals experience shame, whether from self-appraisal or negative sanctions from others, they are motivated to behave more competently in the eyes of others and with reference to normative expectations. Shame is thus an emotion that pulls people to groups and that prompts them to make amends and to do better. It is essential, therefore, to sustain commitments of a low-sociality animal who, at its core, is still an ape.

Similarly, guilt motivates individuals to try harder to meet the expectations contained in values, beliefs, ideologies, and other moral standards of encounters and the more inclusive sociocultural systems in which encounters are embedded. When an individual experiences guilt, whether by self-appraisal of his or her actions in reference to moral codes or by sanctions pointing out the transgression to the person, the experience drives the individual to recommit to moral codes in ways that promote solidarity and continuity.

Without shame and guilt, sanctioning by others would have to carry the entire burden of sustaining group commitments and of social control. But, with shame and guilt, emotions are mobilized that make individuals sanction themselves. Moreover, even when others are not present, such self-sanctioning pushes individuals to behave competently, appropriately, and morally. In this manner, the burden of constant monitoring is shifted from others to the individual, providing a constant internal self-monitoring of activity. Guilt and shame allow persons to be individualistic and, hence, true to their ape ancestry, but it also provides an emotional gyroscope that pulls them into commitments to others, norms, and moral codes.

The speculative part of my argument is that shame and guilt are com-

Table 4.4.   The Structure of Shame and Guilt

RANK ORDER OF PRIMARY EMOTIONS	SECOND-ORDER EMOTIONS	
	Shame	*Guilt*
1	Disappointment-sadness (at self)	Disappointment-sadness (at self)
2	Assertion-anger (at self)	Aversion-fear (about consequences to self)
3	Aversion-fear (about consequences to self)	Assertion-anger (at self)

SOURCE: Data from Turner 1999a, 1999b.

posed predominately of sadness, activated with varying amounts of fear and anger. Table 4.4 outlines what I believe occurs when individuals experience shame and guilt. The dominant emotion is sadness, but the respective levels of fear and anger varying for each emotion. Shame is mostly sadness at self, coupled in order of salience, anger at self and fear about the consequences of actions to self. Guilt is also mostly sadness at self, but the order of anger and shame is reversed, with fear about the consequences to self having higher salience than anger at self. This shifting of the order of fear and anger produces, I think, very different emotions. One (guilt) is oriented to moral codes; the other (shame) is directed to competent performance in accordance with expectations from others and norms. The more moral content in cultural codes, the more likely is guilt to dominate over shame; and conversely, the less moral content, the more shame will be produced relative to guilt. Of course, one can behave both incompetently and immorally, thereby activating both shame and guilt.

My belief is that selection first produced cortical control over emotional outburst, then expanded variants of primary emotions; as these promoted group solidarity and fitness, the neurology of hominids was further rewired to generate first-order elaborations of primary emotions. Then, as enhanced and flexible social bonding using this expanded repertoire promoted fitness, the brain was again rewired to generate second-order emotions like shame and guilt. We can see, to some extent, the footprint of this rewiring. For an expanded emotional repertoire to exist, subcortical areas must grow, as is outlined in Table 4.1, but for guilt and shame to be effective, considerable re-wiring of subcortical and neocortical systems must occur. Moral codes and expectations must be held cognitively, but laced with emotions produced subcortically outside of consciousness. This occurs primarily through the pre-frontal cortex that, some argue, apes do not have, but the important point is that considerable wiring to connect neocortical and subcortical emotional systems has occurred in humans, primarily through connections running through the amygdala and the prefrontal cortex. Indeed, individuals with damage to the prefrontal cortex cannot read emotions in others (Damasio 1994, 1997), and so selection restructured the hominid brain for second-order emotions, and perhaps some first-order emotions such as pride where con-ceptions of self stored in the frontal cortex are integrated with emotions and with reference to others, norms, and moral codes.

Emotional Language

As I emphasized in the last chapter, the association cortices appear to be the neurological substrate for language. These emerged in the transition to vi-sual dominance among monkeys and apes. Monkeys cannot learn human language, as far as is known, but apes can. Thus, not only must association cortices exist, but also the neocortex must pass some threshold in size and complexity to generate the capacity for language. Apes do not use human languages in the wild, but they can learn language in much the same ways as young adults; at maturity, bonobo and common chimpanzees can "speak" via the visual sense modality at about the level of a three-year-old child (Savage-Rumbaugh et al. 1993; Savage-Rumbaugh, Rumbaugh, and Mc-Donald 1985). If emotions were the key to increasing sociality and bonding among apelike hominids, then it is likely that the association cortices mak-ing language possible were used to structure emotions. The fact that chim-panzees can communicate through face and body rather complex instru-mental intentions (such as coordinating a trap for catching young monkeys to eat) indicates that a vocabulary of visual signs could already have been in use among the ape ancestors of humans, thereby giving natural selection a capacity to enhance. These signals are so subtle that researchers cannot read them (Menzel 1971), demonstrating that the ape ancestors of hominids may have already possessed a high level of acuity in using visual vocabularies and, perhaps, even syntax. If such were the case the burden on natural selection to create emotional language would be considerably less since there was an in-place system on which to select.

Young children can recognize emotions at a young age, suggesting that humans are hard-wired to learn and use them. I would argue that, much like spoken language, there is a window of opportunity to learn emotional languages, probably from birth to ten or twelve years of age. After this point, I would hypothesize that it becomes ever more difficult to learn emotional languages. Feral children, for example, often have trouble with spoken language, but I suspect that the real difficulty is in their inability to read emotional languages on which spoken language, at the neurological level, is piggy-backed. Autistic children too have trouble reading emotions in others; and this tells that they have reduced facility with emotional languages, and by extension, often with spoken language as well. There is, I believe, a whole new area of study in emotions: understanding the configurations and sequences of gestures, particularly of the face, that signal various emotional states. Naturally, context and culture determine that gestures signal emotional states, but for first- and second-order emotions, there is a syntax consisting of both sequences and configurations of body responses. Research by Ekman and various collaborators on primary emotions needs to be extended to variants and elaborations of primary emotions; rather than search for universal signals of emotions, research should also concentrate on how culture and context shape the structure of the language.[3] After all, spoken language varies from society to society, and there is no reason to think that emotional languages are any different, although they may have a more hard-wired embedding in the brain than spoken language, which, I believe, evolved millions of years after the emergence of the first emotional languages. In fact, the high degree of variability in spoken language may reflect the lack of hard-wired bases beyond the neurology of making individuals receptive to learning a language, whereas the existence of what arguably appear to be universal syntaxes for at least primary emotions and perhaps some elaborations suggests that the hard-wiring for emotional languages is more embedded than auditory language in the neurology of the brain.[4]

[3] See Ekman 1992a, 1992b, 1992c, 1984, 1982, 1973a, 1973b; Ekman and Friesen 1975; Ekman, Friesen, and Ellsworth 1972.

[4] Noam Chomsky (1980, 1965) might dispute this line of argument. It may be that the auditory language is equally hard-wired, but my sense is that there is more cultural variability in auditory language when compared to emotional languages.

As spoken language was built on the neurological wiring for visually based emotional language, the auditory channel also became increasingly a medium to communicate emotions. After all, it had been the uncontrolled auditory expression of emotions that came under heavy selection to control loud emotional outbursts in more open-country conditions among early hominids; it is likely that this control would be used to modulate emotional states under neocortical control along the auditory sense modality. Thus, in addition to emotional languages along the visual channel, there are elements of emotional language emerging in speech. Recent efforts to understand how frequency of sounds is influenced by social interaction and vice versa indicate that there are clear back channels of auditory emissions that communicate emotions above and beyond the spoken words (Gregory 1999, 1994). Of course, all humans understand the importance of inflection and modulation to communicating the more emotional content of spoken words. It may be, then, that there are also phonemes and syntax for these auditory modulations; this too would be an interesting area for research.

Humans also have a highly developed, although underutilized, sense of touch. This acuity of haptic responses is the result of selection on apes in arboreal habitats, and it is what makes humans able to perform rather fine-grained manipulations with their hands and fingers. Touch is often used to communicate affective states, from the ritual handshake or its equivalent through the pat on the back to the caress of the face. Is there a syntax to these gestures? Is there some kind of metalanguage that structures the relations among emotional signals via the visual, auditory, and tactile sense modalities? I suspect that there is, and this too needs to be researched further.

My goal in this chapter is not to lay out a general theory or even a description of emotional language, but we can make some fairly obvious generalizations. The more two or more individuals employ the same emotional syntax, the greater will be their ability to role take at an emotional level; and the more these individuals can assume the emotional perspective of the other, the more likely are these individuals to achieve a sense of intersubjectivity and to play complementary roles. The more individuals use multiple sense modalities—visual, auditory, and haptic—in self-presentations and in role

---

What is clear, however, is that for both auditory and visually based emotional languages, there is a window of neurological opportunity to learn them; and if they are not learned by early adolescence, normal speech and visual gesturing are not possible.

taking, the greater will be the sense of intersubjectivity and intimacy. Visually based, emotional language will communicate more than either auditory or haptic signals that carry emotions. The more interaction is instrumental, the greater will be reliance on the auditory channel. Conversely, the more an interaction is emotional, the greater will be the reliance on the visual and haptic sense modalities.

In any encounter the force of emotions can always be found, even in highly instrumental interaction where emotions operate as a back channel for auditory gestures. Moreover, this emotional syntax is what binds individuals to each other and keeps them focused on others in an interaction. Even when individuals are being highly calculative and rational, interacting only with others because of perceived extrinsic rewards, emotions bind them, in two ways. One is a back channel of affect that inevitably seeps out. Another is neurology of calculating utilities, which depends on the ability to attach emotional valences to alternatives (Damasio 1994; Collins 1993); thus, the most "cold-hearted" calculation is, in reality, a highly emotional experience. And even when individuals seek to manipulate others with expressive control of emotions, whether holding them in or cynically being disingenuous, emotional languages are in play. When one holds back, this control of expressive behavior is done in a particular configuration and sequence; or when people signal emotions that they do not subjectively feel, this kind of acting is effective because there is a syntax to the gestures emitted that others understand, even though they are being manipulated. Manipulation is only possible because there is a syntax to emotions, and so, syntax is the stuff of deceit and lying. In fact, without this syntax, deceit and lying would be much more difficult since individuals would have to invent a new emotional syntax in each and every cynical interaction. The same would be true for normal interaction; so it is not hard to visualize why selection would wire the brain to be receptive to syntactical emotional structures.

Emotional Dynamics

As we will see, many of the dynamics of emotions in encounters unfold in response to other forces driving encounters—transactional needs, roles, symbols, status, and demography/ecology. Moreover, encounters are always embedded in categoric and corporate units that constrain emotions directly and that also exert indirect influences on emotions through their effects on other

forces—needs, symbols, roles, status, and demography/ecology—driving encounters. We cannot, therefore, explore all emotional dynamics at this stage,
but it is possible to provide some of the core processes that unfold as other
forces drive encounters.

There are, I believe, two critical dimensions of any interaction that constrain and circumscribe the valence and amplitude of emotions (J. Turner
1999b): (1) sanctions and (2) expectations. In all interactions, signaling and
interpreting involve sanctioning. Such sanctions can be either (a) positive
and reinforcing or (b) negative and punitive. Sanctions are used to assure
that individuals do what they are supposed to do, as established by others'
needs, by positions and roles, by cultural norms and moral codes, and by the
demography and ecology of a situation. Sanctions can be either deliberate or
unconscious; all that is essential is for them to be read and interpreted by
others. In each and every interaction, individuals also come with, or soon
develop, expectations about what will transpire; these can be consciously articulated but more often they are implicit. Like sanctions, expectations are
determined by the transactional needs of individuals, cultural norms and
moral codes, positions and roles, and demography/ecology.

Sanctions and expectations are very much constrained by embeddedness
of encounters in categoric and corporate units. When categories are unambiguous, individuals understand the characteristics of members in each category. On the basis of this understanding, people can adjust their expectations and sanctioning activities. Similarly, when corporate units reveal a clear
division of labor, the norms, positions, and roles of individuals are clear; individuals can generally develop realistic expectations and understand sanctioning processes. Thus, embeddedness reduces emotional arousal when categoric and corporate units delimit and specify expectations and sanctions.

SANCTIONING

When individuals mutually present themselves and role take, their respective
gestures operate as sanctions, either reinforcing or questioning each others'
responses. Sanctions could not exist without emotions because, unless a positive sanction arouses variants and elaborations of happiness or unless a negative sanction arouses variants and elaborations of fear, anger, and sadness,
the sanctions have no "teeth" to move an individual. Most sanctions are is-
sued implicitly; it is comparatively rare for people to consciously and deliberately send a positive or negative sanction. Moreover, the reading of sanc-

tions in the gestures of others is both unconscious and conscious. It is now clear that humans possess an unconscious emotional memory system that stores in subcortical regions of the brain (most likely, the hippocampus) emotional reactions to particular stimuli (LeDoux 1996, 1993a, 1993b, 1991, 1987). Thus, individuals often respond to the sanctions of others without conscious recognition of their own responses. Indeed, a person may only become aware of their reaction by role taking with others who can readily observe and react to the activation of subconscious emotional memories. Interaction is, thereby, layered in complex ways. Sanctions can be sent either consciously or unconsciously; they can be received and responded to both consciously and unconsciously; and they can only become clear to an individual during second rounds of role taking in which the first round of mutual gesturing elicits unconscious responses that only become known to an individual through the subsequent reactions of others.

In the distant past, millions of years ago, the big problem for natural selection, if I can anthropomorphize a neutral process, was how to overcome the neurological fact that three primary emotions—fear, anger, and sadness —are negatively valenced and, hence, the motivation for as well as the outcome of negative sanctioning. Negative sanctions alone cannot hold individuals together unless they have innate bioprogrammers pushing them to herd or to form groups. For these reasons selection grabbed emotional areas of the brain such as the amygdala and literally attached layers of cells activating happiness and pleasure, or expanded neocortical areas like the cingulate gyrus that already had layers of cells devoted to bonding and pleasure. Without a high ratio of positive to negative sanctions, solidarity is not possible. Negative sanctions are extremely costly for both the individual sending and the individual receiving them. To use negative sanctions invites negative emotional responses—counteranger, fear and withdrawal, and sadness or further withdrawal by those on the receiving end of these sanctions. Negative sanctioning can also initiate countersanctioning by those receiving negative messages in a cycle that can ratchet up the flow of negative emotions. In contrast, positive sanctions generate variants and elaborations of happiness, particularly pride, which cause those receiving a positive sanction to give back signs of happiness and pleasure that operate as positive sanctions for those who originally emitted positive sanctions. This cycle can ratchet up the level of positive affect, although marginal utility or satiation and fatigue can set limits on how far the emotional "highs" can go. But neurologically, the core mammalian brain is not set up for high levels of positive sanctioning, and so it is not surprising that human limbic systems look jury-rigged for happiness. One implication of this set of evolutionary events is that just below the surface of any interaction is the implicit fear that negative sanctions will be invoked, leading to disassociative outcomes. Humans are extremely alert to visual, auditory, and tactile signs of anger, fear, and sadness; the reason for this, I believe, is that our most primal subcortical wiring is for fear and anger, with additional wiring for happiness beyond mother-infant bonding and sexual encounters being a later evolutionary add-on.

Yet, to sustain solidarity, most sanctions must be positive; and negative sanctions must be mitigated. Second-order emotions like guilt and shame help reduce the power of negative sanctions to disrupt social relations by shifting the burden of sanctioning from others to self, while at the same time motivating individuals to try harder to behave competently and to uphold moral codes. Various first-order elaborations of primary emotions can make the arousal of negative emotions less severe to both those sending and receiving negative sanctions. I would offer another further speculation along these lines. Negative sanctions can be directed in reference to either *pre*scriptive or *pro*scriptive norms and moral codes; and among the hunting-and-gathering bands in which hominids evolved, most moral codes were prescriptive, indicating what people should do. Proscriptive moral codes specifying what individuals cannot or must not do, along with the more severe negative sanctions that their violation invites, are more typical of complex social structures of settled populations where morality gets codified in both law and various ideologies (religious, economic, political). Violations of prohibitions generally invite more severe negative sanctions than prescriptive expectations for what one should do; and so, if this speculation is correct, the dominance of prescriptive codes reduced the consequences of negative sanctioning among bands of hominids because sanctions were not emitted in reference to prohibitions contained in the moral order, but rather to transgressions of what is expected. In fact, for any encounter, most norms and moral codes are still prescriptive, with proscriptive codes usually constituting a background morality emphasizing the inappropriateness of failing to use tact and etiquette or to sustain emotional control.

Attribution processes are always a part of sanctioning. If individuals blame themselves for receiving negative sanctions, they will experience variants and first-order elaborations among fear, anger, and sadness. If the sanctions are severe, individuals will experience shame or guilt, depending on whether the transgression is behavioral incompetence with respect to expectations or a failure to abide by moral codes. If the internal states of others or categories of others are blamed, then anger toward the others and categoric units will increase; the more these others have engaged in active sanctioning, the greater will be the anger emitted by an individual. If the structure or culture of the mesolevel corporate unit within which interpersonal sanctioning occurs is seen as the cause of behaviors that brought sanctions, then an individual will experience generalized and diffuse anger toward this unit and the more in-clusive institutional sphere in which this unit is embedded. However, this anger will be less intense than the anger aroused when specific others in the encounter are seen as the cause of sanctioning or when representatives of cat-egoric units are seen as the cause.

Attribution processes also operate in more positive sanctioning. When an individual sees him- or herself as the stimulus and cause of positive sanc-tioning by others, variants and first-order elaborations of happiness will be experienced; if the individual had been somewhat fearful of his or her ability to perform adequately or meet expectations, he or she will experience pride when receiving positive sanctions. When individuals experience pride, they are likely to emit positive sanctions toward others in a cycle that ends with fatigue, satiation, or termination of the encounter. If others or members of categoric units are seen by an individual as the cause of positive sanctions, then the individual will develop positive but lower-key sentiments toward these others or categoric units and, as a result, be more committed to inter-action with them. If the structure and culture of the corporate unit within which an encounter is embedded are seen by a person as the source of posi-tive sanctions, then this individual will develop lower-key positive senti-ments toward, and commitments to, this unit and the broader institutional sphere within which this mesounit is embedded.

Sanctioning is thus a key to the emotional responses of individuals in en-counters and to their feelings about the meso- and macrostructures in which encounters are embedded. Attribution is one of the important mechanisms mediating the effects of sanctions. As we will see, attributions and emotional outcomes are also influenced by other forces operating in encounters—that is, transactional needs, roles, culture, status, and demography/ecology.

EXPECTATIONS

For any encounter, each participant enters with expectations along many di-mensions, and during the course of interaction, these can change. But, the key dynamic is expectations, per se, because when they are met, individuals experience at least satisfaction and variants of low-intensity happiness; and if they are exceeded, they experience higher levels of happiness and first-order elaborations such as pride. Conversely, when expectations are not realized, individuals experience more negative emotions such as anger, fear, and sadness. The most common emotional reaction to unfulfilled expectations is variants and first-order combinations of anger.

Many studies document this relationship between expectations and emotions. For example, B. F. Skinner observed that pigeons appeared angry when they did not get the food following their conditioned responses. George Homans (1961) elaborated this idea into a "law of distributive justice," arguing that individuals become angry when their investments, relative to those of others, are not proportionately rewarded. Homans (1974) later converted this to an "aggression-approval proposition," with actors giving off approving responses to rewards that were proportionate to costs and higher-intensity happiness for rewards exceeding expectations. On the negative side, individuals became angry when not receiving rewards proportionate to costs and investments. Within the expectation-states literature proper, negative emotions are consistently found to escalate when individuals do not honor the expectations associated with the distribution of status (Ridgeway 1982; Berger 1988; Ridgeway and Johnson 1990). Among symbolic interactionist theories, the affect control approach (Heise 1989, 1979; Smith-Lovin and Heise 1988; Smith-Lovin 1990) emphasizes the arousal of emotions when there is deflection between fundamental sentiments (the expectation) and transient sentiments (the actual experience). In power-status models of emotion (Kemper and Collins 1990), the activation of negative or positive emotions is related to whether anticipated confirmations of relative status or power have been realized.

Thus, there is a clear relationship revolving around the degree of congruity (or incongruity) between expectations and experience. If there is an incongruity between what people expect from others and if the reactions of these others keep individuals from meeting these expectations, negative emotions are aroused; if there is congruity or if others' reactions allow individuals to sense that they have exceeded their expectations, ever more positive emotions are generated. When the number of expectations increases for a person in a situation, it becomes likely that some will not be met, producing variants of anger, but the more all expectations are fulfilled, the greater will be the level of satisfaction-happiness. The more salient expectations in a situation and the higher their intensity, and the less these are met, the more likely will high-intensity variants of anger be generated. Conversely, the more these highly salient expectations are met or exceeded, the greater will be the level of happiness experienced.

As with sanctions, attributions are critical to the flow of emotions arising out of expectations. When individuals attribute the failure to realize expectations to themselves, they experience shame and other variants of sadness; when the failure to meet expectations includes moral content, they experience guilt. When, by contrast, people attribute the success in meeting expectations to themselves and their actions, they experience variants of satisfaction-happiness; and the more their expectations are exceeded, the more intense will be the sense of pride and happiness. If, however, individuals attribute the failure to have experiences correspond to expectations of others, or categories of others, they will feel anger toward these others or to members of the categoric unit that is blamed for the incongruity; and they will develop prejudices toward members of this categoric unit. Conversely, if individuals attribute the congruity between expectations and experience to the motivations and actions of others or to categories of others, they will feel low-level positive emotions toward these others and members of categoric units. If experiences exceed expectations and this occurrence is attributed to others and/or categories of others, individuals will display more intense forms of happiness and will be more committed to relations with these others and mesolevel categoric units. When individuals attribute incongruities to the culture and structure of the corporate units in which an encounter is embedded, they will experience at least disapproval for the corporate unit and, by extension, to the institutional system in which this corporate unit is embedded; the greater the incongruity and attribution, the more intense will variants of anger toward the corporate unit and institutional system become, and the lower will be both individuals' commitment to the culture of these units and their willingness to play roles in these units. When the process works the other way, and the experience of congruity or the experience of exceeding expectations is attributed to the culture and structure of corporate units, individuals will reveal ever-higher levels of happiness and commitment to the corporate unit and the institutional systems in which this unit is embedded, and the greater will be individuals' commitment to the culture of these structures, and the greater will be their willingness to play roles in the corporate unit.

Sanctions and expectations are, then, the mechanisms by which emotions are aroused in encounters. Depending on the attributions about the cause of either negative or positive sanctions or about the level of congruity between expectations and experience, the emotional valences and the flow of interaction will vary, as will the commitments to more inclusive meso- and macro-structures. I have yet to say much about the sources of expectations, or the dimensions along which they vary, but, as we will see, other forces of the encounter—transactional needs, status, roles, culture, and demography—generate varying types of expectations. Moreover, expectations are very much influenced by the embeddedness of encounters in mesostructures. When an encounter is embedded in either a categoric or corporate unit, and the characteristics of members in categories and the structure and culture of the corporate unit are clear, individuals are more likely to adjust their expectations and responses in a realistic direction. As a result, they are more likely to avoid negative sanctions and, in most cases, receive positive sanctions. Thus, interaction with the "boss" (a categoric unit) within a business (a corporate unit) will lead people to develop realistic but different expectations than those for interaction with a wife in a family. Similarly, the sanctions themselves are constrained by categoric and corporate units. For example, a child will be sanctioned differently than an adult, or the sanctions employed in a group will be somewhat different than those in a bureaucracy. Because of the embeddedness, these varying expectations and sanctioning procedures are more likely to be clearly understood by all parties in the encounter.

Defense Mechanism

As natural selection gave hominids the ability to control emotional outbursts, one emergent capacity was the use of defense mechanisms to mitigate the effects of negative sanctions and failures to realize expectations. Individuals will always seek to protect themselves from unpleasant emotions; and the processes involved can be conscious but more typically they are unconscious. Of course, if negative sanctions and failures to meet expectations did not arouse emotions, humans would all be sociopaths; and as a result, the social order would not be possible. Thus, when individuals attempt to protect themselves from pain, this is simply a by-product of being emotionally committed to others and social structures. Indeed, the activation of defense mechanisms occurs not only because individuals are trying to protect self but also because they are trying to maintain social ties and some level of commitment to encounters and the structures in which they are embedded. Just how this kind of defensive regime works is, of course, still a great mystery, even after a century of psychoanalytic and medical research. But, despite the complexity to models of interaction that the analysis of defense mechanisms brings, Freud's (1900) insights into these dynamics should not be ignored. The psychoanalytic tradition thus has much to add to microsociological theory.

If individuals hide their emotions from themselves and/or others, push emotions below the level of consciousness, project their emotions onto others or categories of others, displace negative emotions onto others and categories of others, and engage in other defensive reactions, then the flow of an encounter is affected. How, then, do we get a handle on this new complexity? We cannot ignore defensive actions, as many sociological theories do, because they are so much a part of how individuals respond to each other, but how do we go beyond clinical analysis and incorporate the dynamics of defense mechanisms into a theory of the encounter?

I offer no blazing new insights, but simply some theoretical leads. People can become defensive to negative responses from others or from their own internal dialogue and self-criticism, but the key to activating defense mechanisms is a threat to self. Individuals carry conceptions and emotional dispositions about themselves as object (that is, self-conceptions and identity), and they will act to defend these because incongruity between self-conception(s) and the emotion(s) attached to self is highly unsettling. Self is a person's internal gyroscope, and to experience negative emotions toward self is painful. Thus, it is not surprising that people seek to protect themselves, again through mechanisms that are not fully understood. Still, even when self is not highly salient, people respond defensively when expectations are not met, negative sanctions are perceived, or both. The salience of self in an interaction thus intensifies the emotional reactions, hence the likelihood that defense mechanisms will be activated. Any failure to meet expectations or any experience of negative sanctioning will increase the possibility that defense mechanisms will be used. Moreover, when expectations are not met or negative sanctions are perceived, self becomes more salient and, as a consequence, the activation of defense mechanisms becomes more probable.

What are some key defense mechanisms? Repression is perhaps the most central because it is often necessary to repress negative feelings before other defense mechanisms can be activated. Often, attributions can be used as a defense mechanism because individuals can blame others for their own inadequacies, seeing the internal states and behaviors of these others or categories of others as the cause of negative sanctions or failures to meet expectations. A related defense mechanism is projection, in which a person's emotions are imputed to others, or categories of others, rather than to self; in fact, external attributions can be viewed as a kind of projection. Finally, there is displacement where emotions about self or a set of others are directed at another person or set of others. In general, defensive attribution, projection, and displacement are counterproductive to the smooth flow of an interaction because others will respond negatively to these defensive efforts of a person, giving back negative sanctions that can only force the individual to be even more defensive. Repression also tends to be counterproductive because as individuals repress, the emotions build up and eventually come out in highly amplified form and, typically, in a negative form (extreme anger, high anxiety, and severe sadness). When this occurs, an interaction is breached, and the individual experiences intensified shame and guilt that lead to more efforts at repression that will, in turn, cause an emotional explosion at inappropriate times in the future. A biography filled with such outbursts drains individuals, reducing their modal level of emotional animation except for sudden outbursts of emotion. The goal of most clinical therapy is, of course, to get individuals to see and revisit negative emotions that have been repressed, and at times, such self-talk can be effective in enabling people to remain attuned to the responses of others and of self before pushing them below consciousness, or engaging in attributions, projections, or displacements that only invite negative sanctions from others. Indeed, if individuals are successful in overcoming their pain, they will typically experience pride that can work to tear down the defensive regime. Yet, self-talk itself can become another form of defense when individuals talk around their problems without ever getting at their root causes.

When particular defense mechanisms are chronically used by individuals and reduce the intensity of negative emotions displayed toward others, they become part of the expectations that others have for a person, especially in iterated encounters. These expectations often involve the imputation of a "personality" on the basis of the emotions habitually emitted by a person; indeed, what others see as "personality" is very much the result of the particular way an individual expresses emotions, whether directly or indirectly through the filter of defense mechanisms. For example, if a person reveals a constant although low level of diffuse anger, others will portray this anger as a personality characteristic of the person; if the anger is directed at categories of others, this person will be seen as having prejudices that are to be avoided when interacting with this individual. Similarly, if a person is persistently sad, others will typify the person as morose or in some other terms, seeing this chronic condition as part of the individual's personality and responding in accordance with this attribution. If a person is perceived to be typically anxious or fearful, they will be seen as "nervous" and treated as such by others. And ironically, as others' expectations are confirmed by chronic anger, sadness, or fear from a person, these others will offer more positive sanctions since their expectations are being met, thereby enabling the person to sustain this behavior without further needs to impose a defensive regime. If, however, these relatively low-key and chronic emotions are spiked by sudden anger, anxiety, or deep sadness, then expectations of others are violated, and they will negatively sanction the individual, if only by withdrawal. When this occurs, the person will increase the use of defense mechanisms. As a consequence, individuals who are viewed as emotionally unpredictable will always create tension and strain in an encounter, and in general, people will seek to avoid interaction with them or, if they cannot avoid interaction, to keep it highly ritualized and brief.

Defense mechanisms, when used to respond to minor sanctions and failures to meet expectations can, however, be functional for the flow of an encounter. If each and every real or imagined slight were subject to a counterresponse, interactions would be in a constant state of being breached, forcing individuals to engage in continual repair rituals. Thus, as long as the defensive regime of persons does not let powerful self-feelings drive a defensive regime, ignoring small slights and failures works to sustain the focus and flow of interaction. Such low-key defense is often what we mean by tact and etiquette. Yet, it is often small and seemingly insignificant events that arouse disproportionately spikes of emotions in chronically and highly defensive individuals, leading them to emit emotions toward others that only bring them shame and perhaps guilt for having violated moral codes about tact and etiquette.

Let me offer some tentative generalizations from the above discussion. To the degree that defensive mechanisms have been activated by individuals in response to negative emotions, and particularly so for shame and guilt, their modal level of emotional energy in an encounter will decrease. As a consequence, the flow of affect in the encounter will decline. Conversely, if defense mechanisms are not activated, these individuals will exhibit either anger, fear, or sadness. To the extent that individuals have a long biography of using defense mechanisms in all encounters, their modal level of affect will be low, but punctuated by episodes of high anger, high anxiety, and sudden depression. As a consequence of emotional outbursts, the encounter will be breached, and the individual will be negatively sanctioned, while generally failing to meet expectations—all of which increase shame and guilt that need to be repressed.

Others will typify such persons in terms of highly negative personality characteristics, such as "hothead," "nervous," "afraid of their own shadow," "morose," and "depressing"; others will avoid interaction with these unstable personalities or, if interaction is unavoidable, they will attempt to keep the interactions short and highly ritualized. To the extent that the biography of a person's activation of defense mechanisms allows for consistent expressive control of negative emotions so that chronic but low levels of anger, fear, and sadness are emitted, others will define the personality of the person in terms of these emotional states and interact with them accordingly. If a person continues to meet the expectations contained in this characterization of his or her personality, the person will receive at least moderately positive sanctions, and others will continue to interact with them in iterated encounters.

To the degree that individuals use attributions, projections, and displacements onto others and categories of others as a way to avoid negative self-feelings, these targeted others are likely to negatively sanction the individual and keep him or her from realizing expectations, thus inviting further inappropriate and mistargeted outbursts. Such individuals are likely to carry a diffuse level of anger, punctuated with high-intensity spikes of aggression, which makes others in encounters extremely wary of such a person, thereby limiting interaction to only what is required by the normative structure of the mesounits in which the encounter is embedded. If individuals bypass or repress their shame or guilt from these emotional outbursts, they will exhibit sadness and depression, coupled with diffuse anger punctuated by periodic expressions of high-intensity anger toward others, categories of others, and corporate units. As a result others will be even more reluctant to interact with such persons.

When defense mechanisms are used, attachments to mesostructures become problematic. Those who have projected or displaced their negative emotions onto categoric units and/or the structure and culture of corporate units will reveal lower levels of attachment to mesostructures and the larger institutional system built from these mesostructures. Thus, those with low levels of modal energy as a consequence of repression will fail to generate positive emotions toward corporate units, and if either repressed or otherwise defensive individuals exhibit outbursts of high-intensity anger or anxiety, they will be either angry at, or fearful about, categoric units and the culture and structure of corporate units. They will sever emotional attachments to the mesostructures in which the encounter is embedded, or if they cannot sever ties, they will play roles with distance and cynicism. Diffuse anger has much the same result because individuals will displace their anger to "safe" targets that cannot directly sanction back—that is, the culture and structure of corporate units or distinctions marking categoric units. Thus, diffusely angry individuals are likely to reveal prejudices and aggression toward mesostructures, while often being able to control their emotions in specific encounters toward others who could give back negative sanctions or impede realization of expectations. Still, these individuals will almost always have experiences where "they lose it" and incur negative emotions from others and from self-criticism that they must then "control" through heightened use of defense mechanisms. Diffuse anxiety has much the same effect, but to a lesser degree. Chronically anxious individuals will generally be fearful of corporate and categoric units, but they will often be able to control their anxiety with others in focused encounters, at least most of the time. They can often be quite successful with those they "know," but have great difficulty in controlling anxiety in new kinds of encounters with previously unknown individuals.

These generalizations are only tentative, and perhaps they always will be. So much about defense mechanisms is tied to the unique biography of a person and the particular features of an encounter that it is difficult to make determinative statements of how they influence all encounters. My goal, therefore, is to alert sociologists to the fact they cannot ignore these defensive processes, but it may not be possible to develop firm laws about their operation in encounters.

Conclusions

We are only at the beginning of developing a theory of embedded encounters, and as a result, generalizations can only be tentative. They will need to be modified as more of the dynamic forces shaping the flow of an interaction are introduced. For the present, let me close with a somewhat more formal list of provisional propositions that we can carry forth as the theory unfolds.[5]

I. Emotional syntax increases the capacity of humans to communicate meanings and to achieve a sense of intersubjectivity; the more individuals understand and use a common syntax, the greater will be their ability to role take with each other.

[5] See Turner (1999a) for a more complete statement of these dynamics.

A. The more an encounter is embedded in categoric units, and the more discrete and differentially evaluated these units, the more likely are individuals to understand the appropriate forms of communication with members of these categoric units; and hence, the more likely are appropriate forms of emotional syntax to be employed.

B. The more an encounter is embedded in a corporate unit, and the more explicit are the division of labor and normative expectations, the more likely are individuals to understand relevant forms of communication; and hence, the more likely are appropriate forms of emotional syntax to be employed.

II. Emotional syntax is best communicated via the visual sense modality, followed by intonations and inflections of auditory signals and haptic senses. Thus:

A. The more individuals can see each other, the more likely are they to achieve intersubjectivity through mutual role taking.

B. The more visual contact is supplemented by auditory and haptic signals, the greater will be the sense of intersubjectivity through mutual role taking.

III. The level of emotional syntax displayed by individuals is related to the level of sanctioning and to the degree of congruity between expectations and experiences.

A. The more individuals receive positive sanctions and the more expectations are met or exceeded, or both, the greater will be variants and elaborations of satisfaction-happiness.

1. The more an encounter is embedded in categoric units, and the more discrete and differentially evaluated these units, the more likely are individuals to understand the characteristics of members of these units; and hence, the more likely are they to develop realistic expectations vis-à-vis these members and, thereby, receive positive sanctions.

2. The more an encounter is embedded in a corporate unit, and the more explicit the division of labor, the more likely are individuals to understand the normative expectations on them; and hence, the more likely are they to develop realistic expectations vis-à-vis others and, thereby, receive positive sanctions.

B. The more individuals receive negative sanctions and the less expectations are met, or both, the greater will be variants and elaborations of assertion-anger, aversion-fear, and disappointment-sadness.

IV. Attribution processes influence the emotions experienced and displayed by individuals.

A. The more individuals attribute the receipt of positive sanctions and the meeting or exceeding of expectations, or both, to their own behaviors, the greater will be their sense of satisfaction-happiness; and if self is highly salient, the greater will be their sense of pride if they had some fear about meeting expectations or receiving positive sanctions. Conversely, the more individuals attribute the receipt of negative sanctions and the failure to meet expectations, or both, to their own behaviors, the greater will be their sense of disappointment-sadness. When self is highly salient and when anger at self and fear about the consequences to self emerge to supplement sadness, the greater is the likelihood that individuals will experience shame for incompetence and/or guilt for violating moral codes.

B. The more individuals attribute the receipt of positive sanctions and the meeting or exceeding of expectations, or both, to the actions of others or categories of others, the greater will be their use of positive sanctions and the more likely will they develop commitments toward these others and the categoric units in which the encounter is embedded. Conversely, the more individuals attribute the receipt of negative sanctions or the failure to meet expectations, or both, to the actions of others or categories of others, the greater will be their sense of anger toward others in encounters or toward categoric units in which the encounter is embedded, and the more likely will they develop prejudices toward members of the categoric units.

C. The more individuals attribute the receipt of positive sanctions and the meeting or exceeding of expectations, or both, to culture and structure of corporate units, the greater will be their positive sentiments and commitments to the culture and structure of these corporate units and the larger institutional structure within which these units are embedded and the more likely will they play roles enthusiastically. Conversely, the more individuals attribute the receipt of negative sanctions or the failure to meet expectations, or both, to the culture and structure of corporate units, the greater will be their anger toward the culture and structure of these units, and the less will be their commitments to these units and the encounters embedded in these units, the more role distance and cynicism will they display in playing roles.

V. The arousal of negative emotions generally will invite the activation of defense mechanisms, and the more salient self is in an encounter, the greater is the likelihood that defense mechanisms will be mobilized.

A. The more individuals use repression of negative emotions, particularly anger and fear, the more likely will these emotions cumulate and periodically be released at high levels of intensity and at inappropriate times, thereby inviting negative sanctions from others and frustrations in meeting expectations that activate shame and/or guilt and that force further repression. As a consequence, others in the encounter will be likely to avoid those who exhibit such intense displays of emotions.

B. The more individuals' repression of negative emotions generates chronic, diffuse, and consistently low levels of anger, anxiety, or sadness, the more likely are these low levels of emotion to be characterized as a personality by others that guides the expectations of these others in iterated encounters. As a result, the more likely are such individuals to avoid negative sanctions from others, as long as the amplitude and intensity of the emotions do not suddenly escalate and initiate the processes outlined in V-A above.

C. The more individuals project, attribute, and displace their negative emotions onto others and/or categories of others, the more likely are these others to negatively sanction an individual, thereby forcing further counterproductive use of defense mechanisms, and the more likely are individuals to develop prejudices toward categoric units in which an encounter is embedded.

D. The more individuals project, attribute, and displace any of their negative emotions onto the culture and structure of corporate units, the less committed will they be to the culture and structure of these corporate units and the encounters embedded in them.

FIVE

Transactional Forces

Almost all early theorizing on interaction processes had a conception, if only implicitly, of human motivation. For George Herbert Mead (1934), humans seek to consummate impulses; for Sigmund Freud (1900), individuals try to reconcile id impulses with the reality of culture and social relations; for Alfred Schutz ([1932] 1967), actors have interests that they pursue in trying to achieve a sense of intersubjectivity; for Émile Durkheim ([1912] 1946), people need to feel implicated in groups and to represent their attachments to groups with totems and rituals. And so it would go for others writing in sociology's classic period.

In contemporary theorizing, additional motives have been presumed to drive human action. For example, people are seen as motivated to achieve a sense of trust and ontological security (Giddens 1984), to augment positive emotions and cultural capital (Collins 1988, 1975), to confirm or verify self (Burke 1991; McCall and Simmons 1978; Stryker 1980), to realize profits in exchanges (Homans 1974), to make roles (R. Turner 1962), to achieve a sense of a common reality (Garfinkel 1967), to present a face successfully (Goffman 1959), to experience pride and avoid shame (Scheff 1988), to achieve prestige and power (Blau 1964), and so on.

What all of these theories emphasize, albeit in somewhat different ways, is that humans have *need states* that they seek to fulfill. If these needs are not met, individuals experience negative emotions and, depending on the emotional reactions, will continue to seek fulfillment of need states, or, if they can, withdraw from the encounter. The emotional reactions to the failure to meet needs can become convoluted, however, through attribution processes and activation of other defense mechanisms, as was explored in Chapter 4, but this fact should not obscure the underlying needs that individuals try to satisfy in each and every interaction. How, then, do we get a handle on the most basic needs?

It is essential to answer this question in any theory of interpersonal behavior, because human action is driven by more than culture and social structure alone. A great deal of the "energy" of an interaction is directed toward realizing fundamental and universal *transactional needs*. True, much of the exact substance of what actors seek to accomplish in a situation is often defined by the situation itself and by the culture associated with an encounter, but there are needs that cut across all situations. These needs provide an undercurrent of energy as well as a general direction to interpersonal behavior. In this sense, they drive the flow of interaction more than other socially constructed needs or immediate contingencies of the interaction.

Thus, for an encounter to proceed smoothly and for individuals to experience gratification and positive emotions, certain needs must be met. What are these needs? My answer (J. Turner 2000b, 1988, 1987) is that, at the most fundamental level, there are five transactional needs: (1) to confirm and verify self; (2) to receive positive exchange payoffs; (3) to sense group inclusion; (4) to experience trust; and (5) to achieve facticity. This chapter is devoted to understanding the dynamic force of these needs in all encounters.

Needs to Confirm and Verify Self

LEVELS OF SELF

As Mead (1934) and other pragmatists like William James (1890) and Charles Horton Cooley (1902) emphasized, humans can see themselves as objects in a situation. Beyond this fundamental insight, however, considerable disagreement exists about the nature of *self* or *identity*. Whether conceived as self or identity, some argue that identities are situational and tied to a particular status and role, with the result that individuals are seen to have as many identities as the roles they play (Goffman 1959; McCall and Simmons 1978).[1]

---

[1] Georg Simmel was perhaps the first scholar to conceptualize self in this way, although the idea also resides in George Herbert Mead's concept of "self-image" and Charles Horton Cooley's notion of the "looking-glass self."

Transactional Needs

1. *Verification of Self.* Humans have emotionally valenced and generally implicit cognitions of themselves as certain kinds of persons deserving of particular responses from others. These emotionally valenced cognitions exist at three levels: (a) trans-situational core self feelings about who one is, (b) sub-identities about who one is in general classes or types of situations, and (c) role identities about who one is in a particular encounter. People seek to have all levels of self confirmed by the responses of others, although the salience of any one level can vary.

2. *Profitable Exchange Payoffs.* Humans assess all situations for the available resources and symbols, extrinsic and intrinsic, that can allow them to experience gratification or utility. These assessments implicitly calculate (a) the rewards potentially available, (b) less the costs (expenditures of energy and alternatives forgone), and (c) investments (accumulated costs and commitments) that are measured against (d) a standard of justice or fairness. People seek to gain some profit—rewards less costs and investments measured against a standard of justice—in all situations.

3. *Group Inclusion.* Humans examine all situations for signs from others of their inclusion in the ongoing flow of interaction. People seek to feel that they are part of interpersonal flow.

4. *Trust.* Humans assess all situations for signs that the responses of others are (a) predictable, that others are in (b) rhythmic synchronization, that others are (c) sincere, and that others are (d) respectful of self. People seek confirming responses from others along all of these dimensions.

5. *Facticity.* Humans assess all situations for signs indicating that (a) self and others are experiencing a common world, that (b) the situation is as it appears, and that (c) reality has, for the purposes of the encounter, an obdurate character.

When self is conceptualized as having multiple identities, these identities are typically seen as ordered into hierarchies of prominence and salience; and depending on the situation, individuals make some identities more relevant than others. Other theorists see self as both situational and transsituational, and in these theories, there is a view of (1) a "core self" consisting of conceptions about oneself as a person across all encounters, and (2) a set of "situational identities" or selves representing applications of the transsituational core self to particular settings.

Most theories view self as a cognitive construct, as a set of meanings about who and what one is in a situation or across situations; and most conceive of emotions as being activated as a reaction to whether or not self is confirmed or verified. There is an unfortunate separation of emotion and cognition in such theories, for as Antonio Damasio (1994) and others have clearly documented, cognitions cannot be retained as memories unless they are tagged with emotions from subcortical regions of the brain (see Figure 3.1 in Chapter 3). Thus, self is *always* emotional; one does not have a view of self without emotional valences. Another problem with present-day theories is that the emotional dimension of self is typically portrayed as a global self-esteem variable. True, individuals do evaluate themselves in terms of standards of worthiness, but the concept of self-esteem does not tease out the actual emotions involved. For example, a given level of self-esteem can be the result of variants of different primary emotions as well as combinations of these primary emotions, such as pride, shame, guilt. We need, I believe, to engage in more fine-grained analysis of the actual configurations of emotions that make up self rather than gloss over the complexity of self-evaluation processes with a vague concept like self-esteem. I will only go part of the way in teasing out the complexity of the emotional self in analyzing the emotional valences attached to varying cognitions that individuals have about themselves. Obviously, more work will need to be done to unpack the dynamics subsumed by the notion of self-esteem.

As outlined in Figure 5.1, I see self as operating at three levels: (1) *core self* or transsituational cognitions and feelings about who a person is; (2) *sub-identities* or cognitions and feelings about self in classes of situations generally associated with institutional domains (for example, family, work, citizenship, religion, education, and so on); and (3) *role identities* or cognitions and feelings about self in particular roles. Individuals have powerful needs to confirm all three levels of identity, but by far the most important is the core because this level of self activates the most intense emotions about oneself as a person and about how one should be treated by others. In general, the three levels of self are roughly consistent with each other, although considerable slippage can occur between core self and role identities. For example, individuals can conceive of themselves as highly competent persons, deserving of respectful responses from others, but freely admit that they are incompetent in a particular role. This inconsistency can be tolerated because

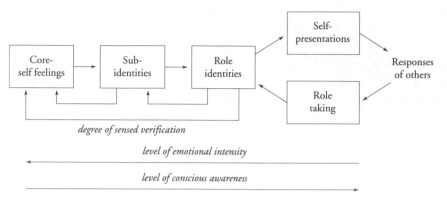

Figure 5.1.   The Structure of Self

the role identities have much lower salience; and this can even be true of roles in key institutional domains, such as the role of parent or worker. If this kind of slippage did not exist, individuals would endure a constant attack on their core-self feelings, and as a consequence, they would activate defense mechanisms to protect themselves in each and every situation. Just how much inconsistency between core self and role identities can be tolerated probably varies for different individuals, but as Peter Burke (1991) has emphasized, a tightly structured self in which all role identities are markers of core-self feelings makes it difficult to confirm self, whereas flexible role identities and low salience can be disconfirmed without necessarily posing a crisis of verification for core self. Sheldon Stryker (1980) has emphasized that when individuals get emotional in roles, this is a sign that a role identity or a subidentity is closely coupled with the deepest self-feelings about oneself as a person. And people who get highly emotional in all of their roles are likely to have too much of their core self invested in too many role identities. Thus, a certain amount of slippage and inconsistency between core self and more situational identities provides insulation against disconfirmation of core self, while potentially offering cognitive and emotional room for defensive strategies to protect the core.

The more core-self feelings are attached to subidentities and role identities being presented in an encounter, the greater will be the needs of individuals to confirm or verify these identities. The more these highly salient identities are confirmed by the responses of others in an encounter, the more likely are variants and elaborations of positive emotions to be experienced by individuals, whereas the less these identities are confirmed by others, the more likely are negative emotions—that is, variants and elaborations of fear, anger, and sadness—to be aroused, and the more likely are defense mechanisms to be activated. As Burke (1991) has emphasized, self is "a control system" in which an individual compares inputs from others against a standard or "comparator" imposed by an identity. When the responses of others are congruent with the comparator, self is verified. When the responses of others are not congruent with the comparator, self is not verified, and under these conditions, individuals experience distress or, in my terms, negative emotions revolving around variants and elaborations of fear, anger, and sadness. In Burke's theory, "distress" is highest when an identity is salient, when the elements of an identity are tightly organized, when individuals are committed to an identity, and when the inputs from others are significant to a person. As individuals experience incongruence, they adjust their outputs in an effort to secure responses from others that confirm the identity. For example, a person who sees him- or herself as highly competent but experiences inputs from others signaling a lack of competence will redouble efforts to demonstrate his or her competence in the eyes of others. Although I see this conception of identity as correct in its broad contours, my goal is to amplify this conception of self as a control system.[2]

VERIFICATION AND LEVELS OF SELF

The emotional reaction of a person to incongruence between presentations of self and the reactions of others varies with *which level* of self is not verified. Failure of a role identity will not cause great distress unless it is seen by a person to symbolize more powerful core feelings. Individuals will not be happy, of course, if a role identity is not confirmed, but neither will they be highly distressed. When subidentities are not confirmed, emotional reactions will increase above those for failure to confirm a role identity, but even here, unless this subidentity is attached to core feelings about oneself, the emotional reactions will not be great as would be the case when core feelings are being disconfirmed. For example, if a person is seen as a "bad worker" by

---

[2] Affect control theory (Heise 1979; Heise and Smith-Lovin 1981) argues much the same thing in the view that deflection (or incongruence) between "fundamental sentiments" and "transient sentiments" sets off efforts to eliminate the deflection, since with deflection, emotions are aroused.

others in a job (the role identity) but work in general (the subidentity) is not important to this person's core feelings, this individual will not feel highly distressed when role and subidentities revolving around adequate perform-ance in a job are questioned by others. In contrast, workaholics, who define their self-worth in terms of their jobs and their ability to work hard, will be devastated when others fail to verify these role- and subidentities in which core self is so salient.

Depending on which level of self is verified or not, then, the emotional re-actions to the responses of others will not only vary in intensity but also in type. On the positive side, when subidentities and role identities of low sa-lience are verified, the individual will experience the low-intensity variants of happiness, such as satisfaction (see Table 4.1 in Chapter 4). When a role- or subidentity that is closely coupled with a person's core self is verified (that is, of high salience), moderate to high levels of happiness will be experienced; and if the person had some fear that they might not do well in a situation, he or she will experience pride. On the negative side, failure to verify subiden-tities and role identities of low salience will generate low-intensity reactions of fear, anger, or sadness. The failure to verify a highly salient identity (that is, involving core self), however, will lead to moderate to high levels of fear, anger, or sadness. Just which of these negative emotions will be felt and ex-pressed varies with attributions and activation of defense mechanisms.

ATTRIBUTION PROCESSES

If attributions for verification of a low-salience identity are seen as the result of the actions of the individual, then the individual will experience low-intensity satisfaction. If a highly salient marker of core self is confirmed and perceived to be verified by virtue of the actions of the person, then moder-ate to high levels of happiness will be experienced; and if there was some fear about whether or not self would be verified, then the individual will experi-ence low-intensity pride. If verification occurs for a highly salient identity at-tached to the core self and if the person perceives his or her actions to have brought about verification, then moderate to high levels of happiness will be experienced. Moreover, if there was some fear about verification, the person will experience high-intensity pride.

If a person attributes verification of an identity to others or categories of others, positive sentiments toward these others or categoric units will be ex-pressed; and the more salient the identity (that is, involving core self), the greater will be the intensity of these sentiments. For example, a worker who realizes that verification of a role identity in a job is largely the result of help from others and who sees that these others are members of a categoric unit will develop positive sentiments toward these others and the categoric units to which they belong. Correspondingly, as people engage in external attributions, the positive emotions directed toward themselves will decline; and the more salient the self under conditions of external attribution, the larger will be the drop in the intensity of positive self-feelings. If the person was worried about whether self would be verified and attributes verification to actions of others or categories of others, pride about self will be diminished and emotions like gratitude toward others and categories of others will increase. For instance, students who attribute their good grades to the help of tutors or teaching assistants will experience and express gratitude to those who helped them and, as a result, will experience far less pride in their grades than would be the case if they saw grades as solely the result of their own hard work. If a person attributes the verification of self to the corporate unit in which an encounter is embedded, then positive sentiments toward this corporate unit and the institutional system in which it is embedded will be evident. The more salient is self in the encounter and the more this attribution continues over iterated encounters, the greater will be the positive feelings and the level of commitment to the corporate units and broader institutional system in which the encounter is embedded. For instance, a college professor who is able to realize conceptions of herself as a research-active star and attributes this success to the organizational structure and culture of the university will develop positive sentiments toward this system, and the longer this attribution continues, the greater will be her commitment to this corporate unit. However, a professor who sees his own actions as largely responsible for verifying self-worth as a star researcher will display less commitment to the university, and indeed, this individual may be highly receptive to new opportunities at other universities (the "prima donna" professor is thus one who attributes success only to self).

Turning to the negative side of emotions and attribution processes, a person who sees the failure to verify a low-salience identity as his or her own fault will experience low levels of sadness, such as disappointment. If self is highly salient, and the person attributes the failure to verify self to his or her actions, then moderate to high levels of sadness will be experienced. If the individual sees his or her actions as incompetent, anger at self and fear of the consequences to self will be aroused, with the result that shame is more likely to be experienced. To continue the example of the professor, a scholar who fails to publish sufficiently and attributes this failure to his actions will be severely depressed.

When external attributions for the failure to confirm a low-salience identity are made, then low levels of anger will be experienced and expressed toward others and categories of others, but the more salient the identity (that is, involving core feelings of self), the greater will be the anger toward others and categories of others seen as responsible for the failure to confirm the identity. Under these conditions, for instance, the professor who failed to get tenure will be aggressive toward colleagues, the department chair, and perhaps even the dean. If the failure to confirm an identity is attributed to the corporate unit in which an encounter is embedded, then a person will express anger toward this unit and the institutional system in which it is embedded; and the more salient the self, the greater will be the anger. Thus, the professor would now display considerable aggression toward the university. As most academics know, those who fail to get tenure often engage in attribution as a defense mechanism. As a result, it is rare for individuals to blame fully themselves for the failure to verify this aspect of self; rather, the failure usually leads to anger and aggression toward others, categories of others, and corporate units like the department or university as a whole. In this way, individuals' subidentity as a scholar and their core feelings of themselves as intelligent and competent are shielded from the harsh reality that comes with the failure to verify the role identity of research professor.

The types of inputs signaling a failure to verify self are also important in determining the emotional reactions of a person. When the inability to verify self occurs without direct or deliberately given negative sanctions from others, sadness and anger will be the dominant emotions experienced, depending on the attributions made to self, others and categories of others, or corporate units. But the emotional stakes are raised when others are seen as deliberately directing negative sanctions toward a person. When individuals blame themselves for receiving negative sanctions from others, and the more explicit these sanctions, they will begin to experience fear about the consequence of their actions, and they will experience sadness at self for their failure. The more salient is the identity subject to negative sanctions, the more intense will be the feelings of sadness and fear, and the more likely will persons become angry at themselves. The more failure to verify self is marked by negative sanctions from others over iterated encounters, the more likely will sadness, anger at self, and fear of consequences be transformed into shame (see Table 4.5 in Chapter 4); and the more salient an identity, the greater will be the sense of shame. For example, if a professor is consistently evaluated by students as a poor instructor in virtually all of his or her courses, then sadness, fear, and anger will all emerge, perhaps at different times, but in the end the negative sanctions provided by student evaluations and students' behaviors in class will increasingly make verification of a teacher identity impossible. As a result, the professor will begin to experience shame, unless defense mechanisms distort the process (see below) or the professor can get out of teaching, perhaps becoming "an administrator." Moreover, the more value premises of the society or evaluative ideologies of an institutional domain become salient to an individual who blames self for receiving negative sanctions that disconfirm an identity, the more likely will a person experience guilt; the more salient was the self, the more intense is this guilt. Thus, an incompetent teacher may not only feel ashamed but also guilty for his or her failure to realize cultural values and educational ideologies.

In contrast, when individuals see the negative sanctions emitted by others as unfair, they will experience both anger toward, and fear of, these others, but anger will be the more dominant emotional reaction; and the higher the salience of the identity, the more intense will these emotions be. The more others are placed into social categories—for example, "students"—the more likely will a person express anger toward, and fear of, members in this categoric unit. Thus, it is often the case that poor instructors blame students as a categoric unit for their teaching problems, alternately displaying anger toward "ungrateful" students and fear about having to face them again. If individuals attribute negative sanctions experienced in an encounter to the larger corporate unit in which the encounter is embedded, they will direct their anger toward the corporate unit and see the corporate unit as responsible for their failure to verify self. Indeed, professors will often blame the size of classes, the lack of instructional support, the recruitment of "lousy" students, and other features of the corporate unit rather than face up to what negative sanctions from student evaluations are saying about their identities.

THE EFFECTS OF EXPECTATIONS

Expectations are key in the emotional reactions of individuals to self-verification processes. As we saw in Chapter 4, expectations in general are what generate emotional reactions; and perhaps the most powerful expectations are those generated by core self, subidentities, and role identities. Much of the power of self to arouse emotions, then, is the result of the expectations that self establishes in an encounter. When people's expectations for verification are met, they experience variants and combinations of happiness; and the more salient the identity, the greater is the intensity of happiness. Moreover, if they had fears about whether or not their expectations would be met, they experience pride. An interesting twist is when expectations are exceeded. In general, exceeding expectations causes individuals to experience moderate to high-intensity happiness and pride if they had doubts of being verified at all. Yet, some research indicates that individuals with low self-esteem (or low evaluation of their abilities in a situation or across situations) will react to inputs from the environment that exceed expectations as a failure to verify self, and as a consequence, they will be distressed (Swann 1987; Swann et al. 1990; Swann, Pelham, and Krull 1989; Swann and Hill 1982), whereas those with high self-esteem will experience positive emotions when expectations for verification are exceeded. Attribution processes are, I believe, important in sorting out this relationship. I would hypothesize that if individuals attribute verifications exceeding their expectations to their own actions, they will experience positive emotions regardless of their level of self-esteem. For example, even students who do not have high global evaluation of themselves as intellects or even as "good" students will nonetheless be happy when receiving a grade that exceeded expectations *if* they see that their hard work led to this grade. But, when attributions are external, differences between high- and low-self-esteem individuals are important. If individuals attribute their success to others or categories of others, high-self-esteem persons will have positive feelings toward others and categories of others, while still experiencing happiness toward themselves. In contrast, low-self-esteem individuals will resolve the incongruence between the low evaluation of their identity and responses from others exceeding expectations by displaying emotions such as gratitude toward others or, alternatively, will seek to attribute the outcome to categories of others or the corporate units in which the encounter is embedded, thereby resolving the incongruence by deflecting verification away from themselves. For example, I have always found that when average or mediocre students get a high grade in one of my classes, they almost always attribute their success to my "great teaching" more than their own hard work (and while I feel somewhat guilty about taking the credit, it is still pleasant to verify a role identity that is often under assault).

When individuals expect self-verification but do not receive it, however, they will experience and express negative emotions. In general, the more individuals expected others to verify self and the more salient the self, the greater will be the negative emotions. If individuals blame themselves for failure at self-verification, they will experience anger at themselves and, if this self-blame holds across iterated encounters, then fear about the future and sadness will increasingly become the dominant emotions, particularly for low-self-esteem individuals. Under these conditions shame is likely to be experienced. When individuals assess their failure against value standards or evaluative ideologies, the mix of negative emotions will cause them to experience guilt; and the more salient their identity, the greater is the sense of guilt.

If actors attribute the failure to receive expected verifications to the actions of others or categories of others, they will reveal anger toward these others and categories of others. If the encounter is iterated with the same outcome, they will display chronic anger toward others and prejudices toward categoric units. And if they blame the corporate unit for their failure, they will display anger toward this unit; if they are forced to stay in disconfirming encounters within this corporate unit, they will develop chronic anger toward the corporate unit and broader institutional system in which this unit is embedded, while feeling alienated and estranged. But over time the external attributions of such individuals often shift toward self, and as a result, their anger is directed at themselves, coupled with sadness at self and fear of the consequences to self that open the door for shame and guilt. For example, my university has a ruthless biomedical program that fast-tracks freshmen through medical school from their freshman year, but, unfortunately, the program takes in three hundred elite students each year for only thirty slots for the final two years of medical school. Most of these students are confident of their intellectual powers and of their ability in student roles to get high grades; and so, most carry high expectations for their eventual success in the program. Yet, with only 10 percent actually making it in the program, most must come to terms with failing to verify their identity and perhaps core-self feelings. Thus, when these students take a sociology course (which they consider beneath them) and then receive the grade "B" or even "A–" (a very negative sanction from their point of view), their reactions almost always involve anger toward the instructor rather than themselves; by virtue of this attribution, they are able to avoid a full disconfirmation of self. But over time as encounters in courses are iterated and their grades fall below those of the small number who will make it through the program, their attributions shift to the program itself and to the larger university for putting them through such cutthroat competition. Indeed, they often leave the university as extremely angry individuals, but at the same time, they also begin to reveal sadness and perhaps even shame as they shift attributions back to themselves. Thus, attributions for failure to verify an identity or a highly salient aspect of core self can shift across time; and there is probably a rough sequence of initially engaging angry external attributions of failures followed over time by a growing awareness of personal failure. As this shift occurs, shame at having failed and guilt at not meeting cultural ideals and institutional ideologies are ever more likely to be experienced.

THE ACTIVATION OF DEFENSE MECHANISMS

A variety of *defensive strategies* can be used to avoid incongruence between an identity and the responses of others. One is selective perception in which the person reads the gestures of others as confirming an identity. A variant is selective interpretation of cues from others such that they are interpreted in a manner at variance with what others intended. Another is to invoke what McCall and Simmons (1978) term "short-term credit" from past confirmations of self to ride out episodes of incongruence. Still another is to switch a new role identity that is more likely to be confirmed. Another is to disavow a particular episode of behavior as not representing one's "true self." And, relatedly, a person can simply disavow the audience of others who fail to confirm an identity.

These defensive strategies can work only in the short run in repeated encounters because persistent use of these strategies will generally arouse anger in others and invite negative sanctions. For short-term encounters, especially those that are not embedded or iterated, these strategies are often employed and allow individuals to escape having to deal with failures in role identities or even subidentities, but if core identities are touched by incongruence, these strategies become, I believe, less viable and effective. More powerful defense mechanisms will be activated in those encounters disconfirming self that cannot be abandoned.

Attribution can be seen as a kind of projection; and as such, this defense mechanism follows the dynamics discussed above. But use of projection of any kind is generally counterproductive because it invites negative sanctions from others. As has already been examined, when active negative sanctioning by others leads to disconfirmation of self, the intensity of the emotions experienced by a person escalate, assuring that their external attributions will lead to more failures to verify self. Displacement has the same consequences as projection because when others are the brunt of the anger, hurt, sadness, fear, and shame of a person, they will negatively sanction this person, unless they are in subordinate positions and cannot fight back with negative sanctions. Thus, one reason that corporate and categoric units are often the targets of projection and displacement is that these units are not people and, hence, are less likely to retaliate. Anger at a company or prejudice against a categoric unit (women, blacks, Jews) is far safer than anger at one's boss or colleagues who are in a position to sanction an individual.

Repression, however, is a more complicated defense mechanism because it pushes from consciousness negative emotional reactions and, depending on how well the repression works, from the purview of others as well. The effectiveness of repression is related to the extent to which individuals must consistently confront failures to verify self. A biography filled with repression of failures to confirm salient role identities will produce a person who is depressed but who, periodically, erupts with either anger or fear. If repression has worked to remove fear from consciousness, then the individual will have episodes of high anxiety and, potentially, a variety of phobias; whereas if a person has repressed anger, then episodes of high-intensity anger and even violent behavior are more likely to occur. When second-order elaborations combining fear, anger, and sadness into either shame or guilt are repressed, a person will be likely to have episodes of all three emotions, whether singularly as spikes of anger, anxiety, or depression or as moments of great shame and guilt. Displacement can accompany repression that erupts into anger, since individuals will often vent their aggression on what are perceived to be safe objects such as a spouse, a subordinate, a categoric or corporate unit. The critical point is that repression is like a compressor that builds emotional pressure, and when the emotions are released, they generally are not proportionate to events in the person's environment. Yet, ironically, as emotional pressures build, a person can appear depressed and sad, revealing a relatively low level of modal interpersonal energy. Repression is costly in terms of the energy expended to sustain control of emotions, and thus it saps the energy available for interaction. Such is particularly likely to be the case where emotions like shame and guilt are repressed since the dominant emotion in each is sadness (see Table 4.4 in Chapter 4).

A further complication is that repression is often incomplete, with a person revealing an ongoing and persistent patina of sadness, aggression, or anxiety; and as noted in the last chapter, if this edge of aggression or anxiety is consistent, it becomes defined as a "personality trait" by others who readjust their expectations and sanctioning practices accordingly. The irony of this adjustment by others is that a person is more likely to have an identity verified as long as the individual behaves consistently. For example, people can be accepted as just assertive, anxious, or low key, as long as repression can keep the lid on high-intensity expressions of the underlying emotions. Under these conditions repressed persons will have their role identities confirmed, although such repression is usually the result of failures in the past and perhaps in the present to have core selves verified.

The particular level of self—that is, core self, subidentity, or role identity—that is unverified thus has important effects on defense mechanisms. If the core self is not confirmed in a one-shot encounter, then defensive strategies can prove effective, but if the encounter is repeated, individuals will have more difficulty in avoiding the incongruence between self and responses of others. For example, a person who considers himself to be a competent worker but who must constantly endure failure to verify this role identity as well as the underlying feelings of core self will have difficulty maintaining expressive control. Thus, when core self is not verified in the present and when disconfirmation occurs again and again, the emotional reactions of a person will intensify, and defensive strategies will generally prove ineffective. More powerful defense mechanisms may be activated, but these will often become counterproductive if they arouse anger and fear in others. Consistent disconfirmation of core self will thus, in the end, cause depression as a person begins to make self-attributions, but if a person has sought to repress these self-attributions, then their depression will be punctuated by episodes of either fear or anger. Core self is, I contend, difficult to change, and so individuals cannot easily redefine their deep-seated emotions about themselves as persons. Subidentities and particularly role identities can be changed and, at the same time, accommodate core-self feelings. Thus, a person who sought to maintain the identity of a good father will, if results prove to the contrary, initially invoke defensive strategies and perhaps even defense mechanisms, but if the failure to verify this identity persists, the identity can be readjusted. Even if the person feels that he is competent in many other spheres, he can contextualize and rationalize this new identity of being a poor parent with other subidentities and core self. For example, parents often accept the fact that their children did not turn out as they had hoped, readjust their identity of parent to one "who made mistakes," and yet still feel highly competent at their core. This is usually accomplished by not only changing the role identity (from good parent to bad), but in order to sustain the core identity, the changed identity is devaluated. Alternatively, a parent can simply make an external attribute to the child who "did not turn out well," seeing the problem as solely the child's fault; and in this way self-blame by the parent can be mitigated. But, if individuals cannot lower the salience of core self to subidentities and role identities, and if they cannot successfully blame others, then they are likely to repress at least some of their self-blame and, as a consequence, feel depressed, anxious, and irritated.

Embedding has effects on the use of defense mechanisms. If, as noted earlier, a person can make attributions to categoric units for the failure to verify self, then self can be protected and the consequences of negative sanctions can be avoided. Such persons, as emphasized in Chapter 4, will reveal prejudice and bigotry, but self will be protected. Similarly, if attributions are made to corporate units, or particular positions in corporate units that, in essence, become categoric units (for example, "it's management's fault") persons can protect self and avoid direct negative sanctioning as long as they maintain expressive control in front of others who have the power to sanction negatively. Thus, the more encounters are embedded in distinctive and discrete categoric units and the more they are lodged in corporate units with a hierarchical division of labor, there are many "safe" objects on which to displace aggression and blame for failures to verify self. In this way, individuals can keep from blaming themselves, at least for a time.

EMBEDDING AND NEEDS FOR SELF-VERIFICATION

Embeddedness also alters the dynamics of self-confirmation by structuring the positions, roles, demography, ecology, and normative expectations of encounters. In general, the more embedded is an encounter in corporate and categoric units, the greater will be the clarity in normative expectations, in the distribution of prestige and authority, in the roles, and in the demography and ecology of the encounter.

Corporate unit embeddedness and self-verification

The structure of a corporate unit varies along several axes: its size, external boundaries and internal partitions, horizontal and vertical divisions of labor, and formality. The culture varies with respect to the application of texts, technologies, values, beliefs/ideologies, and rules of the institutional system in which the corporate unit is lodged. Structure determines the demography of who is present, the ecology of space and the physical props available, the distribution of status, and the nature of roles in the encounter, whereas culture dictates the normatization of categories, frames, forms of talk, rituals, and feelings in the encounter. In general, the larger and the more bounded, formal, and hierarchical a corporate unit, the more clearly defined are demography, ecology, status, and roles; and the greater is clarity of structure, the more clear-cut are the normative expectations for categories, frames, forms of talk, rituals, and feelings. Conversely, the smaller and the less bounded, formal, and hierarchical a corporate unit, the less constrained are demography, ecology, status, and roles; and the less is the clarity of structure, the more ambiguous are normative expectations.

When the structure and culture of a corporate unit are explicit, the range of subidentities and role identities relevant to an encounter is delimited, thereby making it more likely that individuals will present an identity that can be verified. It is only when core-self feelings drive individuals to seek verification of identities outside the culture and structure of the corporate unit that the potential for disconfirmation arises. For example, a clerk in a bureaucracy knows what to do and what role identity is appropriate; if this person presents a variant of the appropriate role identity, then identity is generally verified. But, when core self pushes a person to embellish and expand the role identity beyond what is dictated by the structure and culture of the corporate unit, it becomes increasingly likely that the expectations generated by this identity will not be realized and/or that negative sanctions from others will ensue. For instance, a clerk who also considers himself to be a "ladies' man" (a subidentity) will seek to confirm this identity in the context of work roles and, generally, will encounter trouble in confirming this identity. Similarly, a low-level clerk or manual laborer whose core self contains images and feelings of dominance will perhaps try to be dominant while in a subordinate role; and this person will soon encounter trouble from fellow workers and superiors.

As corporate units become smaller and less bounded, formal, and hierarchical, the range of possible role identities generally expands. Under these conditions, elements of core self and subidentities may be expressed in role identities. If the effort to verify this identity does not violate normative expectations for what is appropriate, the identity is more likely to be confirmed. There is, of course, no guarantee that identities will be verified, only an increased range of possible identities; and if individuals are prudent, they have a chance of receiving inputs verifying their identity. Of course, lack of structure can encourage individuals to reach too far or, equally likely, to be unsure what identities are appropriate; as a result, they will experience disconfirmation.

When identities are not verified, all of the emotional dynamics discussed above come into play. Depending on salience of the identity, the incongruity between expectations and outcomes, the level and source of negative sanctioning, the attributions made, the defensive strategies employed, and the defense mechanisms activated, the emotional reactions will vary in accordance with the patterns examined earlier. Yet, some additional generalization can be offered. If failure to verify self occurs in a highly structured corporate unit with a clear culture, individuals are likely to attribute their failures to verify self or identity to others, categories of others, or the corporate unit as a whole. For when external targets—for example, categoric and corporate units—are conveniently available and cannot, by themselves, negatively sanction a person for attributions, this person is more likely to take this route to protecting self because self-blame is painful and because specific others can fight back when negative attributions are made to them. In contrast, if the failure occurs in a less structured unit, those who have failed to verify self will not have these convenient targets and, thus, will be forced to make attributions to specific others rather than to categories of others or the corporate unit. And yet, these others will generally negatively sanction a person who has made negative external attributions. As a consequence, the rates of self-blame will increase, even as a person continues to blame others. In structured corporate units with an unambiguous culture, defensive strategies are the first line of defense; and only when a failed role identity is a marker of, and closely coupled with, elements of core self (that is, of high salience) will the individual repress negative emotions or displace these emotions onto what are perceived as "safer" targets, if they are available. In less structured units, individuals are more likely to embellish role identities with elements of their core self, and as salience thereby increases, failure to verify a role identity will generally activate defensive strategies and external attributions. When others negatively sanction these strategies, repression becomes more likely because individuals can no longer avoid self-blame through external attributions.

Corporate units can also trap individuals in roles where their identities cannot be verified. The lazy worker who needs money or the unmotivated student who needs a credential are, in essence, unwilling incumbents in corporate structures; under these conditions, some aspects of their identities will not be verified. And yet, they must stay for the extrinsic rewards offered by the unit; under these conditions, failures to verify self will generally activate external attributions to others, categories of others in the corporate unit, or to the corporate unit as a whole. For example, poor students with a core self that they are competent or with a role identity that they can do the work if they "wanted to" will constantly have their identities disconfirmed, leading them to blame the external world. Only after repeated failures and negative sanctions from others will actors begin to take responsibility for their actions, but even here, if the role identity is salient, defensive mechanisms are more likely to be activated than internal soul searching. As a result, in accordance with the dynamics examined above, these students will be more angry than sad.

Categoric unit embeddedness and self-verification

When an encounter is lodged in categoric units, identity processes are altered. An individual with distinctive categoric membership (for example, male, female, young, old) will generally seek to present a role identity that is consistent with this categoric membership. Indeed, when the role identity asserted and the membership in a distinctive categoric unit diverge, self-verification becomes more problematic. For example, if an old man seeks to portray his identity as a "romantic Romeo" in a situation of younger persons, it is likely that the romantic portion of the identity will remain unverified, while the identity of a (dirty?) old man will be verified. Such individuals often employ defensive strategies, particularly selective perception and selective interpretation of cues from others; and if necessary, they will attribute their failures to others or the situation as a whole. The emotional dynamics unleashed by this failure to verify a role identity that clashes with categoric membership will vary, of course, in terms of the effectiveness of defensive strategies, the use of attributions and defense mechanisms, the extent to which expectations established by the identity were not met, and the degree of negative sanctioning received.

   When an interaction is built around categoric memberships and the categories are discrete and clear, then role identities are likely to be more consistent with categoric membership and the respective evaluations of categories. Thus, for example, a man and a woman, a gathering of male ethnics, and other situations where categoric membership is paramount will generally proceed in accordance with the expectations for members of the various categories involved, and as a consequence, role identities are likely to be confirmed unless a person reaches beyond expectations associated with membership in a categoric unit. Some of my African American students, for instance, occasionally complain that they are accused of "acting white" in encounters with fellow ethnics, presumably because they are seen as trying to present an identity that is associated with academic "white demeanor," which their friends refuse to validate. Or, if Asian students move too far beyond their ethnic identity in adopting Anglo demeanor, they will often be seen by fellow ethnics as "whitewashed."

If categories are embedded in a corporate unit and the structure of the corporate unit is formal and hierarchical, then the positions of the corporate unit will diminish the effects of categoric units. Yet, even when the identities associated with categoric units are diminished, they often remain salient in corporate units. For example, as many women in professional careers in corporate units have learned, acting "too masculine" invites negative sanctions, thereby forcing them to forge role identities that are "feminine" and quietly assertive. When membership at positions in a corporate unit and categoric unit are highly correlated, the effects of this correlation increase the salience of categoric unit identities and, as a result, force individuals to present identities considered appropriate for a member of the categoric units. For example, interactions on slave-holding plantations in the South before the Civil War involved a high correlation between position in the corporate unit (that is, slave, owner) and categoric membership (black, white); under these conditions, the power of categoric units to influence which identities can be asserted and which will be verified was even more influenced by categoric unit membership.

When a role identity is associated with categoric membership and when an individual sees this role identity as consistent with core-self feelings, verification produces positive emotional reactions. But, when the role identity is forced on a person by virtue of categoric unit membership and when the core-self feelings stand in conflict with this coerced role identity, individuals will become angry. They are more likely, under these conditions, to attribute their inability to present role identities consistent with their core feelings to others, categories of others, and corporate units in which the encounter is embedded. Yet, if their anger cannot be expressed, then defensive strategies can be pursued, such as overplaying a role identity in a cynical performance. And, as people are forced to sustain this conflict between role identity and core self, eventually they will also come to feel sad and depressed by their inability to present identities consistent with their core self, even if they continue to give cynical performances of this identity. At times, individuals shift their self-conception, but rarely is this shift complete because there will always remain the emotional residue of not being able to verify core self in key roles. As a result, sadness will remain; and if a person is both angry at others for their situation and fearful about trying to present role identities that conform to core-self feelings, then these emotions combine with sadness to produce shame. For example, I suspect that slaves before the Civil War ran the gambit of emotional reactions, ranging from cynical performances of their slave identities to changes of core-self feelings to mixes of anger, fear, and sadness that often produced shame. Similarly today, I suspect that much withdrawal from the "white world" and the anger expressed toward this world by ethnics who are not allowed (by virtue of past and present discrimination) to sustain core-self feelings and subidentities (say, in work and family) is the result of their inability to verify these core feelings and subidentities in roles. Their anger, often accompanied by fear and sadness leading to shame, can lead these individuals to withdraw from the "white world" and move into roles where they can verify their core feelings and sustain viable role identities. But even as they withdraw, the failure to sustain identities in the white world remain, causing them to maintain diffuse aggression toward whites. Moreover, if this failure to present identities consistent with core feelings is evaluated by a person as a failure to realize value standards, then this person may also experience guilt along with shame.

SELF AS THE MOST IMPORTANT TRANSACTIONAL NEEDS

Most symbolic interactionist theories see self and identity as the central dynamic in interaction. I have dwelled on the dynamics revolving around self because I agree with this conclusion. Needs to verify and confirm self at all levels—core-self feelings, subidentities, and role identities—are the most powerful force driving individuals in encounters. When individuals cannot verify self, the emotional reactions are intensified; and the more core-self feelings are attached to subidentities and role identities, the more pronounced are the emotional reactions. Conversely, when identities are confirmed and verified, especially core-self feelings, the greater will be the sense of satisfaction and happiness experienced and expressed by individuals. Because the emotions involved are so powerful, they can become convoluted as a result of defensive strategies, attribution processes, and defense mechanisms.

Corporate and categoric units become key in the verification process because they constrain what identities can be asserted and verified, given one's membership in a categoric unit or position in a corporate unit. People's commitments to categoric units and to corporate structures are very much related to their ability to verify a role identity that is consistent with core self and subidentities; ultimately, the institutional spheres in which corporate and categoric units are lodged will be affected by these commitments. Similarly, the culture of mesostructures in which an encounter is lodged is influenced by self-verification. People will accept normatization and the broader culture of values, beliefs, and norms if they can verify role identities, subidentities, and core-self feelings within the encounter. If they cannot, they will seek to renormatize the encounter and, if unsuccessful, they will withdraw commitments to the culture of meso- and macrostructures.

Needs for Profitable Exchange Payoffs

The cornerstone of all exchange theories is a view of actors as seeking rewards in excess of their costs and investments. *Rewards* can be almost anything that brings gratification or utility, although in most interactions the rewards are symbolic and intrinsic. Naturally, many of the resources and rewards to be distributed in an encounter are determined by the culture and structure of the mesounits within which the encounter occurs. An encounter lodged in one categoric unit (say, all women) and a particular kind of corporate unit (say, business enterprise) presents very different reinforcers than one embedded in diverse categoric units (male, female, and ethnics) within a corporate structure like a social club. Thus, the actual content, substance, and distribution of the rewards cannot be easily theorized since these can be unique to the situation and its embeddedness. Nevertheless, we can develop theoretical principles about the dynamics of exchange payoffs in general.

RESOURCES AND OTHER FORCES IN ENCOUNTERS

We can begin by noting that other forces operating in all encounters circumscribe the rewards that individuals receive. The emotions flowing in an encounter are a powerful resource. When the emotional valences are positive, individuals will receive positive payoffs from such emotions, whereas when the valences are negative, people are less likely to receive profitable exchange payoffs. Of course, other resources besides emotions influence exchange payoffs, and payoffs of these resources will generate the emotional environment of the interaction, as we will explore later. Thus, emotions are both a resource to be exchanged and an outcome of the exchange of other resources. But once aroused, payoffs will be influenced by these emotional resources. Another force in an encounter is symbolic or cultural. Symbols define not only how individuals should behave but also act as reinforcers themselves. In general, when situations are normatively regulated, individuals' expectations are more likely to be in line with the resources that they can potentially receive; as a result, people will receive supportive and rewarding responses from others. Roles are yet another force in interaction. When individuals have their roles verified, they experience positive payoffs in terms of the resources that the role commands and the positive emotions aroused. Conversely, when they cannot establish a viable role for themselves, they experience negative emotions and cannot claim the resources of the role. Status is another force in interaction; and when individuals have high power/authority and prestige, they are in a position to extract from others the resources and symbols reinforcing their position. In contrast, low-power and low-prestige individuals are disadvantaged and, therefore, must rely on the more intrinsic reinforcers flowing among themselves. Subordinates generally seek positive exchange payoffs from each other, trying to keep their costs and investments in interaction with superordinates to a minimum since these latter interactions generally do not offer opportunities for highly profitable exchange payoffs. Demography and ecology are additional forces in interaction. When a situation is composed of equals, individuals will be more likely to receive intrinsic rewards revolving around social approval. Of course, if a subordinate gains high praise from a superordinate or even extrinsic reinforcers like more money from a superordinate, then the exchange payoffs are that much greater. But generally, individuals tend to congregate in space with "their own kind" because the payoffs are more reliable. Only the highly ambitious incur the costs and make the investment for less certain payoffs by pursuing contact with superordinates.

Despite the effects of these other forces of encounters on exchange payoffs, transactional needs are still critical. In almost any interaction, individuals will be highly attuned to symbols and resources that allow them to confirm other transactional needs—for self-verification, for trust, for group inclusion, and for facticity. In particular, the most valuable intrinsic reward for an individual is verification of self, and so, individuals will be highly alert to the symbols and resources that are relevant to self-confirmation. For example, approving responses of others to a person's self-presentations provide intrinsic reinforcement or utility if they verify self, but at times, extrinsic rewards—for example, high salary and corner office—may be necessary to verify self. Whatever is defined as essential to confirm self will be the most important consideration of persons in a face-to-face encounter; and the more salient the self, the more an individual will become attuned to resources and symbols marking self. Just what symbols and resources are relevant to self will, naturally, be defined by the symbols and resources available in an encounter, and as we will see, these are very much constrained by the mesostructures in which the encounter is embedded. In general, the more extrinsic a resource, the less its power to confirm or disconfirm self; but if extrinsic resources such as money or power can be converted into symbols that verify self, the more important will such resources become. For example, while salary and office space have extrinsic reward value in and of themselves, they are often coveted for their symbolic value to confirm an image of a person as successful. Indeed, American academics generally work for only moderate incomes (compared to other highly educated professionals), but a "merit increase" of a thousand dollars or a promotion to a new rank are worth more in terms of what it says symbolically about self as teacher and scholar. Of course, corporate units often overplay this symbolism by giving new, supposedly higher-status job titles without more pay, but this cynical and manipulative use of symbolic reinforcers alone only demonstrates their power to provide positive exchange payoffs.

Other transactional forces for group inclusion, trust, and facticity also influence needs for exchange payoffs, but not to the degree of drives for self-verification. People always seek resources and symbols marking their inclusion in the flow of interaction; they also seek signs of predictability, synchronization, sincerity, and respect from others; and they search for symbols that others share their view of "what is." Without receiving resources or symbols signaling group inclusion, trust, and facticity, it will be difficult for a person to receive positive exchange payoffs.

STEPS IN SEEKING RESOURCES

Individuals thus search encounters for the *available* resources; and on the basis of this effort, they develop expectations for what they should receive relative to their costs and investments in the encounter, measured against a standard of fairness and justice. This calculation is typically implicit, but when payoffs do not meet expectations, individuals can begin to think consciously about why they are angry, fearful, or sad. Mesostructures often determine what resources and symbols are available, and how they can be distributed; and so, as individuals develop definitions of potential resources and symbols, they do so by taking cognizance of the structure and culture of mesostructures.

After this initial scan for the range of available resources and symbols, individuals focus on those resources that can verify self; and depending on the salience of their core-self feelings and relevant subidentities, they project a role identity. While these expectations for self take account of the mesostructure in which the encounter is embedded, they also follow from a person's core self as well as from past interactions in the encounter. This second level of self-generated expectations, then, is more particularistic; the dangers of disconfirmation of self increase because the expectations are defined more by the person than by others and the structure and culture of the mesounit in which the encounter is lodged.

A third level of scanning for resources and symbols is the other transactional needs: group inclusion, trust, and facticity. People implicitly assess— given the culture, structure, demography, and ecology of the situation— what payoffs are necessary to meet these other transactional needs.

Thus, in encounters humans initially (1) scan the structure and culture of the situation (typically as ordered by mesounits) for the resources that are available, then (2) assess what symbols and resources will allow self to be verified, and finally (3) look for the symbols and resources that will confirm needs for group inclusion, trust, and facticity. On the bases of this three-step assessment of resources, individuals formulate expectations about the payoffs that they can and should receive.

COSTS, INVESTMENTS, AND JUSTICE

Expectations for exchange payoffs are also determined by several additional factors internal to the exchange process itself. Individuals seek to gain a positive payoff of resources relative to their (1) costs and (2) investments measured against a standard of (3) justice or fairness. A *cost* is simply the energy expended in securing rewards of a given type and the alternative sources of rewards forgone. An *investment* is the cumulative costs incurred over time in an encounter or iterated encounters and the commitments developed toward others as well as categories of others and corporate units in which the encounter is embedded. A *standard of justice* or *fairness* is a conception, generally implicit, of the appropriate payoffs in light of the costs incurred and investments made. The assessment of costs and investments by persons is also relative to the perceived costs and investments of others. Thus, perceptions of fairness always involve an actor's costs and investments *relative* to those of others.

When individuals incur costs and make investments in an encounter, they expect payoffs to be proportionate in accordance with a standard of justice. If individuals perceive that they have not incurred great costs or made significant investments relative to those of others, they will have lowered expectation for positive payoffs; and indeed, they could even perceive that they will receive negative payoffs (as would be the case, for example, for a poor student who never attends classes or studies, although, as we will see, attribution processes are important in determining the nature of their emotional reaction).

Humans carry in their stocks of knowledge vast stores of information about justice standards, types of situations, and appropriate payoffs in light of costs and investments in diverse situations. Yet, some (Fiske 1991; Cosmides 1989) have argued that there is a hard-wired propensity for humans to assess reciprocity and justice; and this argument holds some credence since our ancestors were under heavy selection pressures to develop mechanisms for bonding. A sense of reciprocity, fairness, and justice would be a highly effective way to bind individuals together in cooperative social relations; and the fact that norms of reciprocity are universal suggests that there may be a neurological basis for them. If there is a hard-wired basis, then much of the burden is taken off stocks of knowledge for storing vast inventories of information. In fact, it may be that humans' neurological wiring for reciprocity and justice operates as a generative force, automatically assessing situations for reciprocity and fairness in terms of perceived resources, costs, and investments. If such be the case, humans do not have to work too hard assessing the fairness of exchange payoffs; our neurology simply drives us to do so. If we think about the matter for a moment, this appears to be what actually occurs because we rarely have to think consciously about appropriate payoffs (unless we are in an explicit negotiation or have not received what we implicitly expected). Instead, we "automatically" feel satisfaction-happiness when payoffs are proportionate to costs and investments in light of justice standards, or we immediately experience negative emotions when payoffs are not proportionate. Humans do not cognitively ponder these matters, unless "injustice" has been done because, I suspect, the capacity is built into our neurology. Imagine, for example, having to calculate consciously the costs and investments in an encounter, while consciously deciding on a justice standard as it applies to payoffs in each and every situation. If we always did this, we would exhaust ourselves and experience cognitive overload; indeed, if you think about those occasions when you actually did make conscious calculations, you will remember, I think, how difficult and time consuming the whole process was.

Like all transactional needs, the need for positive exchange payoffs is loaded with the potential for both positive and negative emotions. Standards of fairness almost always make exchange a moral issue, often involving general value premises and more specific ideologies; and as a result, the failure to realize standards of justice can arouse powerful emotions. Costs and investments determine how these moral standards of justice will operate; standards are raised when costs and investments increase and are lowered when costs and investments decrease. The implicit calculations weighing the relative costs, investments, and payoffs against considerations of fairness create expectations for payoffs among individuals in an encounter. Once expectations exist, they make emotional reactions inevitable since, as we saw in Chapter 4, the force of emotions revolves around expectations.

SELF AND EXPECTATIONS FOR EXCHANGE PAYOFFS

The salience of self is probably the most important factor in developing expectations for payoffs in an encounter. When individuals present a role identity, they are incurring costs associated with alternative identities that could be presented or alternative situations where they could present an identity. Moreover, a role identity can involve considerable investment when linked to an individual's core-self feelings and subidentities. All identities, but particularly core self and subidentities, are investments that have accumulated from the costs incurred in presenting these identities in the past. The more these identities have been verified in past encounters, the greater will be the individual's commitment to them (Stryker 1980). As commitment increases, alternative identities are forgone, as are situations in which these alternatives could have been presented; and so, commitment to an identity is also a measure of a person's investments in an identity. The more commitments to an identity, the more likely are core-self feelings and subidentities to be implicated in role identities presented in encounters. Thus, as self becomes salient—that is, role identities, subidentities, and core self converge—investments increase for an individual; and as investments of self increase, standards of fairness are revised, as are expectations for payoffs. For example, a woman who has presented the role identity of a "homemaker" or "housewife" in the many encounters is likely to see verification of this identity as important to her subidentity about herself as a woman and family member as well as to her core-self feelings about herself as a person. The more this salient role has been presented and verified, the greater the commitment to, and investments in, this identity. As a result, the emotional stakes are raised for this woman in an encounter where this identity is presented because standards of justice have shifted in light of the heavy investments in this identity. Thus, because of its impact on perceived investments as these investments, in turn, influence standards of fairness, the salience of self drives the search for exchange payoffs, while increasing the potential for emotional reactions.

EMBEDDEDNESS AND EXCHANGE PAYOFFS

The culture and structure of mesostructures constrain not just the resources available but also definitions of costs, investments, and standards of justice. People will adjust expectations for rewards in light of expectations associated with categoric units and the structure of corporate units. For example, a student interacting with a professor (as a categoric unit) will have different definitions of costs, investments, and standards of justice than when interacting with a teaching assistant (again, as a categoric unit). The more an encounter is embedded in categoric units, and the more discrete and differentially evaluated these units, the more will the culture associated with categoric units define costs, investments, and standards of justice, and therefore, expectations for payoffs.

Similarly, the more an encounter is embedded in a corporate unit and the more bounded, formal, and hierarchical the division of labor in this unit, the more likely is the culture of the unit to define costs, investments, and standards of justice, and, hence, expectations for payoffs. For example, an assembly-line worker in the division of labor of a corporate unit will have different definitions of costs, investments, and standards of justice than a foreman or executive. It is rare, however, for mesostructures to determine all expectations for payoffs, since transactional needs and other forces in encounters also operate to define costs, investments, and standards of justice.

EMOTIONAL REACTIONS TO EXCHANGE PAYOFFS

Whatever the source of expectations for payoffs, individuals will experience positive emotions when they are confirmed or exceeded, and negative emotions when expectations for payoffs are not met. The more salient is the self in the encounter, the more intense will the emotional reactions be, whether positive or negative. As with all emotional responses, attribution processes and defense mechanisms are an important consideration. When individuals attribute the receipt of rewards meeting or exceeding expectations to their own actions, they will experience ever more intense positive emotions toward self as expectations are exceeded, and if core self was salient, they will experience pride if they had some fear and anxiety over whether or not they could meet or exceed expectations. When payoffs meet or exceed expectations and when individuals engage in external attributions, they will feel and express positive emotions to others, categories of others, or corporate units; and depending on the target of their external attribution, they will be more likely to develop commitments to these targets, particularly if self was salient.

The dynamics of negative emotions are perhaps more interesting than those for positive emotional reactions to payoffs. Individuals will experience negative emotions when payoffs do not meet expectations, but the interesting theoretical question is: Which negative emotion, or combination of negative emotions? Again, attribution processes are the key to answering this question. If individuals attribute their failure to meet expectations for exchange payoffs to their own actions, then they will experience sadness; and if this sadness is accompanied by anger at self and fear about the consequences to self of this failure, then persons will experience shame. Moreover, if these three negative emotions are aroused in reference to failures to meet expectations of a moral standard, then individuals will also experience guilt. However, if individuals make external attributions, the emotional dynamics change. When people attribute their failure to meet expectations to the actions of others, to categories of others, or to corporate units, they will be angry toward these external sources, blaming them for being unfair and unjust. Of course, if others are in a position to fight back, the individual is likely to receive negative sanctions, which only amplify the sense of the failure to meet expectations for payoffs. For this reason anger will be directed toward categories and structures that do not directly sanction negatively those making external attributions.

Defense strategies and mechanisms can complicate these straightforward dynamics. Defensive strategies such as selective perception and selective interpretation can reduce the power of all emotional reactions since the individual will generally perceive that they have met expectations for payoffs; but if these strategies are employed too often and too long in the face of failures, then defense mechanisms are likely to be activated. One mechanism is projection onto others, and this occurs primarily through external attribution processes described above. Another is repression, which allows individuals to avoid anger, fear, and sadness, as well as the second-order elaborations of shame and guilt, but long-term use of repression will generate depression. Displacement of anger can also occur, but like attribution, this will generally invite negative sanctions from others, unless these others are not in a position to sanction. Moreover, external attributions and displacement of anger to social categories will lead to emotionally charged prejudices against categoric units, while external attributions and displacement onto corporate units will lead to a loss of commitment to these units.

As negative emotions toward self, others, categories, and corporate units are activated, the definitions of costs, investments, and standards of justice are rewritten. When individuals do not receive payoffs, their anger, fear, and sadness will increase costs in an encounter at a faster rate than lowered investments and standards of justice. For even as people lower standards of justice and decrease investments their costs have become much higher relative to lowered standards and investments, thereby assuring escalated negative emotions in the encounter. Unless the person can leave the encounter and find alternatives, these costs will continue to escalate, at least for a time. On the more positive side, success in meeting or exceeding expectations for payoffs reduces costs, while encouraging increased investments and raising the standards of justice. Individuals do not feel that they have to expend as much energy and are willing to forgo alternatives (their costs), but as they increase commitments and raise standards of fairness in light of their positive experiences, they become ever more vulnerable to failure in realizing payoffs that meet these escalated expectations. Once short-term capital of positive memories is used up, individuals will have more negative reactions, perhaps at first disappointment but eventually more intense negative reactions at others and self.

Success in meeting and particularly in exceeding expectations for payoffs can thus have the ironical consequence of making actors less likely to meet raised standards for payoffs in the future. As self has become more salient and implicated in commitments and investments, the potential for negative emotional reactions intensifies. Depending on attribution processes and use of defense mechanisms, a person will target others, categories of others, or corporate units as this negative potential is realized. For this reason previously positive relationships can turn suddenly and intensely negative when one party does not receive payoffs in accordance with lower costs, increased investments, and raised standards of justice. A lover's quarrel or a feud between two previously close friends are good examples of these emotional dynamics. However, if repression is used to hide the failure to receive expected payoffs, then sadness and depression become ever more likely, as can be seen by a depressed spouse who will not acknowledge his or her anger but who sees him- or herself as trapped in a long-term relationship where costs are now high and investments considerable, but where payoffs do not meet previously high expectations (these dynamics are aggravated by "romantic love" ideologies that typically keep the standards of reciprocity and justice high, even when individuals lower their expectations).

Needs for Group Inclusion

Humans have needs to feel part of the ongoing interpersonal flow. Contrary to much social theory, I do not think that humans have powerful needs for high solidarity, except in a few special encounters. We are, after all, evolved apes who still retain biological propensities for individualism, autonomy, and mobility as well as flexible, loose, and weak ties. Clearly, natural selection made our ancestors more social, and so, we are probably more social than present-day apes. But humans can also view high solidarity and group cohesiveness as too constraining and repressive; as a result, people are highly selective about encounters in which they have high involvement and solidarity. Still, individuals always need to feel that they are a part of the encounter, and they seek resources and symbolic payoffs marking inclusion. When individuals feel included, satisfaction ensues; and when the role identity presented in an encounter is a marker of core self, inclusion brings moderate to high degrees of happiness. And, if a person had doubts about being included, this individual will experience pride.

Embeddedness in corporate and categoric units generally increases the likelihood that a person will experience a sense of group inclusions. The division of labor in corporate units assures that, at least along the instrumental dimension of encounters, individuals will feel part of the ongoing interpersonal flow. But, in smaller corporate units with a fluid division of labor or in encounters that move from instrumental to social content, inclusion can become more problematic as positions, roles, and norms associated with the division of labor lose their salience. When individuals are members of common categoric units, they are more likely to feel included since they are likely to share experiences and expectations. But when there are differences among categoric units represented in an encounter, individuals belonging to those categories in the minority or those whose categories are not highly evaluated will often feel less included. Thus, embeddedness does not always work in favor of inclusion.

The failure to feel included generates negative responses. Sometimes people experience hurt (a variant of sadness), at other times they are angry, and on still other occasions, they feel fearful. How, then, do we account for these variations? One critical force is attributions. When individuals blame their failure to feel included on themselves, they experience sadness; if they also have anger at themselves and fear about the consequences of being excluded, shame may emerge. The more self is salient, the more likely will a person experience shame. And potentially, if blame on self is seen from the perspective of values and ideologies, a person may also experience guilt.

When external attributions are made to others, categories of others, and corporate units, anger is the most likely emotion to be felt and expressed, although this anger may also be tinged with fear as well. The more self is salient, the greater is the anger felt and expressed toward external targets and, potentially, the more intense is the fear of these targets. When these external targets are categories of others rather than specific individuals, the greater will be the anger toward, and fear of, these categories, and the more prejudiced against these categoric units will the individual become. Similarly, if the target of attributions is the corporate unit in which the encounter occurs, the greater will be the anger toward, and fear of, the corporate unit, and the lower will be the commitment of the individual to roles in the division of labor of this unit. This lack of commitment increases as self had been highly salient. This negative cycle is mitigated by the fact that such corporate units include many work-practical encounters, which make inclusion virtually automatic, but to the extent that the encounter becomes more social, the person may begin to sense a lack of inclusion; and he or she may feel "out of it" and isolated from others in these more purely social interactions.

Defensive strategies like selective perception and interpretation can stave off a sense of noninclusion, as can short-term credit from memories of previous inclusion. If the sense of being out of the flow continues, however, individuals will leave the encounter if they can or, if they are stuck in the situation, they become more likely to activate defense mechanisms. When an encounter occurs in a bounded and formal corporate unit with a clear division of labor, people are more likely to be trapped if they do not feel included, thereby increasing the potential for negative attributions to this unit and for displacement of anger on others and categories of others within this unit. For example, the worker who is always complaining about his boss (whether as an individual or social category) and who is consistently grumpy and angry with those who are not in a position to fight back is likely to have failed to experience a sense of group inclusion (and, no doubt, this person has also failed in self-verification and exchange payoffs). Yet these kinds of defenses only aggravate the sense of isolation from the ongoing flow because others avoid this person, or, if avoidance is impossible, they remain emotionally distant, which, once again, underscores the lack of inclusion. At some point in this process, the defenses break down, and if and when this occurs, individuals may begin to blame self. As they do so, individuals become sad and depressed over the past and even more disconsolate over the likelihood that they will not be part of the interactive flow in the future. Once ostracized, it is difficult to get back into people's good graces, driving people to depression, often spiked by episodes of anger toward others and the mesostructures in which the repeated encounters are nested.

When individuals do not sense inclusion, it becomes ever more difficult to verify self and to receive positive payoffs. As a result, individuals will withdraw self and present a role identity expressing distance and disinterest (Goffman 1961), and they will lower their costs by reducing the modal level of energy put into roles (but not their anger and external attributions) and reduce their investments in the role to the minimum (while redefining their past investments as a waste of time and energy). The surly, private, and lazy office colleague is perhaps the best exemplar of this outcome. Moreover, when a person signals role distance, it becomes difficult to trust this individual and to achieve a sense of facticity, thereby making other need states difficult to meet for both the person and others.

Needs for Trust

Humans have a need to sense that the actions of others are predictable, that others are in rhythmic synchronization (Collins 1988), that others are being sincere (Habermas 1970), and that others are respecting one's dignity. When a person perceives these things, trust of others ensues. Predictability and rhythmic synchronization are the most important needs, because they exist at relatively high levels of activation in all situations, whereas the intensity of needs for sincerity and respect come with more prolonged interactions with others, particularly when self is highly salient. Thus, a relatively brief and low-key encounter, such as paying the cashier for groceries, requires predictability and rhythm, but sincerity and respect can be ritualized in ways that do not really inform the person about the *real* amount of sincerity or respect being offered. Generally, the person does not care unless ritualized respect and sincerity are not displayed by others. But once self becomes salient, or if the interaction is repeated, all dimensions of trust come into play.

When individuals do not derive a sense of trust from the responses of others, not only does the verification of self become uncertain, but so do the prospects for meeting all other transactional needs. Without a sense of trust, people cannot reliably predict exchange payoffs; they have trouble experiencing a sense of inclusion in the flow of the interaction; and they cannot easily develop a sense of facticity. Conversely, when persons experience a sense of trust, all other needs are more readily realized because trust makes self more likely to be verified, exchange payoffs to be profitable, inclusion to be perceived, and facticity to be experienced.

As a sense of trust is achieved, individuals will experience and display positive emotions. The greater is the trust, the more positive are the emotions. If self is salient and a person was anxious about achieving a sense of trust, the emotions will be more complex, ranging from relief and gratitude to pride. Moreover, even when self was not initially salient in an encounter, people will seek to present a role identity that includes elements of core self, or at a minimum, a subidentity as the encounter is repeated over time. The more this identity is confirmed, the greater will be the sense of trust, and the higher will be the commitment to others in the encounter and to the categoric and corporate units in which the encounter is embedded. Trust among employees, for example, increases the flow of positive emotions as each invests more, while at the same time increasing commitments to the categoric and corporate units in which the encounter is embedded. Of course, if trust among employees evolves in an "informal group" as a reaction against categoric and corporate units, then commitments to these mesostructures and their culture will decline and, in the extreme case, will foster rejection of these mesostructures. Indeed, union solidarity in a plant is often achieved by fostering a sense of trust among workers at the expense of commitments to the categoric units (for example, "management") or the corporate unit (the plant or company). So this chain of increasing commitment to more inclusive structures only works when the trust developing in encounters is lined up with the culture and structure of these larger social units.

When encounters are embedded in categoric and corporate units, trust is typically more readily achieved because the expectations on members of categoric units or on incumbents in the division of labor of a corporate unit will be clear. Still, this is only a tendency since encounters always involve unique elements associated with the particulars of the situation and the people involved; as noted above, countersolidarities can work against mesostructures. Indeed, mesostructures are often implicated in attributions for the failure of trust to emerge or be sustained. When individuals cannot generate a sense of trust in encounters, they can make internal attributions to their actions or external attributions to others, categories of others, and corporate units. Most of the time, attributions are made to either self or others because trust is so connected to the degree to which there is predictability, rhythmic synchronization, sincerity, and respect from *specific* others in the *immediate* situation. Failure at this direct face-to-face level is hard to pass off to the corporate unit; it generally must be attributed to failings of self or others, although people do often try to blame it on a social category (for example, "you can't trust young [old] people" or "it's hard to interact with [fill in a targeted minority"]). If individuals cannot develop trust with others in iterated encounters, they will leave if they can or engage in highly ritualized responses if they cannot, especially if the structure of the more inclusive corporate unit requires interaction. Indeed, attributions of personality traits to others with whom it is hard to synchronize interaction or to realize other axes of trust are common. For example, when someone says that it is hard to "get a handle on x" or that "x is a bit weird," this person is generally signaling that the failure to achieve predictability and synchronization has occurred. But when characterizations of a person in more severe terms emerge (for example, "he's an arrogant s.o.b."), this imputation of personality indicates others feel that this person is not willing to be sincere and respectful. As a result, expectations for achieving trust with such people are lowered, and interaction becomes stiff and stylized.

When trust is not achieved, then, individuals will make attributions to the qualities of others or categories of others if they do not blame themselves. When blaming others, they will generally experience low-key irritation rather than intense anger, unless self is highly salient; when self is salient, they will reveal not only anger but, if the other has power, some fear as well. When blaming self, a person may feel low levels of sadness, perhaps some anger toward self, and if the others are important or powerful, fear as well; if these three negative emotions get combined, the individual will experience shame. If a person also senses that moral codes have been violated in failing to achieve trust, this individual may feel guilty. Such sensations of guilt are more likely when smooth interaction with others was essential to meeting evaluative cultural codes. For example, a person who feels "out of sync" with a parent or a spouse may feel not only shame, if this individual blames self, but also guilt about not realizing moral codes about "being in touch" with loved ones. Embeddedness in either categoric and corporate units (such as family composed of age and sex categories or a group of others defined as "friends") will increase the likelihood that the beliefs and ideologies of these units, as they translate more general values, will be salient, thereby increasing the potential for guilt.

Needs for Facticity

Alfred Schutz ([1932] 1967) emphasized that people seek to achieve a sense of intersubjectivity, or the feeling that they share a common world. Later, ethnomethodology elaborated on this idea, emphasizing the taken-for-granted character of interaction and the use of implicit "folk methods" to create an implicit account of reality (Garfinkel 1967). Anthony Giddens (1984) has phrased this process as seeking "ontological security" allowing individuals to feel that "things are as they appear." All of these approaches converge on what I will term *facticity*, or the need of persons to (1) sense that they share a common world for the purposes of an interaction, (2) perceive the reality of a situation is as it appears, and (3) assume that reality has an obdurate character for the duration of the encounter. When individuals do not have this sense of facticity, they become irritated, and especially so if self is highly salient. When needs for facticity are met, people feel satisfied.

What determines, then, the emotional reaction? Early "breaching experiments" in ethnomethodology (Garfinkel 1967) indicated that when an experimenter disrupted efforts by another to achieve a sense of facticity, the latter expressed anger toward the experimenter; thus, when individuals attribute the failure to achieve facticity to the actions of another, they will reveal varying levels of low to moderate anger toward this person. It is rare for individuals to make attributions to self on the question of facticity, nor do people generally blame corporate and categoric units for failures to achieve facticity, although such attributions are possible. My reasoning here is that, like trust, facticity is highly contingent on the actions of individuals *in the immediate situation*, with each person trying to role take with specific others who provide, or fail to provide, cues allowing needs for facticity to be realized. As a result, a person will blame others for their failure to provide the necessary cues; and since mesostructures do not act and signal, they are less likely to be targets of anger over problems with achieving a sense of facticity. Moreover, because self-attributions for failures to achieve facticity are comparatively rare, defense mechanisms are not required to protect self. Thus, whatever the object of external attribution—typically another person—people will become annoyed and irritated toward this object.

When no clear attribution is made for the failure to achieve facticity in an encounter, people experience mild to moderate forms of fear, such as anxiety and concern. They sense that something is wrong and are anxious about the situation, and they will redouble their efforts to achieve a sense of facticity, typically through the highly visible use of rituals to establish a frame (Goffman 1974; J. Turner 2000b). Thus, normatizing (see Chapter 6) is critical to meeting needs for facticity, for without norms, the "reality" of the situation becomes problematic.

When encounters are embedded in corporate or categoric units, facticity is more readily realized. Expectations for categories of others and for individuals in various positions in corporate units are usually understood. The more clear-cut the categories of others, the easier it is to meet needs for facticity because most persons have stocks of knowledge about the characteristics of these categories and what to expect from them in a given situation; this knowledgeability is enough to get them started, with additional information acquired through active role taking with others and the cultural symbols relevant to the encounter. Similarly, the structure of corporate units, especially when they are bounded externally and internally partitioned and when revealing a formal division of labor, provide the base for meeting needs for facticity, again with additional information needed to complete the picture coming from active role taking with others in the encounter and, perhaps, the culture of the corporate unit. Thus, when an encounter is not firmly embedded in a structured corporate unit or unambiguous categoric units, people must work at achieving a sense of facticity. They will actively read all gestures of others, take cognizance of the physical props in the situation, search their stocks of knowledge for relevant cultural symbols, and engage in highly ritualized interaction until what Goffman termed "a footing" is achieved. Once this sense of facticity exists, individuals can relax their sensors and move to meeting other transactional needs.

Without a sense of facticity, all other needs become problematic. Can we trust others when we do not sense any intersubjectivity even if this sense is only at the minimal level of seeing another as a member of a category? Can we feel included in the interpersonal flow? Can we fully understand the relevant resources and symbols to achieve payoffs? Can we verify self when we do not sense the situation as fully real? Facticity is a quiet need in the sense to which people pay relatively little attention, because, typically, it is relatively easy to create this sense. It is only when the interaction is breached or out of sync that people suddenly become worried or angry that the power of this need is exposed. If needs for facticity are not realized, therefore, the interaction will cycle around highly expressive and visible gesturing until individuals can feel that they share a common world, experience the situation in the same way, and believe the world to have obdurate character for the duration of the interaction.

Failure to meet other transactional needs can effect actors' sense of facticity. Failure to achieve expected payoffs, to perceive group inclusion, to verify self, or to sense that others are predictable obviously erodes one's ability to meet needs for facticity. This is especially likely to be the case as the more powerful emotions that are activated with failure to meet other transactional needs increasingly disrupt the interaction. Still, even when people are being emotional about payoffs, inclusion, self-verification, and trust, they are often able to create a sense of facticity. For when actors make external attributions to the internal states of others or categories of others and/or to corporate units, they have a sense of reality about the (negative) character of their targets of attribution. Indeed, facticity is often the only need that can be met in circumstances where other transactional needs are going unfulfilled. For example, a person may say something like the following when self is not verified or expected payoffs are not received: "I know what you are like!; you are just an unpleasant, mean, and disgusting person who loves to screw around with others in situations like this" (granted, an overdramatization). Such statements indicate that a person has a sense of the reality of the situation and others (obviously rather negative), and so the need for facticity is being met, even as meeting other needs becomes problematic. Thus, the very process of attribution can generate a sense of reality.

Conclusion

Humans have at least five basic transactional needs: (1) self-verification; (2) positive exchange payoffs; (3) group inclusion; (4) trust; and (5) facticity. When these are not realized, the encounter ceases to flow smoothly, and in most cases, negative emotions are activated in ways that disrupt and breach the interaction.

Transactional needs are thus very much subject to the emotional dynamics examined in Chapter 4. Needs generate expectations for what should transpire in an encounter. This is especially so in the case of needs for self-verification and exchange payoffs; thus, expectation states become mediating mechanisms in establishing when needs for self-verification and profitable payoffs are fulfilled (and, to a lesser extent, other needs as well). Sanctioning also intervenes. When the responses of others allow a person to meet needs, these responses can be viewed as positive sanctions that, as we saw in Chapter 4, lead to the arousal of positive emotions. A lack of responsiveness on the part of others to an individual's attempts to meet need states can be seen as negative sanctions that arouse negative emotions. At times, individuals will receive deliberately intended negative sanctions from others, especially in their efforts to confirm self and realize positive exchange payoffs, and these arouse negative emotions to a more intense level.

The emotions activated by transactional needs will also vary in terms of (1) the specific transactional need, (2) the attributions made by an individual toward self, others, categories of others, or corporate units, (3) the use of defensive strategies like selective perception and interpretation or withdrawal from the interaction, and (4) the activation of defense mechanisms.

Moreover, the emotional reaction to the success or failure in satisfying transactional needs is influenced by other need states. The degree of fulfillment of one need is dependent on what has transpired in meeting other needs, and vice versa. When one or more other needs remains unfulfilled, the ability to meet any particular need will become more problematic.

Other fundamental forces of encounters—that is, symbols, roles, status, and demography/ecology—will also determine the ability to satisfy transactional needs. The chances of fulfilling any or all transactional needs are highly constrained by the clarity of norms, the distribution of status, the making and verifying of roles, especially those revolving around identity processes, and the composition of individuals, their distribution in space, and their use of physical props.

Finally, the degree of embeddedness of an encounter will influence transactional needs and circumscribe the emotional reactions to whether these needs are fulfilled. Some of the influence of categoric and corporate units is mediated through the power of these mesostructures to circumscribe the content of symbols, the distribution of status, the availability of roles, and the demographic/ecological parameters of the encounter. At other times, as we have seen, these mesostructures become part of the attribution process, providing targets for emotional responses.

Thus, as we approach some preliminary principles on the dynamics of transactional needs, we will have to keep in mind all of these factors. I cannot present final principles at this stage because we have yet to examine all of the forces driving encounters, but at the very least, I can offer some propositions that summarize the complicated arguments presented in this chapter.

I. Humans seek to satisfy basic needs for self-verification, profitable exchange payoffs, group inclusion, trust, and facticity in all transactions. When these needs are met, individuals will experience and express variants and elaborations of satisfaction-happiness, whereas when these needs remain unfulfilled, individuals will experience and express variants and elaborations of sadness, anger, and fear.

   A. The more one transactional need is met, the more likely are the remaining needs to be satisfied. Conversely, the more a transactional need remains unmet, the greater is the likelihood that the remaining needs will not be satisfied, with the possible exception of facticity.

   B. Encounters embedded in corporate and categoric units are more likely to have clear expectations for how transactional needs are to be realized, and hence, transactional needs in embedded encounters are more likely to be satisfied.

      1. The more an encounter is embedded in corporate units, and the more formal and explicit is the division of labor, the more likely are other forces of encounters—that is, emotions, symbols, status, roles, and demography/ecology—to be specified; and hence, the more likely are transactional needs to be met.

      2. The more an encounter is embedded in categoric units, and the more discrete and differentially evaluated these units, the more likely are expectations for others in categoric units to be clear; and hence, the more likely are transactional needs to be met.

II. When needs for self-verification are confirmed by the responses of
others, individuals will experience and express positive emotions;
and the more a role identity is connected to core-self feelings (high
salience) is confirmed, the more intense are these positive emotions,
whereas the less an identity is connected to core-self feelings (low
salience), the less intense are these positive emotions. Conversely,
when needs for self-verification are not confirmed by the responses
of others, individuals will experience and express negative emotions,
and the more an identity is connected to core-self feelings (high
salience), the more intense are these negative emotions, whereas the
less an identity is connected to core-self feelings (low salience), the
less intense are these feelings.

A. The more individuals see their own behaviors as causing verification of an identity and the more attached to core-self feelings is
the identity, the greater will be their happiness, and the more they
had some fear about securing self-verification, the greater will be
the sense of pride. Conversely, the less an identity is attached to
core-self feelings and the less fear they had about securing verification, the less intense will be the positive emotions.

B. The more needs for self-verification are seen by individuals as
the result of the actions of others, categories of others, and the
structure and culture of corporate units, the greater will be the
positive emotions expressed toward these targets of attribution,
and the more these attributions are sustained over iterated
encounters, the greater will be the commitments to others,
categoric units, and corporate units.

1. The more the core feelings of individuals are negative (low
self-esteem), the more likely are these individuals to make
external attributions to others, categories of others, and
corporate units; and correspondingly, the less intense will
be their positive feelings about themselves.

2. The more the core feelings of individuals are positive (high
self-esteem), the more likely are they to make attributions to
themselves; and if they do make external attributions, they
will still sustain positive evaluations of self.

C. The more others are seen by a person as actively offering positive
sanctions in order to verify this person's self, the more likely will

external attributions be made to these others, and the more these positive sanctions from others are sustained over iterated encounters, the greater will be the person's commitment to these others.

D. The more individuals see their own behaviors as causing disconfirmation of their role identity and the more attached to core-self feelings is the identity, the more intense will be their negative emotions. Conversely, the less an identity is connected to core-self feelings, the less intense will be the negative feeling experienced toward self when this identity is not verified.

1. Sadness is likely to be experienced when self-attributions are made.

2. Sadness about self, anger at self, and fear about the consequences to self increase when self-attributions are made and when failure to verify self is perceived to be the result of negative sanctions from others, and the more an identity is connected to core-self feelings under these conditions, the more likely is the person to experience shame.

3. Sadness about self, anger at self, and fear about the consequences to self will increasingly become transformed into guilt as values and evaluative ideologies are invoked in self-attributions, especially under conditions of negative sanctioning from others, and the more identity is connected to core-self feelings, the more intense will be the sense of guilt.

E. The more the failure to verify an identity is seen by individuals to be the result of actions by others, categories of others, and the structure and culture of categoric units, the more intense are the negative emotions expressed toward these targets of attribution, and the more these attributions are sustained over iterated encounters, the greater is the anger toward, and the less will be the commitments to, these others, categoric, and corporate units.

1. The more an unverified identity is connected to core-self feelings, and the more an individual engages in external attributions, the greater is the anger toward the targets of these attributions.

2. The less an unverified identity is connected to core-self feelings, and the more an individual engages in external attributions, the less is the anger toward the targets of these attributions.

F. The more others are perceived by individuals as negatively sanctioning an individual's identity, the more likely will this person make external attributions to these others, and the more these negative sanctions are sustained over iterated encounters, the greater will be the anger toward, and fear of, these others.

G. The more individuals must continue to interact in encounters where they fail to verify an identity as a result of negative sanctions from others, the more likely will these external attributions be supplemented by self-attributions for this failure, unless defense mechanisms are activated.

H. The more an identity is not verified by responses of others, the more likely are defensive strategies to be employed and defense mechanisms activated.

1. The less an identity is attached to core-self feelings and the less others engaged in deliberate negative sanctioning, the more likely are individuals to employ defensive strategies.

    a. Individuals will leave the encounter if they can.

    b. Individuals will engage in selective perception of the cues given off by others.

    c. Individuals will engage in selective interpretation of the cues given off by others.

    d. Individuals will seek to alter their role identity but only if the identity is of low salience (that is, not attached to core self or important subidentities).

2. The more an unverified identity is attached to core feelings about self, the more likely is the activation of defense mechanisms.

    a. Individuals will engage in projection, particularly external attributions to others, categories of others, and corporate units.

    b. Individuals will engage in displacement of negative emotions on others, categories of others, or corporate units.

    c. Individuals will engage in repression of negative emotions toward self.

3. The more projection and displacement generate negative sanctions from others, or are perceived by individuals as likely

to produce negative sanctions, the more likely will repression be activated, and the more repression is sustained over time in iterated encounters, the lower will be the modal level of energy of individuals. And the more intense are the negative emotions repressed, the more likely will low levels of modal energy be spiked by episodes of intense anger, fear, or sadness.

III. When needs for profitable exchange payoffs (rewards less costs and investments measured by standards of justice) are realized, individuals will experience and express positive emotions. Conversely, when needs for profitable exchanges are not realized, individuals will experience and express negative emotions.

A. Individuals will initially scan encounters for the available resources and symbols that can give them profitable payoffs, while successively narrowing this search for resources and symbols that can verify self and that can meet other transactional needs.

1. The more self is salient, the more individuals seek symbols and resources confirming self; and the more their expectations are met, the more intense are positive emotions. Conversely, the less salient is self, the more resources and symbols necessary for meeting other transactional needs will dominate expectations; and the more these expectations are met, the greater will be the sense of satisfaction.

a. The more individuals attribute success in realizing profitable exchange payoffs to their own actions, the greater will be their happiness; and the more they had some fear about receiving these payoffs, the greater their sense of pride.

b. The more individuals experience pride, the more they will give off positive emotions to others that, in turn, become a source of reward for these others who will reciprocate by providing positive payoffs to the individual in an escalating cycle until the encounter is terminated or fatigue and marginal utility set in.

2. The more self is salient, and the less are individuals' expectations for securing resources and symbols for positive exchange payoffs are realized, the more intense are their negative emotions.

a. The more individuals attribute failure in securing positive exchange payoffs to their own actions, the greater will be their sadness and, potentially, their anger at themselves as well as their fear about the consequences of their failure.

   i. When sadness, anger, and fear are all experienced simultaneously, individuals are more likely to experience shame.

   ii. When sadness, anger, and fear are all experienced simultaneously in evaluating self with reference to values and ideologies, individuals are more likely to experience guilt.

b. The more individuals attribute their failure in securing profitable exchange payoffs to actions of others, categories of others, or corporate units, the more intense is the anger toward these targets.

   i. When anger at others produces, or is perceived as likely to produce negative sanctions from these others, individuals will be more likely to blame categoric and/or corporate units.

   ii. When categoric units are blamed, individuals will develop prejudices toward members of these units; and when corporate units are blamed, individuals will lower their commitments to these units and exhibit role distance.

c. The more individuals cannot effectively utilize defensive strategies and the more they remain unrewarded in encounters, the more likely are the defense mechanisms to be activated.

   i. When defense mechanisms are activated, and when individuals engage in projection or displacement onto specific others, negative sanctions by these others or fear of such sanctions will increase. As a consequence, individuals will be increasingly likely to repress their negative emotions.

   ii. When anger, sadness, fear, and their elaborations into shame and guilt are repressed by individuals, their modal level of energy will decline, spiked by periodic outbursts of anger, anxiety, sadness, and, potentially, shame as well as guilt.

B. Categoric and corporate units are more likely to specify for individuals the resources and rewards available as well as the costs and investments necessary to receive rewards in an encounter.

1. The more resources and rewards are specified by categoric and corporate units, the more realistic are individuals' expectations for payoffs in the encounter.

2. The more realistic are individuals' expectations for payoffs, the more likely are they to engage in profitable exchanges with others in the encounter.

C. Other forces operating in encounters—that is, emotional, symbolic, role, status, and demographic/ecological—are likely to specify for individuals the resources and symbols available.

1. The more powerful these forces, the greater is the specification, and hence, the more likely are individuals to adjust expectations for exchange payoffs to realistic levels.

2. The more embedded is an encounter in categoric and corporate units, the more constraining are other forces in encounters and the greater is the specification; and hence, the more likely are individuals to adjust expectations for exchange payoffs to realistic levels.

IV. Humans seek to satisfy needs for group inclusion in the ongoing flow of interaction. Although humans do not need to achieve high degrees of inclusion in most encounters, the greater is this need and the more this need is satisfied, the more intense will be the positive emotions experienced and expressed. Conversely, the greater is the need and the less this need is satisfied, the more intense will be the negative emotions experienced and expressed.

A. The more the core-self feelings of an individual are salient, the more powerful is the need for group inclusion, and hence, the more intense are the emotional reactions, whether positive or negative. Conversely, the less salient are core-self feelings, the less powerful is the need for group inclusion, and the less intense are the emotional reactions, whether positive or negative.

1. The more salient is self and the greater is the sense of group inclusion achieved by individuals, the more positive are their emotions toward self and others; and if they had some fear about achieving group inclusion, the greater is their sense of pride.

a. When individuals feel included, their positive sentiments toward others will allow these others to achieve a sense of inclusion, causing the latter to increase their rates of inclusive signaling in a cycle that ends with termination of the encounter or fatigue and marginal utility.

b. When individuals feel included, positive sentiments toward others and their reciprocation will increase commitments to these others and the mesounits in which the encounter is embedded.

2. The more salient is self and the less is the sense of group inclusion achieved by individuals, the more negative are their emotions.

a. When individuals blame their own actions for the failure to achieve a sense of inclusion, sadness will increase; the higher the salience of self, the more likely are anger at self and fear of the consequences to self to be experienced.

   i. If individuals experience sadness, anger, and fear simultaneously, the more likely are they to experience shame.

   ii. If individuals experience sadness, anger, and fear simultaneously in evaluations of self with reference to values and ideologies, the more likely are they to experience guilt.

b. When individuals attribute the failure to achieve a sense of group inclusion to others, categories of others or corporate units when self is salient, the intensity of anger toward, and fear of, these targets of external attribution will increase.

   i. If individuals experience anger toward, and fear of, a categoric unit, they will exhibit prejudices toward members of this categoric unit.

   ii. If individuals experience anger toward, and fear of, a corporate unit, they will exhibit low levels of commitment to the corporate unit and high levels of role distance.

c. When individuals cannot use defensive strategies and must, instead, remain in iterated encounters where they continually fail to achieve a sense of group inclusion, defense mechanisms are likely to be activated.

i. When projection, including attributions, and displacement of anger onto others result in negative sanctions or are perceived as likely to cause negative sanctioning from these others, repression becomes more likely.

ii. When repression is activated, individuals' modal levels of energy will decline, spiked by periodic episodes of anger and anxiety.

V. When needs for trust are realized, individuals will experience and express low-intensity happiness. Conversely, when needs for trust are not realized, individuals will experience and express low-intensity negative emotions.

A. The more individuals achieve a sense of trust when self is salient, the more likely is moderate-intensity happiness to be experienced and expressed, and the more individuals had some fear about achieving trust, the more likely is low-intensity pride to be experienced.

1. When trust has been consistently achieved in iterated encounters, individuals are more willing to increase the salience of self and, thereby, present identities tied to core-self feelings.

2. The more encounters are embedded in categoric and corporate units, the more likely are expectations for trust to be clear, and hence, the more likely are individuals to achieve a sense of trust; and the more self is salient, the more likely are they to develop commitments to members of the categoric units and the culture and structure of corporate units.

B. The less individuals have achieved a sense of trust in interaction with others, the more likely are they to experience and express low-intensity anger (annoyance) toward others rather than self; the more self is salient, the more low-intensity anger is supplemented by fear.

1. When others are perceived as untrustworthy but cannot be avoided, individuals will be more likely to channel their anger toward these untrustworthy others in highly ritualized and formal modes of interaction, even if informality and sociality are required.

2. When others are not trustworthy and have power, individuals will experience more fear than anger, and they will channel this

fear in even more highly formal, controlled, and ritualized forms of interaction, even if informality and sociality are required.

    c. The more individuals blame their own actions for failures to achieve a sense of trust in interaction with others, the more likely are they to experience and express low-levels of anger toward self, coupled with sadness; and the more powerful are the others with whom trust was not achieved, the more likely are they to experience some fear as well.

        1. The more individuals blame self and experience mixes of sadness, anger, and fear simultaneously, the more likely are they to experience low levels of shame.

        2. The more individuals blame and evaluative self in references to values and ideologies while experiencing sadness, anger, and fear simultaneously, the more likely are they to experience low levels of guilt.

            a. If an encounter is embedded in a corporate unit, the more clear-cut are the values and ideologies, and hence, the more likely is guilt to be experienced when blaming self for the failure to achieve a sense of trust.

            b. If an encounter is embedded in categoric units, and particularly if these categoric units are correlated with positions in corporate units, the more clear-cut are values and ideologies, and hence, the more likely is guilt to be experienced when blaming self for the failure to achieve a sense of trust.

VI. When needs for facticity are realized, individuals will experience and express low-intensity happiness. Conversely, when needs for facticity are not realized, individuals will experience and express low-intensity negative emotions.

    A. The more needs for facticity are realized and the more salient is self, the more individuals will offer low-key and low-intensity positive sanctions to others who, reciprocally, offer low-key positive sanctions in return, thereby increasing the sense of facticity.

    B. The more encounters are embedded in categoric and corporate units, the more clear-cut are expectations about what constitutes reality, and hence, the more likely are individuals to achieve a sense of facticity, and hence, offer low-key positive sanctions to others.

c. The less needs for facticity are realized in interaction with others, the more likely are individuals to blame others rather than self for failure to achieve a sense of facticity, and the more likely are they to experience and express low-intensity anger toward these others, and hence, the more likely are they to sanction negatively these others.

D. The more needs for facticity are not realized in situations where others cannot be blamed, the more likely are individuals to experience a diffuse sense of low-intensity fear (concern).

1. When encounters have not been successfully normatized, the lack of norms decreases the likelihood that individuals can readily achieve a sense of facticity, and hence, the more likely are they to experience low-intensity fear.

2. When interactions are not embedded in categoric and corporate units, individuals are less likely to achieve a sense of facticity, at least initially, and hence, the more likely are they to experience low-intensity fear.

SIX

Symbolic Forces

In early sociological theorizing, Émile Durkheim ([1893] 1984) was probably the most important theorist on the force of culture.[1] For Durkheim, behaviors and social relations are regulated by the "collective conscience" and although this is a rather vague notion, it is generally thought to mean the values, beliefs, and norms of structural units within which interaction occurs. Other theorists hinted at the same force, as when Sigmund Freud formulated the concept of "superego," George Herbert Mead the notion of "generalized other," and Alfred Schutz the idea of "stocks of knowledge at hand." The history of the idea, of course, is less important than the reality: human behavior and interaction are directed by cultural scripts consisting of systems of symbols. The symbols necessary for interaction are stored in individuals' heads, most probably in neocortical areas like the frontal cortex, and most are tagged with emotional content via neuronets running mostly back and forth through the prefrontal cortex to the amygdala and onto other subcortical emotion centers (see Figure 3.1 in Chapter 3). The end result is humans' amazing ability to store vast stocks of knowledge and to retrieve this knowledge for use in a particular encounter.

No one human could possibly have learned every system of symbols and its "meaning" for every context, especially in complex and changing societies; and yet the human brain can somehow invoke relevant symbols for an en-

---

[1] True, some would argue for Max Weber, but Weber never developed *an explicit theory* of the relations among symbolic and interpersonal forces.

counter, even in a novel context. Indeed, it is rare for humans to be at a loss for "what to do"; and even if a situation is new, it does not take long to pick up what is required. Humans are, I believe, hard-wired to match symbols to context because we rarely have to talk to ourselves about how to behave; we implicitly know what is expected. If we are unsure, our brains are programmed to read the gestures of others and contextual cues to find out what is required of us. Alfred Schutz's ([1932] 1967) concept of "stocks of knowledge at hand" best captures this amazing ability of the human brain to make available, typically without much reflection, the necessary knowledgeability.

It may be that humans' amazing ability to assemble relevant cultural symbols operates like syntax for language. The human brain contains the capacity to assemble in accordance with algorithms—both neurological and cultural—the relevant symbols for an occasion. No amount of experience could allow individuals to store, literally, all of the preassembled stocks of knowledge relevant to all situations; rather, there appears to be a generative dynamic that assembles a bundle of symbols for each encounter. Thus, "knowledgeability" is not a warehouse of "finished and completed symbolic goods" but a warehouse of cultural "parts" and perhaps prepackaged subassemblies of symbols that can be rapidly pulled together by the neurology of the human brain for ever-changing encounters.

The Elements of Culture

The concept of *culture* denotes the assembling of information and meanings along a variety of dimensions: (1) general texts that provide interpretations of present, past, and future conditions; (2) technologies that provide information on how to manipulate the environment, both social and biophysical; (3) values that specify at a general and abstract level right and wrong, good and bad, appropriate and inappropriate; (4) evaluative beliefs or ideologies that apply values to particular types of institutional domains; (5) institutional norms translating the values, ideologies, technologies, and texts of a particular institutional domain into general expectations for various classes of actors in this domain; (6) organizational norms that translate institutional norms into specific expectations for members of corporate units and categoric units; and (7) interpersonal norms that apply organizational norms (and by extension all of the other elements of culture going into them) to specific episodes of face-to-face interaction.

These dimensions of culture exist, I believe, in a continual state of regeneration. On the one hand, culture exists as systems of symbols assembled in the past and, to a degree, neurologically codified as memories that individuals carry in their brains and apply as preassembled packages to familiar situations; on the other hand, these memories are assembled by neurological and culturally programmed algorithms for the particular episode of face-to-face interaction. As this assembling occurs, innovation of new combinations of symbols or inventions of new symbols can also transpire, especially if the encounter is new or if old preassembled packages no longer seem to work as well as they once did.

The process of assembling texts, technologies, and values into beliefs and norms at all levels of reality is fraught with potential ambiguity and even more so when encounters are not clearly embedded. Moreover, some situations do not fall clearly within mesostructures and, hence, reside outside the explicit purview of institutional or organizational norms. Without embeddedness, individuals will invent culture as they go along. But even as people create new symbol systems in an episode of face-to-face interaction, they generally rely on the old, reworking elements in their stocks of knowledge to fit new circumstances. For example, a child may never have been to a funeral, but the child has probably been in, or witnessed, encounters involving seriousness and sadness; and this experience gives the brain something to go on as it assembles norms. Or, to take another example, I may not know the protocols for interacting with opera stars backstage, but I do have many relevant scripts—for example, institutional norms on "artists," norms of ritualized encounters among strangers, norms on gender, norms on deference and demeanor, and so on—to draw on as I orient myself to others in this context. Whether familiar or brand new, a *set* of expectations is invoked to guide the interaction as a person makes his or her way in a situation. The process of creating this set of expectations is what I term *normatizing* the encounter. Before much else can occur, then, individuals have to normatize the situation by developing cultural expectations for self and others about how to act and interact.

Normatizing

Too often, the concept of *norms* is considered to be a noun in sociological thought, but it should be conceptualized as a verb, in this sense: individuals

Axes of Normatizing

1. *Categorizing*: The process of developing expectations by virtue of (a) placing self and others in categoric units, (b) typifying the situation in terms of the relative amounts of work-practical, social, and ceremonial activity, and (c) determining if others are to be treated as personages, persons, or intimates.

2. *Framing*: The process of developing expectations by determining what is to be included and excluded for the purposes of interaction, particularly with respect to (a) the values and evaluative beliefs that will be relevant, (b) the persons to be included and their distribution of others in space, (c) the portions of bodies and biographies to be displayed, (d) the stages and props to be used, and (e) the categoric and corporate units to be used as a point of reference.

3. *Communicating*: The process of developing expectations for the forms of talk and nonverbal gesturing to be employed during the course of the interaction.

4. *Ritualizing*: The process of developing expectations for the stereotypical sequences of gestures to be used in (a) opening, (b) closing, (c) forming, (d) symbolizing and totemizing, and (e) repairing the interaction.

5. *Feeling*: The process of developing expectations for (a) what emotions are to be experienced and expressed, (b) what level of intensity they are to be experienced and expressed, and (c) when they are to be experienced and expressed.

are rapidly and, most typically, implicitly assembling systems of symbols to generate expectations in a situation. These expectations are not fixed; they can change or be refined as an encounter proceeds. Thus, the process of generating expectations is active as individuals' expectations for themselves and others are implicitly formulated and refined. Incumbency within a corporate unit with a clear division of labor can greatly constrain this process; or interaction with clear categories of others can move normatizing in a given direction. But despite these and other constraints, normatizing is a continual process, one in which individuals are constantly checking and rechecking expectations. People do this with such ease that they are hardly ever aware of

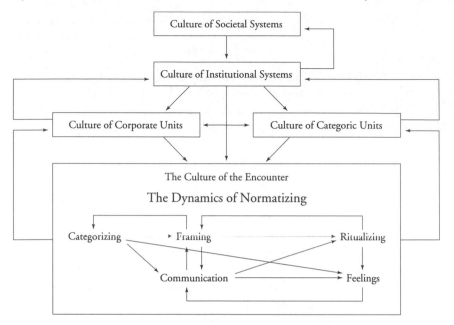

Figure 6.1.   Normatizing the Encounter

what is occurring, but we can become suddenly alert to how much is involved when a situation is breached or is new, forcing us to become more (self) conscious of relevant expectations.

Thus, we need to move away from conceptions of norms as cultural scripts attached to a particular status or guiding a role. The process is much more robust because the cultural script comes from diverse "writers" and the script is constantly being rewritten as individuals interact.[2] How then do we get a conceptual handle on normatizing? My view is that we need to explore the axes along which individuals invoke, use, and develop normative expectations for themselves and others. I think that, at the most generic level, there are five

---

[2] A great deal of sociological theory has addressed the issues that I raise with the concept of normatizing, especially in the recent "cultural turn" in theory. For example, Pierre Bourdieu's (1989, 1984) concept of "habitus" denotes some of what I mean by normatizing. But unlike so much theory in this tradition that, to me at least, glosses over the properties of culture as it intersects with behavior and interaction, I am trying with the concept of normatizing to be more specific and to spell out the dimensions along which culture and action operate.

such axes: (1) categorizing; (2) framing; (3) communicating; (4) ritualizing; and (5) feeling. That is, as an interaction unfolds, its participants use situational cues, often provided by mesostructures, and the gestures of others to assemble from their stocks of knowledge relevant symbols that allow them to categorize each other and the situation, to determine what is to be included and excluded for the purposes of the interaction, to use the proper forms of talk, both verbal and nonverbal, to communicate meanings, to emit rituals at the proper moment, and to feel and express appropriate emotions. When an encounter is normatized along these axes, its focus and rhythmic flow will generally be sustained.

Figure 6.1 outlines in rough form the flow of causal relations among these normatizing dynamics and is supplemented by material that defines each dimension of normatizing. As Figure 6.1 summarizes, however, the process of normatizing is like most social processes in that it is recursive; causal outcomes exert reverse causal effects on the very processes that brought these outcomes about and, as a consequence, potentially change the outcomes. Moreover, most social processes often have closely timed or even simultaneous effects on each other. Thus, Figure 6.1 is not a path diagram because most path diagrams in sociology almost always see causality as flowing one way, from independent to dependent variables, perhaps through some intervening variables. All Figure 6.1 seeks to do is sensitize us to the general configuration of causality, but we could jump into the causal paths at any point and go either forward or backward in time. Also, empirical context can make a difference in which elements of normatizing at different phases of the encounter are more important than others, but I would argue that there is a rough temporal sequence to the process, as is outlined in Figure 6.1 as the diagram flows from left to right.

CATEGORIZING

As Alfred Schutz ([1932] 1967) emphasized, individuals typify each other and the situation, and they often respond to each other as "ideal types" or representatives of a social category. Thus, people immediately place others in a particular categoric unit, or even perhaps several units (for example, Latino female), and on the basis of this designation(s), they form expectations about other(s) and begin to adjust their responses accordingly. At the same time, individuals also categorize the nature of the situation as being of a certain type, and following Goffman (1967), Collins (1975), and my earlier work (J. Turner

Table 6.1. Categorizing Situations and Intimacy

| | TYPES OF SITUATIONS | | |
	Work / Practical	*Ceremonial*	*Social*
PERSONAGES	Others as functionaries whose behaviors are relevant to achieving a specific task or goal and who, for the purposes at hand, can be treated as strangers	Others as representatives of a larger collective enterprise toward whom highly stylized responses owed as a means of expressing their joint activity	Others as strangers toward whom superficially informal, polite, and responsive gestures are owed
PERSONS	Others as functionaries whose behaviors are relevant to achieving a specific task or goal but who, at the same time, must be treated as unique individuals in their own right	Others as fellow participants of a larger collective enterprise toward whom stylized responses are owed as a means of expressing their joint activity and recognition of each other as individuals in their own right	Others as familiar individuals toward whom informal, polite, and responsive gestures are owed
INTIMATES	Others as close friends whose behaviors are relevant to achieving a specific task or goal and toward whom emotional responsiveness is owed	Others as close friends who are fellow participants in a collective enterprise and toward whom a combination of stylized and personalized responses are owed as a means of expressing their joint activity and sense of mutual understanding	Others as close friends toward whom informal and emotionally responsive gestures are owed

LEVELS OF INTIMACY IN DEALING WITH OTHERS

1988), they do so along three dimensions: (1) *work/practical* where individuals are trying to complete a task; (2) *social* or where individuals are engaged in interaction for its own sake; and (3) *ceremonial* in which people are involved in stylized behaviors marking the significance of an occasion, honoring (or dishonoring) another or groups of others. Most situations involve elements of all three, but it is the *relative amounts* of work-practical, social, and ceremonial behavior required that is critical. Once individuals have made an assessment, this too becomes a normative expectation that guides responses.

As people determine each other's membership in categoric units and as they assess the relative amounts of work-practical, social, and ceremonial content required, they also categorize self, others, and the situation with respect to the degree of intimacy expected. Schutz ([1932] 1967) portrayed increasing intimacy or intersubjectivity as moving from categorizing individuals as ideal types to "in-order-to" motives and, then at deeper levels of intersubjectivity, to "because of motives." Following Schutz, but employing a different terminology, these dynamics can be conceptualized as follows: other(s) can be defined as *personages* of a given type (for example, cashier) toward whom little more than polite responses are owed; others can be defined as *persons* toward whom interpersonal responsiveness is required; or others can be seen as *intimates* whose biography, experiences, and feelings are known and are to be taken into consideration during the course of the interaction. Once the level of appropriate intimacy is determined, this also becomes a normative expectation that guides the focus and flow of interaction.

Thus, individuals categorize along three dimensions: (1) categoric units to which self and others belong; (2) situations; and (3) levels of intimacy.

Table 6.1 summarizes in simplified form the nine basic categories that arise from cross-tabulation of levels of intimacy with nature of the situation. These nine categories are, however, supplemented by the categoric unit(s) to which self and others are placed. The greater is the number of categoric units to which a person is seen to belong, the more complex is the categorization of the situation as work-practical, ceremonial, or social, and the more problematic is categorization of others as personages, persons, and intimates. For example, if two African American males of different levels of wealth and status find themselves with only white males of varying levels of wealth and position in a situation that is work-practical but with significant amounts of social content, there may be ambiguity in how these two males should treat each other vis-à-vis the white males. Moreover, the length of the interaction and the number of iterations of the encounter also change the configuration of categories. For instance, a work-practical encounter of personages will, over time, shift to one where more social content is introduced. As this change occurs, others can become persons and perhaps even intimates. Thus, initial categorization only sets early expectations for self and others, and while these will influence subsequent events, categorizations can change as the interaction proceeds. As categories change, normative expectations for appropriate conduct will accommodate the new configuration of categories.

FRAMING

Erving Goffman's *Frame Analysis* (1974) greatly expanded on an idea that had appeared in his work since the 1950s. In the 1950s, Goffman first used the concept of "definition of the situation," and later he began to occasionally employ the term "frame" as a substitute. Goffman's frame analysis went too far, I believe, into the phenomenology of experience; indeed the analysis becomes excessively bogged down in explaining how laminations on primary frames are built up. If individuals really did all that Goffman hypothesized, they would exhaust themselves, even if their neurology allowed them to do much of the work unconsciously. But the idea of a frame is sound because it denotes the processes whereby individuals come to agree, generally implicitly, on the materials that can be included and excluded from interaction during an encounter. Gesturing among individuals communicates what is to be *keyed* or included in the "picture frame" and what is to lie outside the frame. Naturally, frames can change or be *rekeyed* as the interaction unfolds or as it is repeated, especially when other elements of normatizing shift. I want to use these core ideas, then, from Goffman's analysis, but in my own way.

My view is that individuals categorize others and the situation, and on the basis of this initial categorization, framing occurs along dimensions outlined in Figure 6.2. Of course, once frames exist, they reinforce categorization, but perhaps more importantly, changes in categorization often come about as a result of individuals rekeying the frame. Moreover, if it proves difficult to key a frame, the interaction becomes awkward and categorization begins to break down, as does the more inclusive process of normatization. However the frames of an interaction are keyed and rekeyed, this process occurs with respect to the dimensions delineated in Figure 6.2 (J. Turner 1994a, 1988). Individuals in an encounter must generate normative expectations for access to bodies, for who is to be present and who can come and go, for the props to be used, for structure and culture of relevant meso- and macrounits, for

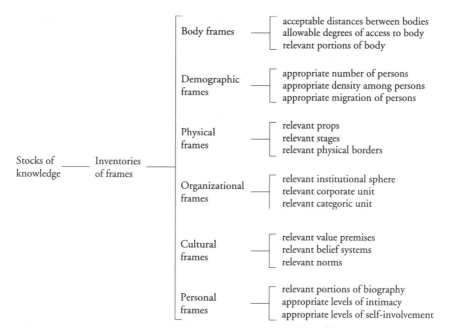

Figure 6.2. General Axes of Framing

cultural values, beliefs, and norms, and for the amount of personal content. When implicit agreements are made along these dimensions, they too become expectations that facilitate the focus and flow of interaction; and once frames are keyed, they are rekeyed through highly ritualized acts (for example, "do you mind if I ask you a personal question"; "can we not talk about this"; "don't go there!"; and many other stylized and stereotypical phrases punctuate interaction as frames are keyed and rekeyed).

Humans carry vast inventories of frames, as well as grammars about how to apply them to varying contexts, how to negotiate and renegotiate frames, how to break frames, how to laminate frames inside or on top of each other, and how to key or rekey frames. Most of the time, people do not have to think consciously about these framing dynamics; they simply "know" what to do. Of course, if an interaction is off track and floundering, we suddenly become aware of the lack of agreed-upon frames; and we soon find that, if we try to impose a frame consciously, it seems awkward and stilted. For example, when a person starts thinking about "what can we talk about," "do I dare broach this," "how should I relate to these people," and so on, they are consciously pondering frames; and once framing is conscious and deliberative, it becomes problematic. Talk and gesturing are usually out of rhythm, at least until its participants agree on a frame. Thus, most framing is done implicitly, somewhat outside of conscious deliberation. When the process becomes explicit, it soon becomes awkward because we are trying to do verbally what our brain does in its own nonverbal ways of processing information. Moreover, without a frame, all other normatizing processes become difficult. Categories do not hold, how to talk and communicate with nonverbal gestures become unclear, what rituals to use and when to use them are ambiguous, and what feelings to experience and express become clouded by anxiety over the lack of a rhythmic flow to the interaction. Thus, while we may not consciously think about framing, we become suddenly acutely aware that something is wrong with the interaction when there is a lack of successful framing.

COMMUNICATION

Humans communicate along the visual, auditory, and tactile sense modalities (and occasionally along the olfactory channel). Nonverbal gesturing is very much influenced by the categorization and framing of the encounter, because these impose normative expectations about how one is to present self, both face and body, to others. Forms of talk are also very much influenced by categories and frames; indeed, when a person talks "out of form" with others, they break the frame and shift categories in ways that often make others feel awkward. For example, a young student calling a senior professor by his or her first name (unless invited) violates categories and frames in ways that make the professor unsure of how to respond. Not just words and how they are spoken, but also the back channel of auditory frequency and information are constrained by categories and frames. When a powerful person interacts with a subordinate, for instance, not only is the talk and body gesturing structured by their respective categories and frames, but so is the pitch, sound frequency, and amplitude constrained (Gregory 1999, 1994).

People not only "talk" along the auditory channel; they also "speak" with body language. People look for a consistency among auditory, visual, and haptic signals, and when they are out of synchronization, the interaction is strained.[3] As I argued in Chapter 4, a visually based syntax of emotions is the

[3] The process will be explored in more detail when we turn to the analysis of role dynamics.

more primary form of communication; as a consequence, humans are highly responsive to body language—use of facial expressions, body continuance, body positioning, and touch—to communicate the more affective side of "talk." Indeed, without communication through visual readings of body language, it is difficult to frame and categorize. People cannot "read" each other, and as a result, role taking and self-presentations become awkward, making all normatizing efforts problematic. Moreover, visually based body language is often more important (because it is more primal) than forms of talk in initially establishing frames and, most certainly, in changing them and in recategorizing.

Thus, when the appropriate form of talk and nonverbal gesturing occur, frames and categories are confirmed. Again, if interactions are prolonged, if new members enter the mix, or if the encounter is iterated, categories and frames may shift, and as a result, so will forms of verbal and nonverbal communication. As forms of talk are established, or reestablished, these become normative expectations for how communication is to occur; and these expectations will guide the focus and flow of the interaction, until frames are rekeyed.

RITUALIZING

When frames are keyed and as forms of communication are understood, rituals keep the flow of interaction in focus and rhythmically on track. Rituals are stereotyped sequences of gestures, mostly talk but body and haptic responses as well. In Figure 6.3, I list what I see as the basic types of rituals that individuals employ in an encounter.

Bracketing rituals open and close interactions and, thereby, help key the initial frames; once these frames have been ritualized, normative expectations for the use of rituals guide the subsequent flow of interaction in the present or in future encounters. For example, rituals open the interaction through verbal greetings, body countenance, body positioning, and haptic responses such as a handshake or pat on the back. Just how these are executed will initially frame the interaction and influence its subsequent flow. Rituals also close the interaction, and the nature of the closing ritual will create an expectation for subsequent interaction. For instance, an enthusiastic verbal send-off, punctuated with touching, and emission of positive affect will set one kind of frame (in American culture) for the next encounter, whereas unenthusiastic movements away from others with little affect or haptic response

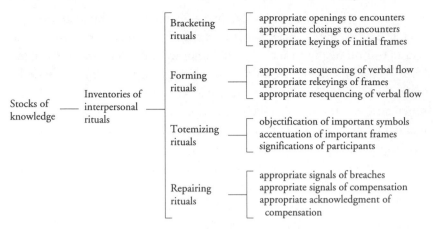

Figure 6.3.   The Dynamics of Rituals

will establish another kind of frame and all that frames influence: categorizing, communication, and subsequent rituals.

Forming rituals structure interaction between openings and closings by pacing and sequencing talk, by rekeying frames and all that they influence, and by resequencing the verbal flow. As rituals structure the flow of interaction, they also create normative expectations for what should transpire now and in the future, until new rituals create different expectations. For example, turn-taking in conversations is highly ritualized through the way that auditory sounds are inflected at the end of a verbal sequence and through the facial and body cues emitted as an utterance is coming to an end. Or, if a person wishes to shift topics or to change the frame, there are highly ritualized ways of doing so, as is the case when someone says "can I talk with you in private" while moving closer, lowering the amplitude and frequency of auditory signals, and perhaps escorting with touch a person out of earshot of others. As the frame is shifted, so must the flow of talk and nonverbal gesturing be resequenced, as is the case when a person communicates private thoughts through hushed and more informal forms of talk among bodies more closely positioned.

Totemizing rituals allow for aspects of the interaction to be reified and seen as an external "thing" symbolizing some aspect of the encounter. Gift-giving, for example, is a totemizing ritual because the gift symbolizes the relationship among individuals. Or, verbal utterances like "I love you" are more than mere expressions of affection, they are stereotyped sequences of talk and associated body gestures that symbolize *the relationship* and require counterrituals such as "I love you too." Of course, there are more obvious physical totems—from badges and clothes to real objects of worship such as a cross—and these operate in the same way: to symbolize the relationship with special significance by an external marker. Just about any aspect of the encounter can be ritually symbolized—another person, a strip of talk, the encounter as a whole, the mesounit in which the encounter is lodged, or particular relationships in the encounter. We tend to think of totems as only physical objects of special significance, but far more frequent are ritualized gestures symbolizing some aspect of the encounter as significant and as having a force outside the persons involved. Even seemingly simple utterances, such as "you tell a great story," "I really like being around you," "let's not upset the boss," operate as totemizing rituals, and once we look for them, they punctuate interaction far more than is commonly realized. Like any totem, they symbolize something about the encounter, others, relations, and situations. The more obvious the totemizing rituals, the more interaction carries heightened emotional valences.

Repairing rituals address breaches to the interaction and seek to redress the negative emotions aroused in self and others. When an interaction is breached, normative expectations are violated and negative sanctions are activated, and this arousal of negative emotions must be controlled if the focus and flow of the interaction is to be maintained. When there is a breach, the initial reaction of others toward the offender is often a highly ritualized reaction—for example, "how could you say that!"—which informs the other of the breach and, at the same time, applies a negative sanction. Often, signals of breaches are nonverbal, as when individuals frown, looked disgusted, look down, or begin to move away, but the matter is typically not left at this stage of a breach. There are also rituals that tell others the appropriate compensations —for instance, "now you take that back!"—and these give an offender a clear opening and avenue for repairing the breach, if this option is chosen. And there are rituals that offer compensation to others by an offender—"I am really sorry," "I don't know what came over me," "I wasn't being very sensitive"—who acknowledges that the breach is his or her fault and offers an apology that allows individuals to get back on track. Indeed, rituals offering compensation are generally followed by further rituals accepting the apology—for example, "oh, that's o.k.," "let's not think about it anymore."

As rituals are used, they have important effects on frames and feelings. Most rekeyings of frames are highly ritualized; as these rituals shift frames,

they alter the forms of communication and, if the shift in frames is significant, categorizations as well. Shifts in frames always change the emotional
valences of an interaction directly as well as indirectly through the effects
of frames on categorization and communication. Erving Goffman's (1967)
work downsized Durkheim's ([1912] 1946) analysis of rituals to the microlevel, but surprisingly, this great insight has not been examined in as much
detail as it might. Rituals rebound in virtually every aspect of interaction,
and yet the complexity of their use has not progressed much beyond Goffman's early insights. Even theorists like Randall Collins (1975) who proposed "an interaction ritual theory" underemphasize the actual nature of rituals; and in Collins's case, the definition of ritual corresponds to Goffman's
definition of the encounter rather than Goffman's conceptualization of rituals. Rituals are critical to the rhythmic flow of the interaction because they
pace and structure this flow, but they also are often the mechanism used to
change the values of other elements of normatization, because rituals are
critical to rekeying of frames and to emotional arousal; and in so doing,
they establish, maintain, or change the normative expectations on individuals in the encounter.

FEELINGS

As we saw in Chapter 4, emotions are central to interaction; and their intensity and valence will reflect the normative or expectation structure of an
encounter. Emotions thus exert their own force on interaction. Because of
this fact, they are almost always regulated by "feeling" and "display" rules
(Hochschild 1983, 1979) as well as by the more general "blueprint rules"
(Ridgeway 1994, 1982) of institutional and organizational systems. What one
is supposed to feel in an encounter and how a person is to display emotions
are dictated by other normatizing processes. Categorization is one source of
feeling rules, since individuals understand the expectations for how they
should express emotions around members of different categoric units and in
different types of situations outlined in Table 6.1. As frames emerge from
categorizations, or are changed by rekeying of a frame, forms of communication and rituals become the vehicles by which emotions are regulated.
Nonverbal forms of communication are the most critical, because humans
are visually dominant; as a consequence, they search faces, bodies, and countenance of other people for what they can tell them about emotions. Auditory signals, especially the back channel of intonation, pitch, and frequency,

also provide emotional cues. And haptic responses, when used to communicate, have large effects on reading emotions. Conversely, nonverbal, auditory, and haptic senses are also the vehicles for self-presentations of emotions to others, sometimes consciously but more frequently unconsciously. Thus, how one feels subjectively is constrained by feeling rules; and how one reveals emotions to others is similarly regulated, although there is almost always some leakage of emotions outside of expressive control.

Feelings change the focus and flow of interaction by virtue of their effects on forms of communication as these feedback and feedforward to other normatizing elements. When an emotion is expressed, nonverbal and verbal communication will reflect this feeling, thereby forcing frames, categories, and rituals to come into line with the emotional valences of the encounter. Of course, if the emotions breach the interaction, then communication will be directed to calling attention to the breach, negative sanctioning, and offers of compensation or apologies, but if a shift in emotional valences does not breach but simply alters the emotional mood of the encounter, then all other sources of expectations must also shift to accommodate these new emotional displays, thereby setting up feeling rules for the new expressive atmosphere of the encounter. For example, if a person suddenly starts crying or otherwise displays sadness, the situation may be breached, but it may also become renormatized. Frames will shift to more concern about a person's inner self; categories will move toward more intimacy and out of work-practical modes (if this was the original categorization of the situation); forms of auditory talk shift intonations and amplitudes to quieter, more affective forms; rituals are directed to displaying concern and caring; and emotions of others become more positive and subdued. All of these changes are marked by highly stereotypical sequences of talk and body movements.

Rituals thus regulate the expression of emotions within the encounter. Rituals have the power to arouse or subdue emotions; thus, as individuals shift emotional valences, they almost always do so in highly ritualized terms. Sometimes people are conscious of the rituals they enact (particularly, if they are being disingenuous), but often the ritual is emitted unconsciously. For example, if someone expresses anger, they will usually do it ritually—for example, "I have a beef with you," "you really piss me off"—unless, of course, the anger moves outside the range of expressive control. Even positive emotions are expressed ritually—for example, "I am so happy," "I am so proud of you," "way to go," "what fun!" Indeed, a high proportion of positive sanctions is expressed ritually through stereotyped sequences of talk and nonverbal gesturing. Fear is also expressed ritually—"I am worried sick," "what am I to do," "he scares me," and similar expressions of fear. Similarly, sadness is often expressed ritually—"I am so down," "It's so depressing," and so on. We may think of these phrases and accompanying body language as mere conventions of talk or even as clichés, but they are stereotyped sequences of gestures for expressing feelings (in American English). Just how, when, and with what amplitude and valence these sequences are uttered is circumscribed by other normatizing processes. Moreover, like any ritual, they arouse the emotion in the person and others; they are not just expressions of raw affect or conversational conventions but signals that are, like any ritual, intended to arouse emotional responses.

Normatizing and Embeddedness

Generating expectations from the elements of normatizing is constrained by the culture and structure of meso- and macrostructures. Individuals rarely have to do a deep search of their stocks of knowledge to pull up the relevant stores of information because most encounters are embedded in corporate and categoric units that, in turn, are lodged in more inclusive institutional systems. Indeed, if encounters were not embedded, normatizing would be difficult and time consuming as actors constantly negotiated over categories, frames, forms of talk, rituals, and feeling rules. Embedding dramatically limits the amount of interpersonal work for parties to the encounter. My goal here is to describe some of the key dynamics of normatizing that follow from embedding.

The broader values of society are translated into ideologies or beliefs as well as institutional norms that, in turn, are further translated into: (a) ideologies of corporate units and normative standards about the relevant and appropriate categories, frames, forms of talk, rituals, and feelings; and (b) evaluations of categoric units as well as expectations for how members of these units should behave. When an encounter is lodged in the corporate units of a more inclusive institutional system—for instance, a meeting in a business enterprise within a capitalist economy—and when the corporate unit is formal and hierarchical with an explicit division of labor, the culture of the corporate unit and, by extension, the broader institutional system are more likely to constrain the normatizing process than when the encounter is outside such units. Even social encounters, not directly related to performance of duties, will be highly constrained by the embedding of the interaction within the corporate unit.

Categoric units also constrain what occurs in encounters, and the more clear-cut, discrete, rank-ordered (in terms of value standards) are the distinctions marking categories, the more likely are the expectations of members in various categories to be understood and, hence, the greater are the effects of categoric units on the interaction in the encounter. The more membership in categoric units is correlated with the division of labor in corporate units—such as boss and workers, professor and students, doctors and nurses—the greater will be the effects of the categoric units. When encounters are not highly embedded in corporate units or when encounters occur outside corporate units, the effects of categoric unit membership increase relative to those of corporate units; as a consequence, the normatizing process will be driven by categoric unit membership. The more clarity, discreteness, and differential evaluation of social categories, the greater will be the effects of categoric units on the flow of interaction. Thus, without the corporate unit's capacity to impose culture on individuals, people will seek an alternative basis for assembling culture to normatize the encounter, and one basis will be categoric units if these are clear. Expectation states research (Berger 1988; Berger and Zelditch 1985) on how diffuse status or transsituational characteristics—such as male, female, black, white—are activated in allocating prestige and the expectations associated with differential prestige supports this conclusion; and so, this effect will be highly pronounced when categoric distinctions are marked and differentially evaluated. This power of diffuse status characteristic will decrease, I believe, as encounters are iterated, especially if they occur outside instrumental activities of corporate units. For as individuals interact over time, categoric membership becomes less salient as individuals "get to know each other," and as a result, encounters are renormatized, especially when the categorization of members in the encounter is outside of, and not correlated with, distinctions imposed by the hierarchy of the corporate unit and its division of labor.

Although normatizing processes are constrained by the culture and structure of mesolevel units, humans are not dupes, blindly conforming to what is required. We are apes, after all, and as such, people will resist too much constraint. Equally significant, the cultural scripts and blueprint rules available to individuals are often not so clear, thereby forcing individuals in encounters to normatize on their own. Moreover, when individuals' need states are not met by a particular configuration of normatization, their negative emotions often force breaches and renormatization of encounters. At times, when renormatization is persistent and widespread across many encounters involving many individuals, the culture and structure of mesostructures are altered. These "bottom-up" processes are, however, generally slow; it takes many iterations involving many individuals to change highly structured corporate units or characterizations in categoric units. Indeed, most rapid change occurs as institutional systems and their culture undergo change. For example, as the economy has become more "high tech," patterns of hierarchy in corporate units, especially among management, have been altered to a more open, casual, and horizontal pattern; this change has, in turn, led to alterations of "corporate culture," which has made encounters more informal in these "new economy" organizations and, increasingly, in "old economy" organizations as well. Similarly, social movements such as these have influenced decisions in the political as well as economic arenas and have altered evaluations of categoric units—say women and minorities—which, over time, will transform the way in which membership in these categoric units influences interaction in microencounters. Yet even if dramatic and rapid changes are typically "top down," this conclusion does not mean that persistent and consistent renormatization at the microlevel will not, over the long haul, begin to change characterizations of categoric units and even the structure and culture of corporate units. In general, when individuals are too constrained by the structure and culture of mesolevel units, their ape ancestry will begin to assert itself at the level of the encounter, pushing for less constraint and more autonomy. Moreover, when individuals' transactional needs go unfulfilled, their anger or perhaps even their sadness and fear will begin to generate pressure for renormatization at the level of the encounter.

Conclusions

Let me begin this conclusion by addressing what is an obvious concern: Have I not extended the concept of *norms* to include what many would consider nonnormative processes? In a sense, I have done just this. But I believe that sociology needs a much more robust and dynamic view of norms that takes us beyond viewing them as the "instructions," "obligations," and "expectations" attached to status positions and guiding role behaviors. Norms are more than this; they are expectations operating at different levels and with respect to very different elements of an interaction. My use of the term *normatizing* tries to capture the dynamic properties of norms as expectations about a broader range of behaviors in encounters—that is, categorization, framing, communicating, ritualizing, and feeling. I am really not particularly radical here, since few would disagree that these behaviors are guided by norms, beliefs, and values. My goal is to make this more explicit and to emphasize that as culture exerts its force on encounters, it does so with respect to basic and fundamental behaviors of encounters that are often overlooked in discussions of norms or roles.

Some preliminary generalizations on dynamics of normatizing emerge in this chapter, although these will have to be refined and restated as the dynamic force of additional properties of interaction are examined.

I. Normatizing interaction increases the likelihood that the encounter will sustain its focus and rhythmic flow. Conversely, the less an encounter is normatized, the greater will be (a) the level of energy devoted to role taking and self-presentation, especially with respect to (b) problems of maintaining the focus and rhythmic flow of the interaction and (c) problems of avoiding breaches to the interaction.

   A. The more individuals can mutually categorize self and others with respect to (a) relevant memberships in categoric units, (b) relative amounts of work-practical, social, and ceremonial content, and (c) level of intimacy, the less problematic will be other normatizing processes. Conversely, the less an encounter is categorized, the less likely are all of axes of normatizing to be established.

      1. The less categorized the encounter, the greater will be the reliance on frames to establish categories.
      2. The greater the reliance on frames to establish categories, the more active will be the use of rituals and forms of talk to key frames.

   B. The more an encounter has been categorized, the more readily are frames keyed and rekeyed; reciprocally, the more frames have been keyed, the more likely will the interaction remain categorized.

   C. The more an encounter has been categorized and framed, the more readily are forms of communication, both verbal and nonverbal, established; reciprocally, the more forms of communication are normatized, the more readily are frames and categories sustained.

D. The more categorization, framing, and forms of communication are accepted, the more likely are norms for rituals to open, close, form, totemize, and repair the flow of interaction to be understood and used; reciprocally, the more rituals are normatized, the more readily are frames, forms of communication, and categories sustained or changed.

1. The less an interaction is normatized, the more frequent will be the use of rituals to establish frames and, indirectly, forms of talk.

2. The more an interaction is breached from whatever source, the more rituals will be used to repair the breach, to rekey frames, and to alter forms of talk.

E. The more expectations for categories, forms of communication, and rituals are understood, the more likely are feeling rules to be accepted; reciprocally, the more the emotional flow of the interaction remains within these rules, the more likely are other axes of normatization to be sustained.

1. The more feeling rules are violated, the more likely will the encounter be breached.

2. The more the encounter is breached by inappropriate emission of emotions, the greater will be the reliance on rituals and forms of talk to repair the breach.

II. The more an encounter is located within an institutional domain and the corporate units comprising this domain, the greater is the likelihood that the culture of this domain and its corporate units will be used to normatize the encounter.

A. The more bounded, formal, explicit, and hierarchical the division of labor of the corporate units in which an encounter is embedded, the greater will be the influence of the culture of this corporate unit on normatization.

B. The more the division of labor of a corporate unit correlates with categoric unit memberships, the greater will be the influence of the culture of this corporate unit on normatization and the more pronounced will be the power of those categoric units correlated with the division of labor.

III. The more an encounter is composed of members of categoric units, the greater is the likelihood the culture of these categoric units will be used to normatize the encounter.

   A. The more clear-cut, discrete, and rank-ordered are categoric distinctions, the greater their influence on normatization.

   B. The more correlated are categoric distinctions, the greater their influence on normatization.

   C. The less correlated are categoric distinctions with the distinctions imposed by the division of labor of a corporate unit in which an encounter is located, the less influential are categoric distinctions on normatization.

   D. The more an encounter is composed of members of categoric units outside of the division of labor of corporate units, the greater is the influence of categoric distinctions alone on normatization.

      1. The more clear-cut, discrete, and rank-ordered are categoric distinctions, the more influential are these distinctions on normatization.

      2. The more instrumental are the activities of members of different categoric units outside the division of labor of a corporate unit, the more influential are categoric distinctions alone on normatization.

      3. The less instrumental is an interaction, and the more prolonged is this interaction among members of diverse categoric units outside of corporate units, the less influential are categoric distinctions on normatization.

SEVEN

Role Forces

The concept of *roles* has been one of the workhorses of microlevel analysis in sociology, although explicit theorizing on roles has declined dramatically during the last three decades. Early on, George Herbert Mead (1934) emphasized a particular aspect of role dynamics—role taking—or the process of reading the gestures of others to assume their perspective and likely course of action. This view of roles as embracing the process of discovering people's dispositions to act, however, was replaced in the early decades of the twentieth century by more structural approaches. In these conceptualizations, roles were seen as sets of expectations associated with positions in social structures (Park 1926) and as behavioral manifestations of these expectations (Linton 1936). This view of roles tends to make them the behavioral adjunct to expectations attached to positions, but other early theorists like Jacob Moreno ([1934] 1953) extended this somewhat narrow view of roles. For example, Moreno distinguished among "psychodramatic roles" whereby individuals play out the expectation of the situation, "psychosomatic roles" where people behave in ways to meet biological needs, and "social roles" whereby individuals behave in ways that confirm the expectations associated with general social categories (what I have termed *categoric units*).

Later, Talcott Parsons (1951) moved the conceptualization of roles back to mere adjuncts to status positions regulated by a cultural system. But there were clear signs of dissent from symbolic interactionism. In contrast to Parsons, Ralph Turner (1962) emphasized the process of "role making" to complement Mead's idea of role taking. For Turner, individuals not only role take; they also orchestrate the emission of gestures or role make in order to confirm self, to realize values, and to achieve goals. This emphasis gave roles a more dramaturgical character in line with Erving Goffman's (1967) approach, but Turner went further than Goffman. He also incorporated ideas that could be found in Alfred Schutz's ([1932] 1967) work: people assume that the signals of others are consistent and mark an underlying role; and with this "folk" assumption, individuals search their stocks of knowledge to discover what role others are presenting, while constantly seeking to verify and reverify that they have imputed the correct role to others.

More recently, role theory has been extended further by Wayne Baker and Robert Faulkner (1991) to emphasize that roles can be seen as resources that allow individuals to gain access to positions in social structure. Rather than being a behavioral adjunct to a position, or simply a packaging of gestures in role making, the ability to play certain roles (in their case, roles in the film industry) enables people to participate in social structures and, thereby, play still more roles. Roles are thus resources to be strategically used to secure positions, play new roles, and receive the payoffs associated with roles. Peter Callero (1994) has expanded on this idea with a view of roles as "cultural objects" that, on the one side, are resources mobilized by active agents and, on the other side, serve as symbolic markers that allow others to comprehend the actions of these agents.

Are these various conceptions of role contradictory? I do not think so because roles reveal all of the features enumerated above: roles are expectations about how people should behave, often associated with social structures or situations; they are the actual behaviors of individuals as they try to meet expectations of a position or social category; they are resources that are used to secure desired outcomes and access to positions in social structures; and they are cultural objects that signify who people are, what they are going to do, and how they should be treated. Thus, rather than see these as contradictory views of roles, they should be seen as complementary. My goal in this chapter is to provide a framework allowing us to use all these dimensions of roles to understand face-to-face interaction.

Phenomenological Dynamics

ROLES AS CONFIGURATIONS OF GESTURES

Ralph Turner's (2002, 1968, 1962) role theory provides many of the key insights into the phenomenology of roles. Humans seek to discover the underlying role that others are playing, and they do so with the implicit assumption that the gestures of others constitute a syndrome of consistent signals marking a role. The principal reason that people make this assumption, I believe, is that they are driven by needs for acticity to perceive that events are as they appear. As a result, individuals are willing to overlook minor inconsistencies in gestures in order to create a sense that others are behaving in understandable ways in a role. I doubt if individuals consciously articulate this sense of role, unless another overplays a role or uses a role to disrupt the flow of interaction, thereby making it difficult for others to realize their transactional needs. For example, a professor who is "too intellectual" to the point of being arrogant and snobbish will make others conscious of the role being presented; or a foreman who is too bossy will make his subordinates aware of the extreme variant of the role being asserted.

Ralph Turner sees this tendency to interpret gestures of others as a syndrome marking an underlying role as a "folk norm of consistency" but I believe that the process has a substantial neurological base. The brain is wired, especially on the right side, for pattern recognition; if the patterns are configurations and sequences of gestures, people seek to find order not just because of transactional needs but also because they are biologically programmed to do so.[1] Human neurology is structured to learn visually based emotional languages as well as auditory languages, and these languages are organized by grammars that pattern nonverbal and verbal signals. In this case of visually based emotional syntax, the patterns are both configurational and sequential; and as I argued in Chapter 3, this is the more primal system. One implication of this conclusion is that the brain is wired to search for patterning in gestures; thus, as the young learn the languages of their culture, they naturally search for syntax. As Mead emphasized, since this ability to read conventional gestures facilitates adaptation to social environments, pattern recognition is positively reinforcing and, hence, likely to remain in the behavioral repertoire of a person. Once there, it is but a short response generalization to use this same ability to discover the underlying roles being made by others in an encounter, especially since finding the role

[1] Classic Gestalt theory is based on this notion of fields, with individuals tending to see patterns of relationships among elements (Köhler 1929; Koffka 1935); later, these ideas evolved into notions of cognitive "consistency," "congruence," and "balance," but the basic idea can be found in early experiments in the 1920s and 1930s.

being played by another increases adaptation to, and cooperation with, this other. Out of these capacities, people act *as if* others are playing an identifying role, at least until they have overwhelming evidence to the contrary.

COGNITIVE INVENTORIES OF ROLES

Ralph Turner (1962) also argues that people carry "loose cultural frameworks" about what the gestures of others mean for discovering roles. I would go a step further and suggest that people carry more fine-tuned frameworks about roles in their stocks of knowledge (J. Turner 1994a). There are, I believe, at least four general types of roles stored in people's stocks of knowledge: (1) preassembled roles; (2) combinational roles; (3) generalized roles; and (4) transsituational roles.

People scan memories for presorted sequences of gestures marking a role, or what I will term *preassembled roles*. The more a role is widely used and the more it is connected to behaviors within corporate or categoric units, the more likely are variants of roles to be already assembled in the human memory system. For example, most people readily know the contours of basic roles like mother, father, worker, policeman, or student as well as variants of these roles such as strict mother, lazy worker, aggressive policeman, or serious student. People also carry images of roles that combine multiple roles, or *combinational roles*, that will fit a particular situation. Thus, when a woman hosts a family gathering, her kinship roles—mother, daughter, aunt, cousin—are for the purposes of the party merged into the role of "host" in which all parties "know" what to expect and how to behave at a hosted family gathering.

People also carry in their stocks of knowledge more *generalized roles* that can become part of a more specific role in a particular situation. For instance, there are syndromes of gestures for being assertive, social and upbeat, gracious, shy, reserved, serious and diligent, and other metabehaviors. These conceptions of generalized behaviors are stored as stocks of knowledgeability and assembled together with the gestures marking a more specific role like father, mother, student, or worker. Additionally, there are *transsituational roles* typically associated with basic categoric units—gender, age, class position, ethnicity, and so on—or with cultural labels—being a sick person, a parolee, a "gang banger," and the like. Men and women, for example, play all or most roles in diverse situations in accordance with membership in their respective categoric units. These generalized roles and transsituational roles carry their own sets of expectations that are assembled with other roles in particular situations, as when a person tries to combine the generalized role of being assertive with the role of a gang member while also playing the role of father.

But not all roles are simply stored as memories; more generative processes almost always operate in role making and role taking. Even preassembled roles must be fine-tuned to a situation or assembled with elements of more generalized roles or transsituational roles. Moreover, people often play unique variants and combinations of roles, forcing others to assemble cues from various roles in order to interpret the actions of a person. For example, a woman college professor who dresses in a sexually provocative way, while displaying the corresponding sexual demeanor as she plays the role of lecturer, forces reassembly by her students of elements from different roles (and, no doubt, by other professors as well). But a role can be imputed to this professor, although unlike the role of professor in general, this variant may not be prepackaged in memory; it has to be assembled on the spot.

Thus, I see humans as carrying in memory rather extensive images of roles and as using their generative abilities to assemble roles. Memories of roles stored in stocks of knowledge and the generative ability to assemble and reassemble roles are not verbally organized in the brain. Humans are far too quick to discover the roles of others; and this speed in assembling could not exist if role taking involved a conscious "internal conversation" using conventional language. Indeed, only when the gestures marking a role become difficult to ascertain do conscious reflection and verbalization of the problem ensue; and once the process is slowed down through self-talk, the search for patterns generally becomes even more awkward and stressful. Thus, the "folk norm of consistency" is, in my view, not a norm but rather a built-in neurological process that uses the brain's nonverbal way of thinking. As a methodological aside, this conclusion helps explain why people's conceptions of roles stored and assembled in the brain are difficult to measure with verbal tests. It is often hard for a person to download, via Broca's area (see Figure 3.1 in Chapter 3), images stored and processed in the "brain's way of thinking" into sequential verbal statements. Even a well-known and discussed role like father or mother is hard to verbalize if asked: What does the role involve? An answer will typically be a list of duties and obligations, but the more subtle demeanor and feeling characteristics of gesturing will be hard to articulate (but not visualize as images). If we ask people more complicated roles—say, "gentle father"—our verbal description will likely seem shallow and incomplete because so much of what marks a role lies outside direct reflection and articulation in speech.

VERIFICATION OF ROLES

Ralph Turner (1962) also stresses the process of role verification whereby a person reads the gestures of others to see if these others have accepted the person's role-making activities. Again, verification is rarely conscious or verbal; most of the time, humans read visual cues that move directly into the way the brain processes information with little conscious thought or reflection. But when individuals sense a problem with verifying their roles and start to question themselves consciously (for instance, are others responding as they should?; have they accepted my behaviors?), verification will tend to become even more difficult as individuals try to orchestrate gestures in a deliberative (and typically stilted) manner. To the degree that self is salient in people's efforts at role making and verification, the more intense will be the emotions when verification fails. The smooth flow of an interaction thus depends on keeping verification implicit; once conscious and deliberative, the interaction becomes strained. Indeed, if we imagine individuals consciously saying to themselves how they will play this role, involving a list of consciously assembled behavioral cues, they will come off as insincere; or if a person engages in considerable thought on what the gestures of others mean, this individual is rarely better off than before thinking about the matter. For example, a depressed person making a self-conscious effort to be happy and upbeat usually cannot bring this generalized role to a more specific role without coming across as acting or otherwise being untrustworthy, primarily because people have high levels of acuity in automatically picking up the fine-grained gestures signaling true happiness. Our brains are wired, once activated by socialization processes, to rapidly read gestures to see if roles being made are genuine. If we think about the matter, social life would be tiring if we had to ponder our role and the roles of others in each and every encounter. True, people rehearse roles, but only if they are exceptional actors can they bring these roles off by practice alone.

In order for roles to be successfully made, others must often let inconsistent gestures go by or reinterpret them as part of an underlying role. As Alfred Schutz ([1932] 1967) probably would have emphasized (if he had directed his attention to the role dynamics), people will give others considerable latitude in offering inconsistent gestures in role making because the costs of not verifying roles are typically greater than the costs of letting things slide. People try to sustain a sense of an obdurate and stable reality, at least for the interaction at hand; and to monitor too carefully and critically the consistency of the gestures given off by others as they role make is sure to undermine meeting this need for facticity.

While needs for facticity initially push individuals to discover each other's roles, meeting all transactional needs is dependent on successful role taking, role making, and role verification. In an encounter, individuals implicitly monitor the responses of others to see if their respective roles have been verified, while constantly checking to see if the initial imputation of a role to others is correct. When one's own role is confirmed and when others' roles are understood, needs for group inclusion, facticity, and trust are generally met; as a result, the interaction can proceed, and a person's needs for self-verification and positive exchange payoffs can be pursued with greater certainty that they will be realized.

If, however, reverification fails, meeting needs for facticity, group inclusion, and trust becomes more problematic, making a person more self-conscious of his or her efforts to (a) assemble a role acceptable to others and (b) search stocks of knowledge to discover the roles being presented by others. Thus, in role making and role taking, the emotional stakes are potentially high because people's mutual verification determines if participants in an encounter can fulfill transactional needs. When these needs go unmet, negative emotions are aroused, potentially breaching the encounter. It is not surprising, therefore, that people selectively ignore inconsistent responses in order to avoid, if they possibly can, activating negative emotional energy in others.

COMPLEMENTARITY OF ROLES

As people role make and role take, they seek to develop roles that are complementary so that they do not work at cross purposes and fail to verify each other's roles (R. Turner 1968). As roles are made and verified over time or in iterated encounters, individuals attempt to create and sustain a consensus over what each person's role entails. This consensus further constrains the range of roles that each individual can present; for even though others will give each other considerable slack, as interactions proceed, people develop ever more retraining expectations for each other's roles as a means to assure that their transactional needs are fulfilled. For this reason it is difficult to change roles, once established, because to break out of a role forces too many readjustments on the part of others whose ability to meet transactional needs may be jeopardized by readjustments of roles. The trade-off for this constraint on a person's latitude in role making is the tacit assurance from others that this person's transactional needs will be realized at current levels if he or she sticks to a role around which complementary roles have been developed.

NORMATIZATION OF ROLES

All of these phenomenological processes are facilitated by normatization of the encounter. When the situation can be categorized in terms of (a) expectations for relative amounts of intimacy owed toward others as personages, persons, or intimates and (b) expectations for relative amounts of work-practical, social, or ceremonial content, the range of roles possible is delimited, making it much easier to decide on what role to make and how to interpret gestures of others in role taking. When categories and frames exist, the situation is even more constrained; additionally, rituals, forms of talk, and feelings are more clearly specified, thereby reducing further the uncertainty over what role to play and how to interpret the gestures of others.

EMBEDDING AND ROLES

Embedding constrains these phenomenological processes not only because of the effects of categoric and corporate units on normatization, but also because (a) membership in categoric units establishes additional expectations supplementing typifications of the situation in terms of intimacy and content and (b) because incumbency in the positions of a corporate unit specifies the roles to be played. Thus, when an encounter is embedded in unambiguous, discrete, and differentially evaluated categoric units, the expectations for how others in a category will behave become more clearly defined, thereby making it easier for members of categories to role make successfully and for others to verify these roles. When an encounter is embedded in a corporate unit with an explicit division of labor, expectations attached to each position (along with the values and ideologies contained in these expectations) are more likely to be understood and, hence, are more likely to circumscribe role making and verifying.

In summary, much of the phenomenology of roles is the result of the neurological capacities of the human brain. Persons seek patterns to the gestures of others in order to impute a role to them; on the basis of this role taking and imputation, they can adjust their role making efforts. Human neurology not only pushes perception to see configurational patterns to gesturing, it also allows people to store vast inventories of role conceptions, to retrieve these stores, and, when necessary, to assemble and reassemble role conceptions to fit new situations. We do this with such ease because these processes generally operate through the brain's way of processing information as images and gestalts. Only when situations become chronically problematic do people begin to reflect and talk about their inability to make or take roles; as they do so, these reflections themselves confound role making and role taking because humans do not normally reflect on roles in their daily encounters, unless something has gone wrong. Transactional needs are extremely important in understanding the phenomenology of roles because to make and verify roles allow needs for facticity and trust to be realized, while increasing the likelihood that self will be verified, that positive exchange payoffs will ensue, and that a sense of group inclusion will be achieved. Once a role has been made and accepted, it is difficult to remake the role because too many cognitive, emotional, and behavioral adjustments may be required of others as they seek to meet their transactional needs. Roles tend toward an equilibrium of complementarity that provides some assurance of each party meeting transactional needs; when individuals try to shift roles, they are perceived to jeopardize the ability of others to meet their needs. Embedding greatly facilitates role taking, role making, and role verification by establishing expectations for members of categoric units and for positions within the division of labor of corporate units; generally, a person seeks to make roles within the range of these expectations, while others use these expectations to interpret patterns of gesturing in role taking with a person and in verifying this person's role making efforts.

Self and Roles

The most powerful transactional need is the confirmation of an identity, and especially so if a role identity is a marker of more deeply seated core-self feelings and, hence, is highly salient to a person. Others are particularly sensitive to the extent to which a person's self is salient in a role because the higher the salience of self the greater are the emotional stakes. When role identities are verified, people feel positive emotions; and when identities are not verified, individuals experience negative emotions in accordance with the dynamics outlined in Chapter 5. If they can, then, others will avoid negatively sanctioning an identity presented by another because negative sanctioning escalates the emotions involved; and people implicitly know that external attributions by a person whose role identity has not been verified will be directed at them, especially when an identity is salient. Even if a person makes self-attributions as a result of negative sanctions, others will have to cope with sadness and, potentially, with anger, fear, shame, and guilt. Whenever negative emotions are aroused, the interaction must be renormatized, thereby forcing others to scramble to find complementary roles that allow them to meet their transactional needs. So, when they perceive self to be highly salient, people try as hard as they can to avoid disconfirming the role-making efforts of a person.

Thus, role taking revolves around interpreting gestures in order to determine which level of self is committed to a role. Are core-self feelings involved? Are subidentities relevant? Or, is only a role identity being asserted? I would postulate that people search for signals about salience along several dimensions. First, the more animated and/or emotionally valenced is a person's gesturing, the more likely are others to sense that core self is salient. Second, the more a person is perceived by others to have invested in a role and the greater this person's costs in playing a role, the more likely are others to see self as salient. Third, the more a role is highly evaluated by cultural standards and the more prestige that a role carries, the more likely are others to perceive that a role is a marker of core self. Fourth, and relatedly, the more a role is seen as a cultural object or totem, the more likely are others to perceive self to be salient in making this role. Fifth, the more power associated with a role, the more likely are others to see self as salient. Sixth, the more a role is imbued with expectations associated with categoric unit membership, the more likely are others to sense salience of self. Seventh, the more a role can serve as a general resource to gain access to other roles or to positions in corporate units, the more others will believe a role to be central to self. Eighth, the more choice and discretion a person has in selecting a role, the more likely are others to see the role as significant for verifying the self of this person. And ninth, the more adequately a person plays a role, the more likely are others to perceive it as important to core self (R. Turner 1968). Yet these are only tendencies, although if a role is seen to carry several of these dimensions, confidence in assuming that the role is important to a person's core self increases. Thus, an individual in a highly evaluated position of power who has worked hard to gain this power over the years (costs and investments) and who is animated and emotional will likely be perceived by others as having core-self feelings tied to verification of his or her role identity. Once this imputation is made, individuals will work to verify this role, if they can, because to disconfirm the role is to disconfirm self, activating the emotional dynamics that come when needs for self-verification are not met.

Not only will others see a role as embodied in self-feelings when these dimensions are evident, so will the individuals making the role. People will be willing to incur the costs and make the investments in roles that bestow power and prestige, that can be used as a resource to gain access to other roles and positions, and that can be played adequately. But this tendency needs to be mitigated by people's implicit calculation of costs, investments, and probability of receiving the payoffs that came with verification. Thus, what is desired is not necessarily what is pursued because the emotional stakes of not verifying a role are high, leading people to avoid making roles that they cannot successfully bring off in the eyes of others.

Roles and Emotions

When roles are successfully made and verified by individuals, transactional needs for facticity, trust, group inclusion, self-verification, and exchange payoffs are generally realized; as a result, individuals experience and express positive emotions. Conversely, when roles are not successfully made or verified, people's basic transactional needs are not being fulfilled; and they experience and express negative emotions. Humans implicitly sense that roles are the principle vehicle through which their needs will be met, and it is this implicit understanding that makes people highly attuned to the underlying role that others are presenting, and it is what makes their ability to verify a role so important. While failure to have a role verified will, by itself, arouse emotions, the real power of roles resides in their connection to transactional needs. As the principle mechanism for meeting transactional needs, role making, role taking, and role verification have enormous significance in interaction. For this reason the failure to verify a role, even seemingly unimportant ones, can generate emotional reactions. When verified, the interaction stays on track and reveals a positive emotional flow, whereas when roles go unverified, the encounter is rife with negative emotional overtones that can go in many different directions depending on which needs, or configuration of needs, go unfulfilled.

Because people implicitly recognize the importance of role making and verification for transactional needs, they also understand that the emotional stakes are potentially high. If the role making efforts of a person are verified by others, this person will emit positive sanctions, thus making others disposed to continue seeing a person's gestures as marking an identifiable role that they can verify. Thus, the positive sanctions emitted by those who have their roles verified operate as an incentive to others to verify roles in the first place, and to keep on doing so. On the negative side, people will work hard at verifying a role ignoring, if they can, inconsistencies because their failure to do so will invite both anger toward and/or fear of them. Even if the person blames him or herself for the failure to verify a role, others must deal with this person's disappointment and sadness. All negative emotions expressed by a person raise the costs for others, especially if they cannot leave the encounter. Moreover, as negative emotions are expressed by a person toward these others, meeting their own transactional needs can be jeopardized. There are, then, both positive and negative incentives that bias individuals to verify and confirm each other's role, if possible.

Generally, when needs for facticity, trust, and group inclusions are met, people experience low-intensity positive emotions, whereas when these needs are not fulfilled, low-intensity negative emotions—annoyance, concern, disappointment—will be aroused. As these three transactional needs are realized, it becomes more likely that individuals will meet transactional needs for self-verification and positive exchange payoffs that can arouse more intense emotions, whether positive or negative. Again, people implicitly recognize that needs for self-verification and positive exchange payoffs will generate more intense emotional reactions; as a result, they make exceptional efforts to assure that these two needs will be realized in order to avoid the costs of negative emotional valences in the encounter. Indeed, others will be particularly sensitive in their role taking as they search the gestures of others to assess the extent to which core self-feelings are salient and to determine what exchange payoffs are expected from the role that another is making.

When a role identity is a marker of subidentity or core-self feelings, its verification will cause a person to experience positive emotions toward self and express positive emotions toward others and, potentially, the categoric and corporate units in which the encounter is embedded. When a person has a role confirmed, he or she will be happy; if this person sees others, categories of others, or the structure and culture of corporate units as responsible for verification, positive sentiments will be expressed and commitments made to specific others and more inclusive mesostructures. Others will receive positive sanctions; categoric units will be the subject of positive prejudices; and the division of labor, culture, and structure of corporate units will be viewed in positive terms. The more a person had some fear about confirming a role identity in which self is salient, the more likely will pride be experienced, and if a role carries high moral evaluation, the sense of pride will be even greater.

The emotional dynamics become more complicated when roles are not successfully made and verified, because the failure to realize different transactional needs arouses somewhat varying configurations and valences of negative emotions and because defensive strategies and defense mechanisms are activated. Failure to verify a role also disrupts efforts to achieve facticity, because it is difficult to sustain a sense of an obdurate reality when roles are not clear or complementary. When roles do not allow facticity, individuals typically blame others for not confirming their role or, if others' roles are unclear, for making it difficult to interact with them. When a person's self is salient in a role and when this person has failed to have his or her role verified, anger will be directed at others but fear of them may also increase. Similarly, if others have not made their roles clear to a person whose self is highly salient, the latter will fail to have his or her role verified because the gestures of others are difficult to interpret. As a result, anger toward these others and some fear as well will be evident; for without being able to verify the roles of others, a person's self is in jeopardy, even if others are not intentionally refusing to verify this person's role.

Moreover, because needs for facticity are so contingent on the responses of specific others, individuals do not generally make external attributions to categoric or corporate units, although it is possible to make an attribution to a categoric unit if the person being blamed is a member of a clearly defined social category. The inability to satisfy needs for facticity does not usually generate self-attributions, and such is the case for the verification of roles as it bears on facticity. Thus, what will generally be evident is low to moderate levels of anger, like annoyance, frustration, or irritation, coupled with low-to-moderate intensity fear (such as concern, mild anxiety, or distress).

Failure to verify a role also influences needs for trust, since when one's own role or those of others cannot be verified, it is difficult for a person to sense that the actions of others are predictable, that these actions are in sync with those of the person, and that others are respecting a person's dignity. Again, the most likely emotional reaction is anger at others who are seen as not responding appropriately, either in terms of confirming one's role or in being clear about their own roles. If self is highly salient, fear of the situation may increase because a person's role identity is now more important and because verification depends on confirming responses of others. And, like failures to realize needs for facticity, people do not generally blame themselves or categoric and corporate units because trust is so directly related to how the responses of specific others are interpreted.

Failure to make and verify roles immediately stymies needs for group inclusion, because it is difficult to see oneself as being included in the ongoing interpersonal flow when one's roles are not being verified vis-à-vis complementary roles being made by others. As a result, people will always experience some fear (typically anxiety) when they cannot feel part of the ongoing interpersonal flow; and if self is salient, this reaction will be more intense. Failure to achieve a sense of group inclusion invites attributions. If a person blames self for the inability to sense inclusion, fear will escalate and, generally, be accompanied by disappointment-sadness at self and anger at self. If these emotions are simultaneously experienced and mixed, the person may also experience shame as well as guilt when a role personifies cultural values and ideologies. If, however, individuals make external attributions and blame others, categories of others, or corporate units for the lack of success in verifying roles and realizing a sense of group inclusion, they will experience and express anger toward these targets. Of course, external attributions toward specific others revolving around negative emotions almost always invite counternegative sanctioning, with the result that people often shift the blame to safer objects and develop prejudices toward categoric units, while displaying low commitments to corporate units through role distance, cynical performance of roles, and hostile attitudes toward the unit and its culture.

Failure to make and verify a role producing positive exchange payoffs will arouse anger because people's initial response is to make external attributions and, thereby, to blame others, categories of others, or corporate units. If self is blamed, however, a person will experience sadness, anger at self, and fear about the consequences of failure to self; and as these emotions are experienced simultaneously and mixed, shame and guilt (if a role is a marker of values and ideologies) become more likely.

Failure to verify a role identity generates varying emotional reactions depending on the degree to which core-self feelings are salient. The less salient core feelings, the less intense is the level of emotional arousal, whereas the more salient is self, the more emotions shift to moderate and intense variants and, potentially, to powerful first- and second-order elaborations. When self is not highly salient, the emotional reaction to the failure to verify a role identity will be relatively mild. If individuals blame themselves, they will experience disappointment at their actions; and if they also have some anger at themselves and fear about the consequences to self, they will experience mild shame as well as low-level guilt if a role is a marker of values and ideologies. When self is not highly salient and individuals make external attributions, they will experience and express toward others low-intensity anger, such as annoyance; and when others can negatively sanction back, this anger will be directed at the categoric and corporate units in which the encounter is embedded.

As self becomes more salient, however, the emotional reaction to failure in verifying a role identity increases. When a person accepts responsibility for the failure, sadness at self, anger at self, and fear of the consequences to self are more likely to be simultaneously activated, causing a person to feel ashamed and, if moral codes inhered in the role, to feel guilt as well. When others are blamed, a person will express more intense anger toward these others; and if the latter fight back, the interaction can degenerate very rapidly. Or, if the person cannot leave the interaction, negative attributions to categoric and corporate units are more likely to be made, causing the individual to develop prejudices toward categoric units and low commitments to the division of labor and culture of the corporate unit in which the encounter is embedded.

Like all negative emotional reactions, particularly those where self is implicated and salient, defensive strategies and defense mechanisms are more likely to be activated when roles are not successfully made or verified. When role making and verification are problematic, a person may simply employ defensive strategies, selectively perceiving and interpreting the gestures of others, using short-term credits of previous success in making the role, or simply leaving the encounter. When these defensive strategies do not work and when self is salient, defense mechanisms are ever more likely to kick in. The most likely defense mechanisms are external attributions and displacement revolving around anger toward others, categories of others, and corporate units. Since others can fight back and negatively sanction a person, the longer this person sustains external attributions and displaces anger, the more likely is the individual to shift anger to safer targets, typically developing prejudices toward categoric units and hostility toward the division of labor and culture of corporate units. Repression of emotions is more likely when self is highly salient, when failure to verify a role or roles is chronic, and when a person experiences all three negative emotions as well as second-order elaborations—that is, disappointment at self, anger at self, fear to self, shame, and guilt. Repression will generally lower the level of modal interpersonal energy displayed by an individual, usually in the form of role distance or cynical performance of a role; yet, short episodes of anger, anxiety, depression, shame, and guilt will also break through the neocortical sensors.

Conclusions

Interaction is very much influenced by the force of roles. Humans carry rather fine-grained conceptions of roles in their stocks of knowledge, and they reveal amazing capacities to assemble images of roles when role making, role taking, and role verifying. Most encounters are embedded in corporate and categoric units, which set expectations and delimit the range of roles possible in an encounter. More fundamentally, transactional needs and the emotions that these needs can arouse are generally realized by successful role making, role taking, and role verification within categoric and corporate units. Role dynamics are the primary vehicle through which these needs are fulfilled; because of this connection, emotions can be positive or negative depending on how successful individuals are in their role making, role taking, and role verifying activities. At this point, I cannot present these dynamics in their full context in relation to other forces driving interaction, but let me offer some preliminary hypotheses that summarize the argument in this chapter.

I. Humans carry in their stocks of knowledge conceptions of (a) specific roles, (b) combinations of roles, (c) generalized roles, and (d) trans-situational roles, which they implicitly use in role making, role taking, and role verification. When the gestures of individuals are perceived to be consistent and to mark an underlying role, individuals' efforts at role taking, role making, and role verification will be more successful.

    A. The more gestures of all individuals in an encounter are seen to be consistent and to mark underlying roles, the more individuals can mutually impute roles to each other and verify these roles; as a result, the more likely are roles to reach an equilibrium of complementarity. The more this equilibrium is realized, the more difficult will it be for individuals to change their respective roles.

B. The more an encounter is embedded in a corporate unit, the more likely are the roles available to participants to be specified by the culture and division of labor of this unit; and hence, the more likely are individuals to perceive the gestures of others as consistent, and as a result, the more likely are they to impute roles to each other and to verify these roles.

C. The more an encounter is embedded in categoric units, the more likely are the expectations associated with categoric unit membership to delimit and impose roles on individuals; and hence, the more likely are individuals to perceive the gestures of others as consistent, and as a result, the more likely are they to impute roles to each other and to verify these roles.

D. The more an encounter is normatized, the more likely are expectations for roles to be mutually understood; and hence, the more likely are individuals to perceive the gestures of others to be consistent, and as a result, the more likely are they to impute roles to each other and to verify these roles.

II. When individuals can successfully make their respective roles as well as verify the roles of others, their transactional needs are more likely to be realized, causing them to experience positive emotions.

A. The more salient are transactional needs, the more individuals will implicitly perceive the high costs to both self and others in failing to meet needs; and hence, the more likely are they to allow others to make and verify their respective roles.

1. The more the gestures of others are seen to be consistent and mark an underlying role, the more likely are needs for facticity, trust, and group inclusion to be realized; and hence, the more likely are individuals to experience and express low-intensity positive emotions.

2. The more individuals can achieve a sense of facticity, trust, and group inclusion, the more likely are needs for self-verification and positive exchange payoffs to be realized; and hence, the more likely are individuals to experience and express moderate to intense positive emotions.

B. The more a person's core-self feelings are perceived by others to be part of a role identity (high salience), the harder they will try to verify this person's role in order to avoid negative emotional reactions from this person; to the degree that others succeed in verifying the role, the more likely will the person experience and express the positive emotions that come with role verification.

1. The more a role is played competently and emotionally by a person, while being seen by others to involve costs and investments, to have high cultural evaluation, to have power and/or prestige in corporate units, to be associated with categoric unit membership, to mark cultural objects, and to be a resource, the more likely are others to perceive that the self of a person is highly salient.

2. The more individuals experience the positive emotions associated with verification of their role identity, and particularly when core self is salient, the more likely are they to experience positive emotions toward themselves and to express positive emotions toward others who, in turn, will reciprocate in a cycle of positive affect that ends with fatigue, saturation, or termination of the encounter.

   a. The more an individual had some fear about successfully making a role in which salience of self is high, the greater is the sense of pride experienced when this role is verified.

   b. The more a role personifies value standards and ideologies and the higher the salience of self in this role, the greater is the sense of pride experienced when this role is verified.

3. The more individuals experience the positive emotions associated with verification of their roles and the more verifying responses are perceived to come from members of categoric units, the more likely are individuals to hold and express positive sentiments toward all members of these categoric units.

4. The more individuals experience the positive emotions associated with verification of their roles and the more these roles are associated with positions in a corporate unit, the greater will be individuals' positive sentiments toward, and commitments to, the division of labor and culture of the corporate unit.

III. When individuals cannot successfully make and verify a role, the less likely are transactional needs to be realized, causing them to experience negative emotions.

    A. The less needs for facticity of an individual are realized in role making and verifying, the more likely is low-intensity anger to be directed at others for their failure to verify a person's role or for their failure to make their roles clear; and the more self is salient in the encounter, the more intense will be this anger, and the more likely will the individual also experience mild fear of others.

    B. The less needs for trust are realized in role making and verifying, the more likely is low-intensity anger to be directed at others for their failure to verify a person's role or for their failure to make their roles clear; and the more self is salient in the encounter, the more intense will be this anger, and the more likely will a person also experience mild fear of others.

    C. The less needs for group inclusion are realized in role making and verifying, the more likely is fear to be experienced by a person; and the more self is salient, the more intense will this fear be.

        1. The more a person blames self for the failure to realize group inclusion, the more likely are sadness at self and anger at self; and the more fear, sadness, and anger are experienced simultaneously, the more likely is a person to experience:

           a. shame for not behaving with sufficient competence to feel included; and

           b. guilt if a role is a marker of values and ideologies.

        2. The more a person blames others, categories of others, and corporate units for the failure to realize group inclusion, the more likely is anger to be expressed toward these targets; and the more others are in a position to fight back with negative sanctions, the more likely are categoric units and corporate units to be blamed, causing a person to develop prejudices toward categoric units and to lower commitments to corporate units through role distance, cynical performance of roles, and hostility toward the unit as a whole and its culture.

    D. The less needs for positive exchange payoffs are realized in role making and verifying, the more likely are:

1. anger at others, categoric units, and corporate units if these are blamed for the failure to receive expected payoffs; and
2. anger at self if a person accepts responsibility for the failure to receive expected payoffs, coupled with sadness and fear of the consequences to self for this failure. The more these are experienced simultaneously, the more likely is a person to experience:

   a. shame at incompetence to receive appropriate payoffs; and
   b. guilt if a role is a marker of values and ideologies.

E. The less needs for self-verification are realized in role making and verifying, the more likely are low-intensity emotional reactions when self is of low salience; and if an individual can employ defensive strategies (selective perception and interpretation, termination of the encounter, or use of short-term credits), the emotional reaction will be of even lower intensity.

1. The more a person blames self for failure to make and verify a role of low salience, the more likely is the person to experience low intensity sadness; and if the person is also angry at self and fearful about the consequences, the person will also experience:

   a. mild shame for not behaving competently; and
   b. mild guilt if a role is a marker of values and ideologies.

2. The more a person blames others, categories of others, or corporate units for the failure to make and verify a role of low salience, the more likely is the person to express low-intensity anger at others; and if others sanction negatively this external attribution and if the person cannot leave the situation, attributions will shift to low-key prejudices against categoric units and low commitments displayed through role distance and cynical performance of roles attached to the division of labor of corporate units and the culture of these units.

F. The less needs for self-verification are realized in role making and verifying, the more likely will emotions shift to moderate and high-intensity levels in accordance with the pattern delineated in E-1 and E-2.

G. The less needs for self-verification are realized in role making and verifying, and the more salient is self, the more likely is the activation of defense mechanisms.

1. The more defense mechanisms are activated, the more likely will external attributions be made in accordance with the pattern delineated in E-2.
2. The more defense mechanisms are activated, and the less external attributions can be made (because others can fight back and negatively sanction and/or because a person cannot leave the situations), the more likely is repression of negative feelings toward self.

    a. The more repression revolves around sadness, anger at self, and fear of the consequences to self, the more likely is a person to repress shame at the inability to verify self in a role and guilt if moral codes are marked by a role.
    b. The more shame and guilt are repressed, the more likely is a person to reveal low modal levels of emotional energy, punctuated by episodes of higher-intensity anger, fear, sadness, shame, and guilt.

EIGHT

Status Forces

In retrospect, it is surprising that early microlevel theorists failed to conceptualize the dynamics of positions in social structures. George Herbert Mead ([1934] 1953) emphasized the process of role taking, leaving the discussion of "society" rather vague; Alfred Schutz ([1932] 1967) similarly stressed the process of intersubjectivity without paying much attention to social structure; Émile Durkheim ([1895] 1938, [1893] 1984), despite his strong advocacy for studying "social facts" and for visualizing structure as the number and nature of interconnections among positions, did not pursue this view in detail; and Sigmund Freud (1900) did not examine social structure beyond clinical analysis of ego and superego processes or beyond grandiose pronouncements about the constraints of "civilizations." Indeed, except for Jacob Moreno's ([1934] 1953) pioneering use of sociograms or except for early anthropologists' (Linton 1936) and sociologists' (Park 1926) conceptualizations of status and roles, the notion of interrelations among positions was not well developed in early-twentieth-century sociology. Only more modern approaches such as expectation states theory and research offer a dynamic conception of status, but even here the concept is limited to differences in the prestige or authority of individuals in task-oriented groups. Even Goffman (1983, 1967), who recognized the embeddedness of encounters in gatherings and social occasions, failed to offer much detail about the structure of these beyond discussion of roles, stages, props, and fixed equipment.

As a consequence of this neglect to incorporate the analysis of structure into much microsociology, the term *status* has ambiguous meanings. For some status denotes a position within a social structure; for others the term connotes honor and prestige alone; for still others status refers to both authority and prestige. These respective definitions need not be contradictory, but the different uses of the term require conceptual clarification. For my purposes, *status* is a position, occupied by an individual, standing in relationship to at least one other position, occupied by another person. Status positions reveal a variety of properties, and the most interesting dynamics of status are to be found in the variations of these properties.

One property is the clarity and discreteness of status positions. Some positions are explicitly demarcated from others, as is the case of mother and father in a family and supervisors and subordinates in a business, while at other times, the clarity of status is not so clearly defined, as is evident with the status of being an acquaintance. Thus, a critical property of status is its clarity vis-à-vis other status positions. Another property of status positions is their connection to each other, or what might be termed their *network properties*. Positions can vary along several dimensions of connectedness, including "density" (degree to which all positions are connected to each other), centrality (extent to which a particular position is a path to all other positions), equivalence (degree to which two positions are located at similar places in the same or different networks), brokerage and bridges (extent to which a position stands between two or more subsets of positions). While all properties of networks among positions can be important (Burt 1980), I will emphasize the density and equivalence of positions. A third property of status is the amount of power and/or authority attached to a position. A fourth property of status is the prestige and honor that accompanies a position. A final key property of status that influences all of the others is the embeddedness of positions in corporate and categoric units.

The Clarity of Status

THE PHENOMENOLOGY OF STATUS

When people role take, they also seek to discover the status of others, and when they role make, they attempt to signal their status vis-à-vis others. Indeed, role taking and role making are constrained by the positions that self and others occupy, and because of this fact, people seek to "know" what status they and others have. Phrases like "I don't know where I stand with her" are verbal confessions that a person does not know his or her status and role in relation to the position and role of another. If individuals cannot determine their respective status positions, they have difficulty not only in role making, role taking, and role verification but also in meeting transactional needs for confirmation of self, profitable exchange payoffs, group inclusion, trust, and facticity. Since these needs drive people's behaviors, they push each person in an encounter to discover the status of others. With understanding of each participant's position, the appropriate identities are more likely to be presented and verified, the resources and range of potential exchange payoffs are more likely to be recognized, the markers of group inclusion are more likely to be understood, the facticity of the situation is more likely to become clear, and the way trust is to be achieved is more likely to be specified. For example, when a student enters an encounter with a professor, the respective positions will indicate (a) how self should be presented and confirmed, (b) what range of resources and possible payoffs are possible, (c) what markers of inclusion are to be used, (d) what constitutes the reality of the situation, and (e) how predictability, sincerity, respect, and other dimensions of trust are to be achieved. Conversely, when status is not clear, interaction becomes strained. For instance, a professor who attends a student social gathering will often feel uncomfortable, as do the students, because everyone is unsure of their relative positions. Do classroom positions dominate, or does the position of party-goer dominate? Or, is there some mix among the positions of professor, student, and party-goer? In any case, it will be more difficult to establish clear expectations, to play roles, to normatize the situation, and to meet transactional needs.

Thus, when individuals successfully place each other in a position, not only are transactional needs more likely to be realized, but moreover, other forces driving encounters are likely to be channeled in ways generating viable sequences of interaction. With mutual understanding of positions, the expectations and sanctions appropriate to individuals in various positions become more readily understood, thereby keeping the emotional flow of the encounter within bounds and on track. For example, if a person places another in the position of good friend in a social encounter, expectations for how such a person should behave are clear as are the appropriate modes of sanctioning. The same would be true for the position of husband-wife, worker-supervisor, or professor-student. With mutual understanding of positions comes knowledge of how to role make and what to look for in role taking. A person who is put into the position of friend knows what role he or she should play, while implicitly becoming alert in role taking to gestures emitted by the other signaling the alter role of friend. Normatizing is also greatly facilitated by understanding positions; developing expectations for categorizing self and others, framing the situation, selecting forms of communication, using rituals, and displaying appropriate feelings are now more readily achieved. Finally, with knowledge of positions, the demography and ecology of the encounter are understood and used in appropriate ways.

Thus, when individuals can put each other in clearly defined and discrete positions, the interpersonal flow of the encounter will proceed smoothly. Clarity of positions is more than a property of status; it is what individuals seek if they are to feel comfortable in the interaction. With clarity, other forces in the encounter can be channeled, and transactional needs can be realized. What conditions, then, increase the clarity of status? I see two conditions as critical: (1) embeddedness and (2) iterations.

EMBEDDEDNESS AND CLARITY OF POSITIONS

When an encounter is embedded in a corporate unit, positions become more explicitly defined by the culture and structure of the unit. The more formality and hierarchy evident in the division of labor, the more likely is the status of individuals to be clear. As a result, the emotional flow, the roles, the symbols, and demography/ecology of the encounter will be channeled, and the way to meet transactional needs will be better understood and acted on.

When an encounter is embedded in categoric units, the diffuse status characteristics operating in the encounter will be known to all, and the more these characteristics are discrete (for example, male-female), the more likely are they to influence the interpersonal flow of the encounter. If diffuse status characteristics are differentially evaluated, their effects will be that much greater. Even more graduated characteristics (for instance, years of education, age, income, pigmentation of skin) can be converted into more nominal categories (such as educated-uneducated, young-old, rich-poor, black-white) that are differentially evaluated. To the extent that this conversion into discrete categories is possible, the effects of these diffuse status characteristics will increase. Furthermore, if differentially evaluated status characteristics are correlated with each other (say, black-male, young-student), the effects are not just combined; they are amplified beyond their additive effects alone and exert even more influence on the interpersonal flow of the encounter.

The most interesting aspect of embeddedness is the intersection of status in corporate units and diffuse status characteristics flowing from categoric

unit membership. The basic relationship between status in corporate and
categoric units is, I believe, this: the more formal and clear-cut the division
of labor, and particularly so when the division of labor is also hierarchical,
the greater is the relative influence of status in corporate units over status in
categoric units. Thus, the effects of diffuse status characteristics are reduced
when the division of labor defines status for individuals in encounters. Conversely, the less embedded is an encounter in a corporate unit or the less explicit is the division of labor in a corporate unit, the greater will be the relative effects of diffuse status characteristics. Without the division of labor in
a corporate unit to define status, individuals will, by default, rely on diffuse
status characteristics, particularly if these are discrete and differentially evaluated. For example, an interaction between a man and a woman will be much
more influenced by these diffuse status characteristics when the interaction
occurs outside a corporate unit or when it occurs in a corporate unit with a
fluid division of labor. But, as the status of these two individuals is marked
by their respective positions in the division of labor, the effect of diffuse status characteristics declines, and the salience of status in the division of labor
of the corporate unit increases. Rarely are the effects of diffuse status characteristics completely eliminated by the division of labor (as the persistence
of gender, ethnic, and age discrimination in most businesses attests), but the
power of categoric membership is mitigated.

When membership in a categoric unit is correlated with status in the hierarchical division of labor of a corporate unit, the influence of diffuse status
characteristics increases. Thus, when women in a business corporation were
primarily clerks and secretaries, while only men were managers, the effects of
being a man or a woman were amplified by their correlation with the hierarchical division of labor. Similarly, when positions in the division of labor are
highly correlated with a diffuse status characteristic, the distinctions among
both types of positions are made more discrete. As a general rule, when categoric unit membership is correlated with the division of labor, especially when
the division of labor is hierarchical and when diffuse status characteristics are
nominal as well as differentially evaluated, the power of diffuse status characteristics and positions within the corporate unit are amplified beyond what
each would be alone. For instance, because slaves were all black (except for a
few white indentured servants) and virtually all masters were white in the
pre-Civil War south, the correlation of a diffuse status characteristic with the
hierarchical division of labor reinforced and amplified the salience and power
of status in the division of labor of the plantation system (a corporate unit)

and in the demarcation and evaluation of the categoric units (blacks versus whites). Thus, individuals do not always "average" evaluations of status from varying sources; when statuses are correlated, their effects are multiplicative as each draws attention to the other and magnifies the salience of the respective evaluations of status in corporate and categoric units.[1]

When diffuse status characteristics are consistently associated with inequalities in authority and prestige in encounters within corporate units, this association can lead to "status beliefs" that become part of the broader culture of a society. As Ridgeway (2001, 1998), Ridgeway and Erickson (2000), and Webster and Hysom (1998) have argued, this association of status characteristics and inequalities in authority/prestige at the microlevel can, over iterated encounters in different contexts, generate ideologies that harden differential evaluations of diffuse status characteristics, with these beliefs becoming expectation states guiding each and every encounter. For beliefs to spread, however, a consistent association of inequalities of positions with diffuse status characteristics is essential, as was the case with slaves. Should expectations generated in one encounter in a corporate unit be countered by the lack of association of diffuse status with inequalities of positions in another, status beliefs cannot gain a foothold and spread. But, once in existence, such beliefs are difficult to break down, as the history of civil rights or the history of the women's movement documents.

When the division of labor is horizontal, diffuse status characteristics will have greater influence than when the division of labor is vertical. Thus, interaction between blacks and whites at the same position in the division of labor or even in different positions that reveal no differences in authority will be more constrained by categoric unit membership than by corporate unit membership. This effect will increase to the extent that diffuse status characteristics are differentially evaluated. For example, interactions among equals within a business corporation will be more influenced by the age, gender, ethnicity,

---

[1] Expectation states theory argues that multiple status characteristics are combined to form an aggregated expectation for self and others. Moreover, this combining involves a process of combing positive status information into one set, negative into another, and then summing the values of the two. Although data support this argument, my point is that when the values of status information are consistent in either a positive or negative direction, more than summing occurs. There can be multiplicative effects. See Wagner and Turner (1998: 456–57) for a review.

and other differentially evaluated characteristics than by the specific positions of individuals at the same level in the division of labor, although these effects will often decline the more the encounter is iterated (see next section).

Oftentimes, a position within a corporate unit becomes itself a categoric unit. The president of a corporate unit like a business or a university is often converted into a social category; and when such categories are differentially evaluated, they influence interaction like all diffuse status characteristics. Thus, when a university president interacts with others outside the university, his or her place in the division of labor often becomes a status characteristic that others use in role taking and role making. Indeed, individuals often try to convert positions in the division of labor into categoric units, since such placement will facilitate the interaction. For example, when I interact with students, it is far easier to define them as a social category—that is, "students"—than it is to visualize their place in the division of labor of the university as freshmen, sophomores, juniors, or seniors (or to place them in diverse student roles). Similarly, it is easier for rank-and-file military personnel to define higher-level officers as "the brass" and, thereby, to interact with them as members of a categoric unit than it is to treat them in terms of their exact place in the hierarchical division of labor (as generals of various stars or as captains, colonels, and the like). I suspect, to illustrate further, that people ask those whom they are just getting to know about "their job" (for example, "What kind of work do you do?") because it allows them to place people in categoric units stemming from their position in an important corporate unit and, on the basis of this placement, to adjust their responses. I might speculate further that the more corporate units form the structure and culture of an institutional system (such as a business corporation, family, church, school), the more likely are positions within the division of labor of these corporate units to be converted into categoric distinctions and, as a result, to influence the responses of individuals to each other in an encounter.

TIME AND ITERATIONS

The effects of status change over time as an encounter is iterated with the same or approximately the same individuals. As a general process, the initial effects of hierarchy of positions in corporate units and of differential evaluation of diffuse status characteristics flowing from categoric units decline over time. This decline is greater for diffuse status characteristics than hierarchy in corporate units.

Individuals often develop positive sentiments of liking in repeated interactions. Early on, George Homans (1951) argued that among equals, rates of
interaction over time increase the mutual liking of individuals, but Homans
qualified this generalization by arguing that this effect is undone when there
are authority relations between individuals. By extension, I argue that the
more individuals interact and develop positive sentiments toward each other
(as individuals are able to meet their transactional needs, play roles, and normatize encounters), the less will be the effects of status distinctions that were
salient during initial encounters among individuals. For example, the more
whites interact with blacks at the same point in the division of labor in a corporate unit, the less relevant are these categoric distinctions in shaping the
flow of interaction. And, despite the fact that diffuse status characteristics
may be differentially evaluated, these differences will decline over time. Even
when the interaction is more passive and vicarious (as is the case with media
presentations of those from different categoric units), this effect can be observed, although to a much lesser degree since these interactions are not face
to face and do not, therefore, pull other forces driving encounters into play.

Similarly, there is ample evidence that even when authority exists between
high- and low-status individuals in corporate units, more positive sentiments will emerge (contrary to Homans's conclusion) as the interactions are
repeated. But we must immediately make some qualifications.

First, as expectation states theory emphasizes, status orders (of authority
and prestige) become expectations for performance that guide the flow of interaction; once established, these expectations are difficult to change. But I
would argue that most research in this tradition generally examines short-
term experimental groups, and, therefore, I am not sure that these data explain longer-term chains of interaction, unless more general status beliefs
have emerged in the broader culture. There will be, I believe, two contradictory tendencies in iterated encounters: one for the expectation states to hold
and thereby maintain differences in authority and prestige, and another for
the effects of interaction to create new positive sentiments that mitigate the
power of initial expectation states. The initial expectation states may endure,
but they will lose some of their power to control subordinates' responses over
time. As individuals all behave in accordance with expectation states, positive
emotions will be mutually expressed by those high and low in status, and
ironically, as these sentiments are expressed over time, the salience of hierarchy will decline (although rarely disappear).

Second, the way in which authority is used or prestige is invoked influences whether the effects of status differences in corporate units will recede over time. If superordinates in a corporate unit use their authority and prestige to (a) deny subordinates the ability to realize their transactional needs, especially for self-verification and positive exchange payoffs, (b) frustrate subordinates in their efforts to meet expectations carried over from previous encounters, (c) persistently impose negative sanctions on subordinates, (d) push subordinates into ever-changing roles, and (e) force subordinates to constantly renormatize across encounters, then interactions will harden status differences rather than reduce them. Thus, the arousal of negative sentiments in subordinates will increase the salience of hierarchy, assuring that the flow of interaction will be guided by inequalities of status.

Third, when subordinates can mobilize their resources to challenge authority or abusive practices of superordinates, they can reduce the effects of hierarchy or, at the very least, regulate it. For example, unionization of workers can be seen as a way to regulate and delimit the use of authority. Still, even as subordinates get angry or even when they can fight back, the hierarchy in the division of labor is still pushing the flow of interaction; indeed, the hierarchy has become ever more salient even as individuals try to change it. Thus, whatever the outcome of conflict, the very emergence of open conflict will harden distinctions and arrest the emergence of positive sentiments over iterated encounters.

Fourth, much of the apparent reduction of hierarchy is just that: apparent. It is in the interests of subordinates to present positive sentiments to superordinates in order to mitigate the exercise of authority or imposition of prestige; and it is in the interest of superordinates to seem pleasant so as to lower the costs (anger and resentment by subordinates) in imposing their authority or in receiving honor and deference. Indeed, the emergence of positive sentiments is often the result of good acting more than genuine sense of affection, indicating that authority or prestige in the division of labor is still highly salient.

These four qualifications perhaps obviate the generalization that positive sentiments emerge over iterated encounters. Still, I argue that there are pressures for more positive sentiments to develop; and once emergent, these sentiments reduce the salience of inequalities in status on the flow of interaction. Of course, there is no guarantee that this fragile state will emerge or persist, but there is a tendency for the salience of inequalities to decline over repeated encounters.

Again, the intersection of status in corporate and categoric units reveals some interesting dynamics in iterated encounters. If differentially evaluated diffuse status characteristics emanating from categoric unit memberships are correlated with inequalities in the division of labor in a corporate unit, the power of all status differences to structure the flow of interactions will not be mitigated over time. For example, if all managers are males and all subordinates are females in a corporate unit, then iteration of the encounter will reinforce and amplify the effects of diffuse status characteristics (men and women), with this amplification of status characteristics serving to reinforce the hierarchy of authority in the division of labor, and especially so if generalized status beliefs emerge from consistent association of positions in a hierarchy with differential evaluation of diffuse status characteristics (Ridgeway 2001, 1998). Conversely, if the hierarchy in the division of labor is uncorrelated with categoric unit membership (as is the case when males and females are equally distributed in positions of authority and subordination), the effects of diffuse status characteristics will decline over time as encounters are iterated, and so will the effects of authority but to a lesser degree (assuming, of course, that the authority is not used in the ways enumerated above to enhance the salience of status).

If a position in the division of labor is converted to a diffuse status characteristic, this characteristic will have more relevance during initial encounters than in later ones, particularly in interactions outside the corporate unit. For instance, if the position of president of a university is converted to a status characteristic that influences encounters outside the university, this effect on the flow of interaction will initially be great and then decline thereafter. However, expectation states research finds the opposite to be the case, visualizing the effect of the prestige of university president as setting expectations that allocate prestige and authority in groups. How, then, can we reconcile these contradictory predictions? The groups studied by expectation states researchers are generally task groups; thus, when a diffuse status characteristic is seen by participants to an encounter as task relevant, the allocation or authority and prestige will hold as long as the group remains instrumental. But as encounters are iterated, ever more social content is introduced into the flow of interaction. Therefore, more generally, I would hypothesize that the more repeated encounters turn on social rather than instrumental content, the less will be the hold of the initial allocation of prestige and authority associated with a diffuse status characteristic on the flow of interaction. Thus, in iterated social encounters outside a university, the status of university president will, over time, become less salient in structuring the flow of interaction outside the university. While there may be an initial allocation of prestige and authority to a person like a university president in social encounters, these will be likely to decline over time, although there will be a subtle residue and undercurrent of the prestige associated with the high evaluation and authority of the position of president. Thus, expectation states stemming from inequalities in task performance are not obliterated, but they will be dramatically reduced when encounters become more social, or are social at the outset.

Thus, there will always be, I believe, a tendency for iterated encounters to reduce the effects of differentially evaluated status characteristics and the hold of positional authority in a corporate unit, except under certain conditions: (a) the status distinctions from categoric units and those in the hierarchical division of labor in corporate units are highly correlated; (b) the encounter remains instrumental with little social content; (c) those in positions of authority and prestige engage in practices that impose authority and prestige, thereby arousing negative emotions among subordinates; and (d) conflicts have erupted that harden the lines of authority. But when these conditions do not prevail, the hold of status on how individuals interact will be reduced.

As the hold of inequalities in status decline, however, the clarity of status will also decline. When managers become friends with those over whom they have authority, when males and females interact as equals, when ethnic minorities and those of the more highly evaluated majority spend time together in the same positions, and when interactions are repeated, the power of both status in the division of labor of corporate units and diffuse status characteristics emanating from categoric units will generally decline, unless (a), (b), (c), and (d) above are operative. This diminution (although rarely elimination) of status reduces the clarity in the positions of individuals vis-à-vis one another. Individuals will then be forced to rely more on the other forces of the encounter—emotional, transactional, roles, symbols, and demography/ecology—to sustain the encounter.

Why would individuals act in ways mitigating the effects of status when it forces them to live with somewhat more ambiguous attributions of their respective positions and, thereby, requires them to engage in more interpersonal effort? Part of the answer resides, I think, in human biology. First, humans are apes who are still driven by their ape ancestry to prefer individualism, autonomy, mobility, and most significantly, low levels of inequality and hierarchy. If monkeys were our more immediate ancestors, we would, no doubt, prefer interactions structured by inequality. Inequalities of status would rule, even beyond the predictions of expectation states research. But we are apes, and as apes, humans chafe against constraints, especially those imposed by hierarchy. Second, although humans are not *highly* social in most situations, prolonged interactions in repeated encounters will arouse positive emotions; and once these are consistently aroused across encounters, they do increase sociality and solidarity as memory pathways and emotional centers of the brain become conditioned to positive affect from specific others. Moreover, positive affect and solidarity are more readily sustained without explicitly order-giving and -taking or implicit threats of negative sanctions. As a consequence, once aroused and reinforced across repeated encounters, the positive sociality becomes a more powerful force than the expectation states associated with authority and prestige unless, of course, the conditions sustaining inequalities (enumerated earlier) are in play. Moreover, arousal of positive sentiments becomes a new kind of "affective expectation state" whose violation (through use of authority and negative sanctions) would set off negative emotional arousal (as indicated in Chapter 4 and suggested by Joseph Berger [1988]).

Ironically, as the clarity of status declines, the risks and problems for individuals increase. Individuals will have to adjust expectations, but these will remain somewhat ambiguous and uncertain because the new sociality is typically accompanied by some expectations from the old inequalities. When expectations are uncertain, breaches and negative sanctioning become more likely, thus activating negative emotions along the pattern described in Chapter 4. Individuals will also have to deal with more uncertainty in meeting transactional needs. They will have to work harder at presenting role identities that verify self; they will have positive exchange payoffs but these will always be somewhat precarious because of the background of status inequalities that have been mitigated but not eliminated; they will have a greater sense of group inclusion with the flow of positive sentiments but the potential for this to be disrupted by the exercise of authority by superordinates remains a possibility in the minds of subordinates; they will have a new sense of facticity, receiving more respect and sincerity but this will be achieved against a backdrop of potential unpredictability and loss of trust stemming from the potential use of authority or imposition of prestige by superordinates. Individuals will also have to work harder at normatization, since categories of self, other, and situation will need to be adjusted, as will frames, forms of talk, rituals, and feelings; and because of the implicit uncertainty that inequalities could potentially be reasserted, subordinates will live with two sets of norms, those structuring the flow of the new sociality and those memories of the old formality and inequality. Individuals will have to pay especially close attention to the demography and ecology of the interaction, especially who is present, what props are used, how space is occupied and other features of demography/ecology, because these become important markers of the new sociality and reminders of the older inequality. Thus, there will be a tension in the new, more social relations; so, there are hidden costs to this sociality, but still, humans cannot help themselves, if iterated interactions drive the encounter in ways mitigating the inequalities of prestige and authority in corporate units and the differential evaluation of categoric units.

As a result of this increased ambiguity, the emotional stakes become higher and potentially more volatile. As noted above, people develop expectation states about the reduced salience of authority and prestige differences and about the increased flow of sentiments of liking. When these are violated, more negative emotions are likely to be aroused because all other forces driving the encounter are disrupted: needs will go unmet, roles will not be verified, and normatization will collapse or revert back to older patterns. Thus, there are benefits to knowing where you stand in a hierarchy that specifies the terms of group inclusion, trust, and facticity, even if this sense of inclusion, trust, and facticity makes people vulnerable to negative sanctions, forces them to play subordinate roles, present self in a subordinate way, condemns them to less valuable and more costly exchange payoffs, requires them to use formal talk, makes them engage in rituals marking subordination, and requires them to suppress their true feelings. But this very list of "costs" associated with certainty in inequalities indicates why individuals who descended from apes prefer the informality and sociality of reduced inequality, even if these must be purchased at increased uncertainty.

In general, when expectations for more informal and social relations among equals have developed, it almost always acts by superordinates that breach these expectations. This action can result from a simple interpersonal mistake increasing the salience of inequalities once again to an explicit effort to prevent informality from going too far. As a result, subordinates in corporate units or lower-prestige categoric units will almost always make external attributions to the superordinate who violates expectations. As a result, subordinates will: (1) express anger toward a superordinate, and if they cannot express this anger openly, they will do so when out of reach of superordinates; and (2) experience some fear because of what reassertion inequalities mean for future encounters. Individuals may also experience sadness for what has been lost, but I would hypothesize that the dominant reactions are anger toward and fear of those who have reestablished inequalities. Thus, guilt and shame are far less likely because of these external attributions that arouse anger and fear. The more individuals must readjust expectations, receive negative sanctions from superordinates, make and verify new roles, present revised selves, lower expectations for exchange payoffs, and renormatize future encounters, the greater will be their anger and fear.

Status and Networks

Status positions are generally connected to each other by ties. The nature of the ties can vary, but in general they involve the flow of resources from one position to another. In most face-to-face interactions, the resources are intrinsic, revolving around the emotions associated with other driving forces in the encounter. When transactional needs are met, roles are verified, norms are clear, and status is understood, individuals will experience and express positive emotions; and although other resources can be involved, the currency of most face-to-face interactions is emotion. For example, even when we purchase a product and have an encounter with a cashier where money is the extrinsic resource connecting the positions of cashier and customer, far more important for the flow of interaction is the emotional undercurrent stemming from the ability of each party to meet transactional needs, play roles, and abide by norms specifying categories, talk, frames, rituals, and emotional displays. Even in this fleeting encounter, the emotional resources are still what connect the two positions, as is immediately evident when one party behaves in ways that violate transactional needs, appropriate role behavior, or norms. Under these conditions, amazingly powerful expressions of anger are likely to be experienced, and perhaps expressed by the offended party, indicating that there is an undercurrent of emotion connecting these two positions. For this reason "emotion work" is emphasized to employees in retail sales and other work situations (Hochschild 1983, 1979).

The analysis of networks in sociology is a highly refined and technical subdiscipline.[2] I do not intend to delve too deeply into this literature, but rather I will offer the key generalizations about the dynamics flowing from the nature of connections among positions. I will focus on two properties of networks: (1) density and (2) equivalence.

---

[2] For overviews, see Wasserman and Faust 1994; Maryanski and Turner 1998; · Wellman 1983; Marsden and Lin 1982; Burt 1980; Holland and Leinhardt 1979.

THE DENSITY OF TIES

Density denotes the degree to which the number of ties among positions reaches the theoretical maximum of all positions being connected to each other. The more dense are the ties among positions, the greater will be the effects of status on the *initial* flow of interaction. Thus, when ties are dense, each position will be examined along several dimensions: the prestige of the position, the authority of a position, the roles appropriate to a position, the norms guiding those in a position, and the transactional needs to be realized in a position. Connectedness increases the salience of positions, then; and the more connected by ties are all positions, the more likely are all dimensions of status to be taken into account by individuals during early iterations of an interaction. Compare, for example, an interaction with a clerk to that of family members. The tie with the clerk is brief; moreover, the customer is not connected to all of the other ties (with other employees, the manager, the union, and the like) of business. As a result, the customer pays only scant attention to the details of the status of clerk, and vice versa, unless the clerk or customer behaves inappropriately. In contrast, members of the family are highly attuned to all aspects of status—authority, prestige, norms, emotions, need states, and roles—because these positions are all connected to each other. Much of this increased attention to all aspects of a position is, of course, the result of iterations of encounters.

As I emphasized earlier, however, the salience of positional authority and prestige as well as differentially evaluated diffuse status characteristics will have a tendency to decline, despite the pressure of expectation states to sustain status inequalities. Thus, density of positions will generally increase rates of interaction over time, and as encounters are repeated, the effects of iteration in reducing the salience of initial authority and prestige in corporate units and/or differential evaluation of categoric units (discussed above) will begin to kick in, eroding the power of these initial expectation states and shifting them toward more informality.

Individuals are more likely to find themselves in dense-tie situations in small corporate units, like a family or work group, whereas those in categoric units are less likely to be connected by ties unless they are congregated in a corporate unit. Thus, fellow family members or workers are more likely to occupy connected positions than are women or men as a whole. This is an obvious point, but it nonetheless makes a great deal of difference to the flow of interaction. When a member of a minority interacts with a member of a majority, the interaction proceeds along the expectations associated with their respective categoric units or diffuse status characteristics, at least initially. But when members of a family interact, the ties are much more robust, revolving around emotions operating at many levels. Connectedness involves more emotion and raises the emotional stakes for all those who participate. For this reason individuals remain highly attuned to all those in a dense network. Indeed, gossip is but one manifestation of the fascination of individuals to those in their close networks (especially gossip about emotions); and in fact, the receipt of gossip often becomes a key emotional resource sustaining ties in the network. The more an encounter is embedded in a small corporate unit, then, the more likely are ties among positions to be dense; as a result, the greater will be individuals' attention to the properties of each status position and to the forces—that is, emotions, transactional needs, roles, norms, demography/ecology—converging on each position. As a result, the emotional velocity flowing through ties will be high, or potentially high when a breach occurs.

In larger corporate units, however, the overall density of ties will decrease since it is impossible for all positions to be connected to each other, especially on an emotional level; as a consequence, encounters among those in diverse positions will rely on the expectations inhering in the formal and hierarchical structure of the corporate unit to guide the flow of interaction. Participants will be most attuned to differences in the authority and prestige of their respective positions; and on the basis of these properties of status, the interaction will proceed in a highly stylized manner involving little emotional connection between participants. Within a larger corporate unit, of course, more dense ties will merge in various subunits or cliques; encounters among people in these positions will involve more dimensions of status beyond authority and prestige. In cliques, status characteristics will be more important, at least initially, as will perceptions of the needs of incumbents, the roles they make, the way they normatize, the sanctions they use, and the emotions they feel and express.

EQUIVALENCE

Status positions reveal "equivalence" when they stand in the same relationship to other positions. For example, the position of mother in one family holds the same relationship to children as the status of mother in another family. Or, a worker in one factory has much the same relationship to the foreman and other supervisory personnel as a worker in another factory. Again, like all concepts in network analysis, equivalence has several more precise definitions.[3] However, the general argument is that people in equivalent positions will typically share similar orientations because they must interact with other positions revealing the same characteristics. People in equivalent positions will, therefore, have normatized their relations with others in similar ways; they will have played similar roles; they will have realized transactional needs in a similar manner; and they will have experienced similar emotions.

When people in equivalent positions interact, this similarity in their relationships to other positions changes the dynamics of the interpersonal flow. Even when they have no previous connection, they will generally not interact as strangers; instead, they will often relate to each other in ways more typical of individuals at the same positions in dense social networks because they have been in equivalent networks. They will pay less attention to authority and prestige considerations and more to (a) diffuse status characteristics (at least initially), (b) role-playing styles, and (c) transactional needs in fine-tuning the interactive flow. For example, when students from different universities gather, they have much in common because they generally have been at equivalent positions at their respective universities; as a result, they will tune into diffuse status characteristics (most typically, gender, ethnicity, and perhaps age), watch for variants of the student role that others make for themselves, and seek to meet each other's transactional needs for self-confirmation, positive exchange payoffs, group inclusion, trust, and facticity. All of this attunement of responses will be relatively easy because of their equivalent positions. The same is true for any encounter among those in equivalent positions; and if these positions are also part of a dense network, the effects of equivalence will be that much greater.

EMOTIONAL AROUSAL IN NETWORKS

The potential for emotional arousal increases with breaches in the interaction among individuals in dense networks or among those in equivalent positions in the same or different networks. The person who breaches the flow of inter-

---

[3] I am using the term in line with Lee Douglas Sailer's (1978) notion of "regular equivalence," which, I believe, is superior to Harrison C. White's and colleagues' (1976) notion of "structural equivalence."

action in a dense network or in one composed of structural equivalent positions will violate expectations, fail to meet others' transactional needs, disrupt roles, and force renormatization; as a consequence, emotions will be aroused.

Attribution processes are important in how emotions play out among incumbents. If individuals blame themselves for the breach and the network is composed of relative equals, they will experience sadness, anger at self, and fear about the consequences to self; and if these emotions are aroused simultaneously, they will experience shame as well as guilt if moral codes are invoked in self-evaluations. If the person blames others for the breach in a dense network or one composed of structurally equivalent positions and the network is composed of relative equals, anger toward others is likely; and if categories of others are blamed, then a person will experience and express anger toward members of these categories, while developing prejudices toward members of these categories.

As noted earlier, if the network is composed of unequals and a higher-status person is blamed for the breach, individuals will experience anger toward this person and will express this anger with those of equal status. They will also experience fear of the higher-status individual who has breached the interaction, and particularly so when the higher status revolves more around authority than prestige. If the superordinate can be typified as a category (such as the "boss," the "brass," the "suits," and so on), prejudices will develop for members of this categoric unit.

Sometimes individuals will blame themselves for breaches in dense networks in which a superordinate has breached the interaction; under these conditions, these individuals will experience escalated fear, anger at self, and sadness, which can become shame and guilt. For example, women often blame themselves for arousing the anger of their abusive spouses; or students blame themselves if a professor becomes mad at them. But, as emphasized earlier, individuals will generally tend to make external attributions rather than self-attributions for breaches of the interpersonal flow with superordinates under conditions of high density, even if they cannot openly express their anger and fear.

Expectations and Status-Organizing Processes

During the last four decades a set of theories, variously known as expectation states theory or status-organizing theories, has proliferated from the core ideas originally developed by Joseph Berger (1958) and colleagues (Berger and Conner 1969).[4] The essential idea, one that appears throughout the pages of this book, is that much interaction is organized around expectations that constrain how individuals respond to each other. Early work focused on the expectations generated by performance in task groups, with those making the most contributions to the task receiving positive evaluations that, in turn, establish expectations for future performance. More generally, the theory predicts that those with high authority and prestige are expected to behave more competently, creating expectations that, in essence, become self-fulfilling prophecies guiding the responses of those high and low in authority and prestige. Moreover, diffuse status characteristics brought into the group have this same effect, especially if these characteristics are differentially evaluated. All of these dynamics have been incorporated into my theory thus far, but we can add some further refinements emerging from the ongoing research program on expectation states.

One idea is the notion of multiple status characteristics. For expectation states theorists, individuals are seen as combining several status characteristics, to the extent they are relevant in an encounter. Moreover, actors combine positive information into one set of expectations and negative information into another, and they sum the two sets of positively and negatively evaluated information (Berger, Rosenholtz, and Zelditch 1980; Norman, Smith, and Berger 1988). Once this process has been initiated, each additional piece of information has less effect on the overall evaluation of a person. Thus, as expectations begin to emerge, new information has less and less power to alter expectations, which is one of the reasons why these expectations endure.

Another idea from expectation states is justice. Considerations of justice are tied to the expectations associated with evaluations of different status positions. Cultural evaluations of status positions establish a "referential structure," which sets expectations for the resources that those in differentially evaluated positions should receive (Ridgeway and Berger 1988, 1986). When individuals do not receive the resources or rewards appropriate to the cultural evaluation of their status, they will experience a sense of injustice, as will others in the encounter. Moreover, if several referential structures are activated in an encounter, these will be combined to produce a kind of metaexpectation for payoffs and for receipt of resources. A further implication is that when ref-

[4] For useful overviews, see Berger et al. 1977; Webster and Foschi 1988; Berger and Zelditch 1998, 1985; Wagner and Turner 1998.

erential structures are consistent in a given direction, inequalities will increase in the interaction since there is no contradictory information that must be averaged. Conversely, the more inconsistent are referential structures for a status, the more will the combining process reduce the inequalities of status as positive and negative evaluations are subtracted from each other.

Yet another idea is that when actors meet expectations stemming from broader cultural values as these apply to status characteristics, differences in authority and prestige among individuals are more likely to be seen as right and, hence, legitimated. Once legitimated, the expectations for the present and future encounters will be more stable, becoming moral standards specifying what should or ought to be.

What then can we take from these well-researched ideas? First, when an encounter is embedded in corporate and categoric units, referential structures differentially evaluating status are more likely to be present and unambiguous. As a result, expectations will be more powerful since they carry the values and beliefs of the broader culture as they define and evaluate different positions within the division of labor of corporate units or different categoric units. For example, the position of professor within a university has a clear evaluation because broader cultural values are translated into more specific ideologies of education that, in turn, are applied to various positions within the university as a corporate unit. As a result, referential structures are clear and consistent, thereby making expectations more explicit and powerful in encounters involving college professors. Similarly, encounters between slaves and their holders in the pre-Civil War South were guided by powerful ideologies associated with these categoric units (that is, black and white), with the result that the power of differential evaluations of categoric units was that much greater. Thus, the more embedded an encounter, the more likely are referential structures to be clear; and the more they are used to differentially evaluate status positions, the more powerful are the expectations guiding the flow of interaction.

Second, when embedded, differential evaluations are more likely to be consistent since they are organized by ideologies translating and attaching value premises to positions in corporate units and categoric units. This consistency gives more power to expectations and increases the likelihood that participants to an encounter will behave in terms of expectations and, as a consequence, legitimate differences in prestige and authority now and in the future. As expectation states theory predicts, consistent expectations will increase inequalities. Conversely, the less embedded an encounter, the more likely are referential structures to be inconsistent, thereby decreasing inequality as positive and negative sets of evaluations are subtracted from each other.

Third, embedding increases the probability that standards of justice will be tied to differential evaluations of status. Correspondingly, other forces influencing justice—investments and costs, for example—will contribute less to the assessment of whether or not the distribution of resources to individuals is fair and just. In essence, the differential evaluation of positions in corporate units or membership in categoric units defines what individuals should receive in exchange payoffs and in other sources of rewards. Thus, a president of a corporation is allowed to receive extraordinary compensation by virtue of occupying this position, even if his or her performance has not always met expectations for corporate profits. Similarly, a low-level bureaucrat is given low compensation even if this individual makes important contributions to the success of the organization. In general, these differences are seen as just because of the evaluations associated with these positions. Similarly, for most of the twentieth century, it was seen as just (or, at least, not questioned in most encounters) that women and men should receive different wages for the same job, simply by virtue of the differential evaluation of men and women in work contexts. (Of course, the obvious injustice of this situation became a critical issue in the women's movement, but it took the mobilization of counterideologies to begin to break the hold of older ideologies rooted in patriarchy; and when the counterideology was combined with the older ideology, the resulting inconsistency of referential structures began to reduce inequalities as expectations were altered and as legitimation of inequalities came unraveled.)

A number of generalizations can be drawn from the above discussion. The greater the differences in prestige and authority of individuals in an encounter, the more they create expectations for performances; hence, the more likely are these differences to be sustained if individuals meet their respective expectations. Such is particularly likely when expectations are clear and consistent and when no new status information is introduced (and even if it is introduced later it has less effect than information introduced earlier). Embedding of encounters in corporate and categoric units increases the salience of values and beliefs of the broader culture as these are translated into ideologies attached to status positions; in so doing, embeddedness increases the clarity and consistency of expectations, making their legitimation more likely and giving them more power to influence the flow of interaction. Given the operation of the forces described in these generalizations, how would the status order ever be changed, once these processes are in full swing? There are several countervailing processes that are underemphasized in expectation states research.

One is the effects of iterations and time, as emphasized earlier. As encounters are repeated, new noninstrumental information is introduced as people come to know each other, thus decreasing the power of differences in prestige and authority associated with task behaviors. Furthermore, individuals can change a status order over time by presenting self in nonthreatening ways as ever more competent, thus shifting the evaluations of status (Ridgeway 1994, 1982). Another is the inconsistency of expectations for status, even in embedded encounters. It is rare for status information to be completely consistent: bosses are often incompetent; diffuse status characteristics can counter the evaluation of positions in the division of labor in a corporate unit; new individuals to encounters can shift the distribution and evaluation of status characteristics; changes in the structure of corporate units or social movements challenging older evaluations of categoric units can force reevaluations of status; and so on. Thus, expectations are rarely so consistent as to serve as a straightjacket on behaviors in encounters. Yet another countervailing force is the fact that most encounters are not so embedded in either corporate or categoric structures that evaluations of status are inexorable. Face-to-face interaction always involves unique assessments of others, outside of their membership in categoric units or their positions in corporate units. Such is ever more likely to be the case when interactions are iterated and begin to reduce the salience of differences in prestige and authority. Still another force is that positions in the division of labor or membership in categoric units are often somewhat ambiguous, especially in less task-oriented encounters; this lack of clarity in the respective positions of individuals makes expectations for their behaviors unclear, thereby forcing status-organizing processes to be constructed as the encounter unfolds. And, at least one more additional force is the power of emotions. A status order that denies individuals their ability to meet transactional needs will, in the end, be challenged. Moreover, a status order that does not clearly define expectations assures that, for at least some individuals, expectations will not be met, thus initiating negative emotions that can change the status order. Thus, the vast literature on expectation states provides us with a set of tendencies in the organization of status around inequalities in prestige and authority; and although these tendencies are an important dynamic property of encounters, there are countervailing tendencies arising from other forces guiding the flow of interaction.

Conclusion

Humans seek to discover each other's respective positions because, once these are known and understood, the interaction is more likely to proceed smoothly. Like role taking, participants to an encounter engage in "position taking," assessing their status relative to that of others and, on the basis of this assessment, adjusting their behaviors accordingly. Without information about status, the burden of keeping the flow of the interaction going falls on other forces driving encounters. Thus, individuals are highly motivated to discover status because, when known, other forces driving encounters are circumscribed. In this chapter, I have emphasized three dimensions of status as critical to the flow of interaction: (1) the clarity of status positions; (2) the network properties of positions; and (3) the expectation states dynamics of status-organizing properties. My goal has been to indicate how these properties influence the flow of status dynamics. Below, I offer some tentative generalizations about these processes:

I. The greater is the clarity of the respective status positions of individuals in an encounter, the more likely are (a) appropriate expectations and sanctions to be understood, (b) transactional needs, especially for self-confirmation and positive exchange payoffs, to be realized, (c) normatizing of categories, frames, forms of talk, rituals, and emotions to be achieved, (d) role making, role taking, and role verification to be successful, and (e) demography and ecology of the situation to be understood. Conversely, the less clear are individuals' respective status positions, the less likely are (a), (b), (c), (d), and (e) to be readily achieved; and hence, the more interpersonal work required of all individuals in the encounter and the more likely is the encounter to be breached.

A. The more embedded is an encounter in corporate or categoric units, the more likely are the respective status positions of individuals in an encounter to be clear. Conversely, the less embedded are individuals' respective status positions, the less likely are they to be clear.

1. The more an encounter is embedded in a corporate unit, and the more formal and hierarchical the division of labor in this unit, the more likely are the respective positions of individuals in encounters to be clear.

2. The more an encounter is embedded in categoric units, and
   the more discrete or nominal and differentially evaluated the
   diffuse status characteristics associated with membership in
   categoric units, the more likely are the respective positions of
   individuals in encounters to be clear.

   a. The more graduated status characteristics can be converted
      into nominal ones, the more likely are the respective posi-
      tions of individuals in encounters to be clear.

   b. The more correlated are diffuse status characteristics, the
      more likely are the evaluations of these characteristics to be
      amplified above and beyond simple additive effects alone.

3. The more formal, explicit, and hierarchical is the division of
   labor of a corporate unit, the greater will be the influence of
   evaluations and expectations associated with positions in
   this corporate unit over those expectations associated with
   membership in categoric units.

   a. The more categoric unit membership is correlated with the
      hierarchical division of labor in a corporate unit, the more
      influence will categoric unit membership have on the flow
      of interaction.

   b. The more positions in the hierarchical division of labor are
      correlated with differentially evaluated categoric units, the
      more likely are evaluations of both to be amplified above
      and beyond simple additive effects alone.

   c. The more the diffuse status characteristics associated with
      categoric unit membership are consistently associated with
      inequalities in prestige and authority within corporate units,
      the more probable is the emergence of status beliefs empha-
      sizing this association, and the more these beliefs are con-
      firmed in encounters over time and across different corporate
      units, the more likely are these status beliefs to become part
      of the culture of the broader society and, thereby, to influence
      the flow of interaction in all encounters.

4. The more the division of labor in a corporate unit is horizontal
   (as opposed to hierarchical) or the more ambiguous is the
   division of labor, the greater will be the initial influence of
   diffuse status characteristics on the flow of interaction over

positions in corporate units, especially if these diffuse status characteristics are nominal (or can be converted to nominal characteristics) and differentially evaluated.

B. The more individuals occupying either different positions in the hierarchy of a corporate unit or revealing membership in discrete and differentially evaluated categoric units interact across iterated encounters, the less salient will be the effects of these status positions on the flow of interaction in an encounter, unless those with higher authority and prestige (a) deny subordinates the capacity to meet their transactional needs, (b) violate subordinates' expectation states carried over from previous encounters, (c) push subordinates into ever-changing roles, (d) persistently impose negative sanctions on subordinates, and (e) force subordinates to renormatize each and every encounter. Under these conditions, negative emotions are aroused among subordinates, with these emotions hardening status differences between super- and subordinates.

1. The greater the level of conflict between super- and subordinates, the more likely are conditions (a) to (e) in I-B to prevail.

2. The more an encounter remains purely instrumental, pushing aside social content, the more likely are status distinctions to remain salient and impose inequalities in expectation states guiding the flow of interaction.

3. The more correlated are positions in the hierarchical division of labor in a corporate unit with membership in nominal and differentially evaluated in categoric units, the more likely are inequalities of status to reinforce and amplify each other, and, hence, the more likely are status distinctions to remain salient and impose expectation states guiding the flow of interaction.

4. The more emotions, whether positive or negative, are aroused between super- and subordinates across iterated encounters, the more these emotions become expectation states that guide the flow of interaction.

   a. The more negative emotions have been aroused, particularly under conditions specified in (a) to (e) in I-B above, the more likely are subordinates to make external attributions and blame superordinates, thereby arousing anger and fear among subordinates, with such emotions becoming expectation states that guide the subsequent flow of interaction.

b. The more positive emotions have been aroused in the absence of the conditions specified in (a) to (e) in I-B above, the more likely are individuals to relax the constraints of status inequalities in ways that enhance the positive flow of emotions, with such emotions becoming expectation states that guide the subsequent flow of interaction.

   i. The more formal authority and prestige in the division of labor and the more differential evaluations of categoric unit membership decline in salience, the less clarity of positions and, hence, the more ambiguity and uncertainty individuals confront. The more ambiguous situations, the more interpersonal effort required of individuals to sustain the focus and flow of interaction.

   ii. The costs associated with increased interpersonal effort are, however, mitigated by the flow of positive emotions that (a) shift expectations and sanctioning to the positive side, (b) allow individuals to present and verify selves beyond simple role identities, (c) offer a range of positive sentiments as resources in positive exchange payoffs, (d) define group inclusion through solidarity-producing positive emotions, (e) enhance mutual respect and sincerity, (f) normatize categories around unique assessments of individuals as persons or even intimates in interactions with more social content, more personal frames, more informal modes of talk, and more use of rituals to produce and sustain positive feelings.

II. The more dense are the ties connecting status positions, the greater will be the salience of status during initial phases of the encounter; but to the degree that density increases rates of interaction, it will reduce the initial effects of inequalities of authority and prestige in corporate units or of differentially evaluated diffuse status characteristics stemming from categoric unit membership in structuring expectations and the flow of interaction, unless conditions (a) through (e) in I-B above prevail.

   A. The more dense are the ties connecting status positions in corporate units, the less salient will differences in authority and prestige become over time if none of the conditions in I-B (a) through (e) prevail, and the more salient will informally generated expectations for positive emotional flows stemming from each individual's ability to meet his or her own unique configuration of transactional needs, to make and verify roles tailed to these needs, and to normatize the interaction in ways encouraging informality and positive feelings.

1. The larger the corporate unit, the less dense is the overall network of ties and, hence, the more reliance on differences in authority and prestige, unless the interaction is repeated over time (thereby increasing informality and the flow of positive emotions).

2. The larger the corporate unit, the more likely are subdensities or cliques to emerge, activating the effects of density in reducing the salience of authority and prestige associated with the inequalities in the division of labor and increasing informality and the flow of positive sentiments.

3. The more an encounter is embedded in categoric units, the less likely are relations among members of different categoric units, especially differentially evaluated and discrete units, to be dense; and hence, the more likely are differences in diffuse status characteristics to remain salient, unless the interaction is iterated, thereby increasing the informality and flow of positive emotions.

B. When interaction occurs among individuals in structurally equivalent positions, the more likely are their common experiences to guide the flow of the interaction; and hence, the less salient will be inequalities in status (if any), and the more salient will diffuse status characteristics, role-playing styles, and perceptions of each other's transactional needs become in normatizing the encounter.

1. The more interaction occurs among individuals who have been in structurally equivalent positions, the more likely will they develop positive sentiments toward each other, even if embeddedness in corporate and/or categoric units now marks differences in status.

2. The more interaction occurs among individuals in structurally

equivalent positions in the same network within a corporate unit, the greater will be the effects of structural equivalence on the flow of interaction.

c. Unless conditions (a) through (e) in I-B prevail, density and equivalence will increase the likelihood that expectations will be met, positive sanctions will be employed, transactional needs will be realized, roles will be played and verified, and norms will be understood and accepted, while at the same time creating the conditions for the arousal of more intense negative emotions should expectations be violated through breaches in the flow of interaction.

  1. The more individuals blame themselves for breaches in dense networks of equals or in networks composed of structurally equivalent positions, the more they will experience sadness, anger at self, and fear of the consequences of their actions; and if these emotions are experienced simultaneously, individuals will experience shame as well as guilt if moral codes are invoked.

  2. The more individuals blame others in dense networks of equals or in networks composed of structurally equivalent positions, the more likely are they to reveal anger toward these others; and if these others are members of distinctive categoric units, the more likely are they to develop prejudices toward members of this category.

  3. The more networks are composed of unequals and the more higher-status individuals are blamed for breaches by lower-status incumbents in the network, the more likely will the latter experience anger toward and fear of higher-status individuals, and the more likely are they to express their anger and fear to those in equivalent positions. The more higher-status individuals are perceived to be members of a categoric unit, the more likely are lower-status individuals to develop prejudices toward members of this category.

  4. The more a network is composed of unequals and subordinate individuals blame themselves for breaches, the more likely are these subordinates to experience escalated sadness, anger, and fear; and the more these are experienced simultaneously, the more likely are these individuals to experience shame as well as guilt if moral standards are invoked.

III. The more unequal is the relative status of individuals in an encounter, the more likely are these differences to be codified into expectations for the role performances of those high or low in authority and prestige; and as a result, the more likely are individuals to engage in role performances that meet the expectations associated with their status.

A. The more embedded is an encounter in a corporate unit revealing inequalities in authority and prestige in the division of labor, and in turn, the more embedded is this corporate unit in an institutional domain, the more likely are the values of the broader society to be translated successively into institutional ideologies and ideologies of the corporate unit such that positions in the corporate unit carry high levels of evaluational content that serve to legitimate inequalities and to give expectations a moral component. Conversely, the less embedded is an encounter in a corporate unit and the less embedded is the corporate unit in an institutional domain, the less likely are values of the broader society to be translated into ideologies legitimating inequalities.

1. The more expectations associated with inequalities of status have a moral component, the more likely are referential structures to emerge legitimating inequalities in rewards associated with high- and low-status positions, thereby making inequalities seem fair and just to both super- and subordinates.

2. The more expectations associated with inequalities of status have a moral component, the more difficult to change are expectations associated with positions or individuals in these positions.

B. The more an encounter is embedded in discrete and differentially evaluated categoric units, and the more these differences in evaluation incorporate broader cultural values or institutional ideologies, the more salient and powerful is the evaluation of distinctive categoric units. Conversely, the less clear and differentially evaluated and/or the less differences in evaluation incorporate cultural values or institutional ideologies, the less salient and powerful are the evaluations of membership in categoric units.

1. The more categoric unit membership carries a moral evaluation, whether positive or negative, the more likely are inequalities of evaluation to seem legitimate for both low and highly evaluated categoric units.

2. The more expectations associated with membership in categoric units carry moral evaluation, the more difficult to change are expectations associated with membership.

c. The more encounters are iterated, even under conditions of moral evaluation of differences in expectations for high and low positions in corporate units or for high and low evaluations of membership in categoric units, the greater is the opportunity to change expectations associated with positions and/or individuals in positions, unless the conditions (a) through (e) in I-B are operative.

d. The more inconsistent or ambiguous are expectations for status in encounters, the greater is the opportunity to change expectations associated with positions and/or individuals in positions, even if conditions (a) through (e) in I-B are operative.

e. The less embedded is an encounter in either a corporate or categoric unit, the less likely are expectations to carry moral content, to be consistent, and to be clear; as a result, the greater is the opportunity to change expectations associated with positions and/or individuals in positions, even if conditions (a) through (e) in I-B are operative.

NINE

Ecological and Demographic Forces

Some of the most visible features of an encounter are place and space, architecture and props, number and diversity of interactants, and physical density among participants. Indeed, understandings among individuals about what these ecological and demographic features of the encounter "mean" are critical to all other forces driving face-to-face interaction. It is difficult to meet transactional needs, to establish expectations, to normatize, to play roles, and to assign status without "knowing" what a locale means, what space denotes, what props and architecture signify, what the number and density of people present suggest, and what the characteristics of people dictate. The salience of these features is even greater when individuals are first gathering and getting to know each other.

Thus, without the guidelines provided by the meanings that individuals attach to the demography and ecology of a situation, a much greater burden is placed on those individuals forming the encounter. They must actively role take and role make; they must expend more effort in categorizing each other, in establishing frames, in using proper forms of talk, in engaging rituals, and in deciding on the right emotional tones; they must work at learning how each other's transactional needs are to be realized; and they must often work at discovering each other's status.

Erving Goffman (1959) was one of the few sociologists to recognize the significance of ecology and demography on interaction. My goal in this chapter is to extend his insights into how these forces shape the flow of face-to-face interaction in encounters. I will begin with the effects of ecology on interaction.

The Ecology of Encounters

In all interactions, individuals use their stocks of knowledge to assemble information about at least three dimensions of ecology: (1) the meaning of space; (2) the meaning of various objects arrayed in space; and (3) the meaning of partitions of space. For example, when students enter a classroom, they hold somewhat different meanings for a large lecture hall as opposed to a smaller classroom; they understand how the objects (desks, tables, chairs, lecterns, media equipment, blackboards, and so on) change the flow of interaction; and they will understand the partitioning of the classroom from the outside world as well as the regions on the inside, such as stage. All of these features may seem so obvious that we do not recognize their significance in circumscribing students' expectations (and those of professors as well), students' efforts at meeting transactional needs, students' understandings of their roles and status, and students' normatization of the situation. I can remember how anxious I was as a freshman at the University of California at Riverside in 1960 as I walked into my first large lecture class with theater-style seating (known locally as LS 1500); I had never been in a classroom of this type, and I did not know what to do. Indeed, I hovered in the back row for several lectures just to understand what it all meant—the slope of the seats, the norms about how to fill in the middle seats of rows, the professor so remote behind a pedestal, the use of microphones, the procedures for asking questions, the way to take notes, and so much more. Other theater-style experiences—movies, plays, school assemblies—did not easily generalize to this new setting, at least for me; and so I found myself role taking, observing, imitating, and scanning very actively just to figure out how one acted in this type of classroom. Perhaps I had been sheltered, but it is only when we are unsure about the ecology of a situation that we become aware of how important it is in shaping the other forces guiding an interaction.

How, then, can we theorize the force of ecology? One obvious generalization is that when individuals understand the meaning of space, objects, and partitions, the flow of the interaction will proceed much more smoothly than when they do not. When some or all individuals do not carry adequate information in their stocks of knowledge about the ecology of an encounter, they will expend considerably more cognitive, emotional, and interpersonal energy in role taking, in position or status taking, in normatizing, and in figuring out how transactional needs are to be realized. In the absence of ecological meanings, then, people will have to rely on other forces driving an interaction.

Eventually, ecological meanings will emerge but not without effort. Conversely, when individuals know what space, objects, and partitions mean, these meanings cut down on the range of options for emotional expression, for meeting transactional needs, for normatizing, for role making and taking, and for status. When a situation can be "regionalized" through mutual knowledge of what ecology means (J. Turner 1988), the complexity of the encounter is thus reduced, allowing individuals to select emotions, roles, status, norms, and needs from a smaller set of options. As a result, much less interpersonal work has to be performed, thereby making the encounter more viable.

A second generalization stems from ecological embeddedness of an encounter in a corporate unit with a clear division of labor marked by the spatial distribution of individuals, by props, and by regions. The more the division of labor in a corporate unit is correlated with ecological arrangements, the greater will be the effect of both on other forces driving an encounter. For example, when I take the elevator to what is termed "the fourth floor" or top floor of the administration building where the chancellor's and executive vice chancellor's offices are located, I have adjusted expectations by the time I exit the elevator, catalogued ways to meet needs, normatized the encounter to ensue, shifted my role to being more professional, and become exceedingly conscious of my status. During the thirty-plus years that I have been repeatedly making this trek, I have also made adjustments as the ecology on the "fourth floor" has changed. For example, the offices of the chancellor and vice chancellor were once rather modest, not much bigger or better than my own; the outer areas of these offices were cluttered with equipment, desks, and people in a somewhat chaotic and crammed way. Now, with extensive remodeling in fine woods, etched glass, and reduced clutter, the imperial chancellor and vice chancellor hold forth, and I have adjusted accordingly the way in which I approach them in encounters. Recently, a new fast elevator was installed (the old one was extremely slow, a seemingly semiotic statement about the speed of decision making); and this newfound speed has shifted my meanings about how things are done on the fourth floor. Thus, to the degree that the division of labor in a corporate unit is organized ecologically, individuals will usually have a better understanding of what they can expect, what roles they can play, what positions they can occupy, what needs they can meet and how, and what norms are relevant. Recently, business corporations have recognized the importance of ecology in their efforts to reduce the vertical division of labor by creating open office layouts, encouraging more informal interactions and, presumably, more creativity and productivity; as individuals come to understand the meanings of these new layouts, the dynamics of encounters have indeed shifted, diminishing heavy-handed use of authority, encouraging more relaxed role enactments, categorizing individuals as persons, shifting to more informal forms of talk, adjusting frames to include more personal and biographical contact, using informal rituals to sustain these frames and informal forms of talk, and allowing more emotion (within limits) to be displayed.

Another generalization about ecology comes from its relation to categoric units in which an encounter is embedded. When membership in categoric units is highly correlated with space, partitions, and props, ecology works to sustain the salience of categoric unit membership. For example, when women were in the "secretarial pool" and men were elsewhere in an organization, this segregation in space by partitions and props only highlighted women as a categoric unit. Similarly, when I walk across my campus and see various ethnic groups gathered separately around "their own" tables and benches, the salience of their ethnic identity is reinforced within the encounter and to those observing it from the outside. Fortunately, in recent years, I now see migrations of different ethnics to each other's regions for occasional talk and conversation, giving me hope that the ecology of ethnicity at UC Riverside is beginning to break down.

Ecology also influences the demography of an encounter, and before examining these demographic forces, I should offer some generalizations. The amount of space will influence the density of people copresent; thus, the smaller is the space in which an encounter occurs, the more will ecology drive the effects of density on an encounter. Partitions also influence the demography of an encounter by closing off or opening opportunities for individuals to make eye contact and migrate so as to be in direct interpersonal contact. Thus, the more confined is the space and the fewer are partitions dividing the space, the more likely are encounters to be formed and sustained.

The Demography of Encounters

The number of people copresent in an encounter dramatically influences its dynamics. Since talk is slow and sequential, only one person at a time can command the attention of others along the verbal track, although individuals can visually read the gestures of several others at a time or in rapid succession in ways not possible along the auditory channel. Thus, even when only one person is speaking, the nonverbal emotional cues so essential to the smooth flow of the interaction can be used to keep nonspeaking individuals in contact. Still, there are limits to how many others' gestures can be read at the same time; as a result, the larger the number of people in an encounter, the more difficult it becomes to sustain a common focus and mood. As the number of people increases in an encounter, individuals will eventually segment or differentiate into subencounters where the vocal and visual focus can be more readily sustained. Additionally, people are likely to begin migrating from one encounter to another as the number of individuals in one encounter grows (as in a cocktail party), especially when a large encounter begins to break up into a series of more focused subencounters.

However, a small space that is partitioned from the outside presents a potential obstacle to the breakup of the encounter because as density increases, it is easier to sustain a common focus and, moreover, to monitor and sanction those whose attention wanders. Additionally, there is often insufficient space to create the necessary physical separation to form subencounters. Nonetheless, as anyone at a dinner party knows, the conversation usually breaks up into subencounters among those sitting near each other; and so, there must be other forces, such as embedding in corporate units and authority systems in these units to sustain a common focus and mood, as I will explore shortly.

Diversity also changes the dynamics of an encounter. Diversity can come from membership in distinctive categoric units or from different positions in the division of labor, or both. The more discrete or nominal are categoric units, and the greater is the range of membership in these distinctive units, the more people will have to work at sustaining the encounter, particularly when categoric units are differentially evaluated. An encounter of diverse ethnics, ages, and genders will generally force people to expend considerably more interpersonal energy in assessing expectations, in discerning sanctions, in assessing others' and meeting one's own transactional needs, in normatizing, in determining status, in role making, and in role taking in order to sustain the focus and flow of interaction. And the more diverse categoric units are differentially evaluated, the greater will be the energy expended in keeping the encounter on track. Such is particularly likely to be the case when encounters occur outside the division of labor of corporate units, since without the structure and culture of the corporate unit to override categoric distinctions, each individual will have to become acutely attuned to their respective differences.

When an encounter is embedded in a corporate unit with a clear division of labor, however, the structure and culture of the corporate unit provide additional cues about how individuals are to act; as a result, people will generally interact more in terms of the dictates of the corporate unit than membership in diverse categoric units. Even when categoric unit membership is highly correlated with the division of labor in a corporate unit (thereby highlighting differences in categoric units), interactions will still be structured more by status in this division of labor than by categoric distinctions, although the latter do not disappear. It is just that the division of labor provides a default alternative to individuals, allowing them to escape at least some of the complexity of interacting with diverse categoric units. The more clear-cut, hierarchical, and formal is the division of labor, the greater will be its power to override the effects of categoric unit membership.

Other processes are constrained by the embedding of encounters in corporate units. When encounters are in embedded corporate units with a clear, hierarchical, and formal division of labor, it is typically easier to sustain the focus of attention even as the number of participants increases, especially if high-status individuals are asserting their dominance. Moreover, not only will the formation of subencounters be less likely, but so will migrations to and from the encounter. Such is particularly likely to be the case when there is high density, but the effect of authority will be sustained even as density decreases. Of course, if there is a history of conflict between super- and subordinates, or existence of a counternormative culture, one way of showing disrespect will be to conduct side encounters even as high-status individuals hold the floor (as most professors in large classes soon experience). Still, these encounters will not usually revolve around full engagement because those in authority as well as subordinates are likely to monitor and sanction subencounters that become too intrusive. For example, although at times I have had to sanction a subencounter in a large lecture class, other students are more likely to impose the first sanctions and, thereby, make it unnecessary for me to do anything.

Thus, corporate unit embeddedness will typically mitigate against the effects of larger numbers, wide spaces, and categoric unit membership, particularly when the division of labor is hierarchical and formal. Under these conditions, expectations, sanctions, needs, norms, status, and roles are dictated by the structure and culture of the corporate unit, making it easier to sustain a common focus of attention, to limit migrations, to attenuate the formation of subencounters, and to overcome at least some of the effects of categoric unit membership.

Not only does the status structure and culture of a corporate unit impose itself on an encounter, but also individuals are likely to seek knowledge of this structure and to rely on it to guide them in determining what should be expected, how sanctions are to be meted out, how needs are to be met and how normatization is to proceed, and how roles are to be made. Unless status differences are abused by superordinates and arouse negative emotions among subordinates, it is always much easier for individuals to rely on the division of labor to direct emotional, transactional, normative, status, and role forces than to start from scratch and become too dependent on categoric unit membership to organize responses. People are lazy in this sense: they prefer certainty over uncertainty in encounters, unless the certainty is abusive. There is, then, a bottom-up attention by individuals to cues from corporate structures that can make their work in an encounter easier.

Yet, not all interactions occur among unequals in corporate units. Among those at the same place in a corporate unit or in structurally equivalent positions in this unit, there will usually be a high degree of homophily as well as dense ties or at least cliques of dense ties. Under these conditions, individuals are likely to rely more on diffuse status characteristics in encounters, at least initially, and on informally generated prestige than on the structure and culture of the corporate unit to guide the flow of interaction. So, the more similar or equivalent the positions of individuals, and the more dense their ties, the less effect will the formal structure of the corporate unit have on the flow of interaction in encounters, and the greater will be the effect of diffuse status characteristics and informally generated prestige arising from differences in performances of either task or social activities. These effects will, however, decline as the encounter endures and is iterated.

Conclusions

Ecological and demographic forces are powerful in virtually all encounters. Much of the reason for this power is that these forces provide cues about what to expect, what sanctions are to be used, what emotions are to be aroused, what needs are to be met and how, what norms are to apply, what status characteristics are relevant, and what roles are to be played. When these cues are unclear or absent, other forces driving an encounter must be mobilized to a greater degree, making the encounter more work for its participants and, potentially, creating problems in meeting expectations, imposing and receiving sanctions, meeting transactional needs, establishing norms, playing roles, and marking status. When any one or combination of these forces is rendered problematic by ecology or demography, the dynamics revolving around negative emotions summarized in previous chapters are set into motion. Conversely, when ecology and demography provide guidelines and cues that make the operation of these forces nonproblematic, the emotional reactions will be positive in the ways described in earlier chapters.

We are now nearing the end of the book, with one chapter to go. In this final chapter, I will need to take the many propositions developed in the previous nine chapters and, somehow, make the theory more parsimonious. If I ended the book with all of the propositions from Chapters 4 through 9, the theory would be unmanageable, although any set of propositions summarized at the end of each chapter can be considered hypotheses that, I believe, are testable. Before moving to this consolidation of principles in the next chapter, however, let me close this chapter with a final list of propositions that will have to be incorporated into the theory.

I. All encounters occur in space, use physical props, and rely on partitionings of space. The more individuals understand the meanings of space, props, and partitions, the less cognitive, emotional, and interpersonal energy they will expend and the more likely are other forces driving the encounter to be given direction. Conversely, the less individuals understand the meanings of space, props, and partitions, the more they must work at sustaining the encounter and the less direction given to other forces driving the encounter.

   A. The more an encounter is embedded in a corporate unit and the more clear-cut, formal, and hierarchical is the division of labor in this unit, the more likely is the ecology of an interaction to reflect this division of labor and the more likely are individuals to understand the meanings of space, props, and partitions.

   B. The more an encounter is embedded in categoric units and the more categoric unit membership is correlated with the ecology of an encounter, the greater will be the effects of categoric unit membership.

   C. The more the ecology of an encounter is determined by the division of labor of a corporate unit and the more clear-cut, formal, and hierarchical is this division of labor, the greater will be the effects of the culture and structure of the corporate unit over those of categoric unit membership, although this effect is diminished somewhat when members of the same categoric units are segregated in space and when they use different props.

II. The larger is the number of individuals in an encounter and/or the greater is their diversity, the more problematic is the maintenance of a common focus of attention and common mood; and hence, the greater is the ritual energy devoted to sustaining the boundaries of, and the flow of interaction in, the encounter.

   A. The larger is the number of individuals in an encounter, the greater the likelihood that

      1. the encounter will segment or differentiate into smaller encounters; and

      2. the participants in the encounter will migrate to new encounters.

   B. The more diverse are the participants in an encounter, the more salient will status, symbolic, and transactional forces in the encounter become and the more they will guide efforts to sustain the encounter.

III. The more an encounter is embedded in a corporate unit, and the more categoric distinctions are correlated with the division of labor in this corporate unit, the less powerful are the processes described in II and II-A.

   A. The more an encounter is embedded in a corporate unit, and the larger, more formal, and partitioned is the division of labor in this corporate unit, the greater is the likelihood that

      1. the goals for the division of labor will sustain the focus of attention, especially when this division of labor assigns leadership positions; and

      2. the division of labor will limit migration and formation of new encounters.

   B. The more categoric units correspond to the division of labor in corporate units, the more pronounced are the effects in III-A(1), III-A(2), and the greater is the likelihood that

      1. the division of labor within the corporate unit will direct the operation of status, symbolic, and transactional forces; and

      2. the salience of outside status, symbolic, and transactional forces will decrease.

Microdynamics

When humans interact in face-to-face encounters, certain dynamics are unleashed. I have conceptualized these dynamics as forces driving the interpersonal behaviors of individuals in certain directions. Although these forces constitute a distinctive level of reality, their values are constrained by the particular mesostructures in which they are embedded and, by extension, the macrolevel institutional systems of societies and intersocietal systems. Thus, a theory of microdynamics must include analysis of meso- and macroprocesses. The many propositions offered at the end of each chapter seek not only to document the operation of each microdynamic force, but also to highlight the fact that these forces operate within the culture and structure of corporate and categoric units at the mesolevel of human organization. In this last chapter, my goal is to strip away some of the complexity and redundancy of these propositions so that the theory can be stated more parsimoniously.

Interaction is a complicated process, and as I seek to make the theory more parsimonious, I must simplify—perhaps too much so—in order to communicate the general line of argument. For more details, it is still necessary to refer to the propositions that conclude each chapter on the forces driving face-to-face behavior. Some will argue, of course, that interaction cannot be reduced to a few simple laws, but I would suggest that unless we seek the laws of interpersonal behavior, sociology will not advance as a science. True, the laws that I propose are general and abstract, covering with a few statements the complexity of interpersonal behavior. Specialists in each of the areas covered by these principles will naturally see these principles as gross glosses, although this criticism is muted by the more detailed propositions offered for each force. Still, my goal has been to present a "grand theory" of microdynamics that tries to capture the robust nature of interpersonal behavior. For many, this kind of general theorizing is not the way to go; indeed, most theorists at the microlevel develop more specialized theories. But at times it is useful, I believe, to see how we can combine, synthesize, and extend the many interesting theories that have been developed on microsocial processes. I am a generalist, and quite proud of this orientation to theory.

Emotional Dynamics

All face-to-face interaction is emotional. Natural selection made humans emotional, and as I have argued, emotional syntax is the primal and primary language of our species. Humans are highly attuned to emotions, especially along the dominant visual sense modality, because their use in forging bonds among our low-sociality hominid ancestors was the key to survival. Indeed, the ancestors of humans are the only lineage of apes to have survived to the present day in open-country savanna. Naturally, as auditory languages were piggybacked onto the neurological wiring for emotional syntax, emotions could also be expressed via this modality. Humans' acute haptic senses could also be used to augment the flow of emotions via the visual and auditory channels in face-to-face encounters. All other forces driving encounters are shaped by emotions; so a theory of interpersonal behavior must begin with an examination of emotional dynamics.

Humans can generate, display, and read a wide variety of variants and elaborations of primary emotions. In general, humans experience positive emotions—variants and elaborations of satisfaction-happiness—when their expectations are met and when they receive reinforcing sanctions from others. Other interpersonal forces are critical to generating these positive emotions because they establish the very expectations that drive emotional reactions. Need states, norms, roles, status, and demographic/ecological conditions create expectations for what should occur. When people's transactional needs are realized, when they can successfully normalize a situation, when they can make and verify roles, when they can understand their respective status, and when they can understand the meanings of demography and ecology, they will experience and express positive emotions. Once expressed, these emotions become positive sanctions to others who are likely to return the favor. This process will generate a positive emotional cycle until fatigue or marginal utility sets in.

Attribution processes are an important part of all emotional reactions. When emotions are positive, individuals can attribute their success in meeting expectations and receiving positive sanctions to themselves, to others, to categories of others, or to corporate units; and depending on the attributions made, the flow of positive emotional energy shifts. When self-attributions are made for success in meeting expectations and/or receiving positive sanctions from others, individuals feel positive sentiments toward themselves; and when they attribute their success externally to others, categories of others, or corporate units, they express positive sentiments outwardly and become more committed to others, categories of others, and corporate units.

Natural selection worked, I believe, to jury-rig the neurology of hominids to initiate these cycles of positive emotions because they are so essential to maintaining the social order. Indeed, for a low-sociality animal without genetically driven propensities to form strong local groups or to herd, these cycles of positive emotional energy were, and are today, essential to generating and sustaining social solidarity. Selection had to overcome not only the propensity for low sociality evident in all apes, but it also had to confront a biological fact: three of the four primary emotions are negative and, as a result, are not likely to be useful in generating solidarity unless their power could be muted, mitigated, or transfigured toward solidarity-generating outcomes. Fear, anger, and sadness can disrupt social relationships; so these negative emotions had to be managed if a low-sociality ape was to be more social. Elaborations and combinations of positive with negative emotions were one way to mitigate the raw power of negative emotions (see Tables 4.3 and 4.4 in Chapter 4). Generating the capacity to combine sadness, fear, and anger to produce shame and guilt was yet another route that selection took to transfiguring negative emotional energy into emotions that force individuals to monitor and sanction themselves for inappropriate behaviors with respect to each other or to moral codes. In these ways, the potential harm of cycles of negative emotional energy to social relations was mitigated and channeled toward social bonding.

Yet, because human neurology is structured to generate three potentially powerful negative emotions, interpersonal behavior always reveals the potential for negative emotional arousal. Again, like positive emotions, other forces driving the encounter are critical because when expectations for meeting transactional needs, for establishing norms, for making and verifying roles, for establishing status, and demography/ecology are not realized, negative emotions are immediately activated. Indeed, humans are biologically hard-wired to be attuned to negative emotions, perhaps more than positive ones because these can so easily disrupt the fabric of an encounter. Humans are attuned along two channels: one for sensing when expectations are realized, and another for hints of negative sanctions. Attribution processes are also critical to understanding negative emotional energy in encounters, and they are often important in mitigating the raw power of negative emotions. When people blame themselves for the failure to meet expectations or for receiving negative sanctions, they feel sad. This sadness can be coupled with fear about the consequences of this failure and anger at self. When these three negative emotions are combined they produce shame for the failure to behave competently and, if moral standards are invoked, guilt as well (see Table 4.4 in Chapter 4); and as these emotions are aroused, the power of negative emotional energy is turned inward toward self-sanctioning.

It is when external attributions are made that negative emotional energy can become highly disruptive. External attributions arouse anger toward others and, at times, toward categoric and corporate units. When others are powerful or can fight back, this anger may be transformed into prejudices toward categoric and corporate units, thereby reducing somewhat the power of mutual anger of individuals standing face-to-face. Negative emotions are unpleasant to a person and, as a result, they are often displaced and projected on to others, but like external attributions, these invite counteranger and may initiate an escalating cycle of negative anger in an encounter. Repression can also work to protect the individual and the integrity of the encounter in the short run, but repressed individuals will generally use considerable energy to keep negative feelings out of consciousness, thereby lowering their modal level of emotional energy, whether positive or negative, in encounters. Moreover, cortical sensors often fail, leading to highly intense episodes of negative emotions that can disrupt an encounter and make the individual feel shame and guilt for their emotional outbursts. Repression can only be effective in the long run if the person can sustain consistent emotional demeanor across all encounters (usually at enormous emotional and physical costs to the health of the individual).

Can we now take these emotional dynamics and boil them down into an elementary principle? The more complex principles sit at the end of Chap-

ter 4 and can be viewed as a more refined set of hypotheses. But let us see if
we can present the essential elements of principles on emotional energy.

(1) *The Principle of Positive Emotional Energy.* When individuals' expec-
     tations for transactional needs, for normatizing, for making and
     verifying roles, for establishing status, and for using demography/
     ecology are realized in an encounter and/or when they are recipients
     of positive sanctions from others, these individuals will experience
     and, depending on the attributions made, express positive emotions
     toward self, others, members of categoric units, or the structure and
     culture of corporate units.

(2) *The Principle of Negative Emotional Energy.* When individuals' expec-
     tations for transactional needs for normatizing, for making and
     verifying roles, for establishing status, and for using demography/
     ecology are not realized and/or when they are the recipients of
     negative sanctions from others, these individuals will experience
     and, depending on the attributions made, express negative emotions
     toward self, others, members of categoric units, or the structure and
     culture of corporate units.

     A. When individuals blame themselves for their failure to realize
         expectations or for receiving negative sanctions, they will expe-
         rience sadness; and if they also experience anger at self and fear
         of the consequences of their actions, they will experience shame
         as well as guilt if moral codes are salient.
     B. When individuals blame others for their failure to realize expecta-
         tions or for receiving negative sanctions, they will experience and
         express anger toward these others, but if these others are powerful
         or can fight back, they are more likely to (1) target safer objects
         (less powerful individuals, social categories, or corporate units) or
         (2) repress their anger.
     C. When individuals blame members of categoric units or corporate
         units, they will express anger toward these units and develop
         prejudices toward them.
     D. When individuals repress their negative emotions—whether
         sadness, anger, fear, shame, or guilt—they will display lowered
         levels of emotional energy, punctuated by sudden and dispro-
         portionate outbursts of the negative emotions that have been
         repressed.

Motivational Dynamics

Face-to-face interaction is energized by more than emotions. Humans have transactional needs that they seek to realize in all encounters. These needs push behavior in certain directions and, at the same time, activate emotional responses. The most powerful of these transactional needs is the one for self-confirmation, and when core-self feelings are salient in an encounter, an individual's energy is directed at verifying and confirming this self. Depending on the degree of verification, various emotional reactions will ensue. Moreover, just how other needs are to be met is very much influenced by self when it is salient. For example, when core-self feelings are on the line, the most relevant resources to be exchanged are the signs of confirmation and the emotions that follow. Similarly, group inclusion takes on renewed urgency when exclusion will be seen as an attack on self. Likewise, the self-respect element of needs for trust assumes more significance when core self is salient, and facticity will become increasingly problematic when people do not see others as sharing their sense of who they are.

Just as other transactional needs are shaped by self, so are other forces driving the interaction. When core self is salient, role making and verifying take on new intensity as does acknowledgment of one's status; the ecology of place and use of props marking self become ever more important; and the normatization of categories, frames, rituals, forms of address, and feelings is oriented to self-confirmation; demography of who is present can carry significance for individuals' self-definitions; and the affective responses to confirmation or disconfirmation underscore the significance of self-oriented expectations and sanctioning for people's emotional well-being. Thus, self is a kind of master need; it drives just about all aspects of an interaction.

When core-self feelings or subidentities are less salient, other transactional needs take on more significance and drive the flow of interaction. People become more alert to exchange payoffs, per se, outside of what they say about self; group inclusion is no longer a test of self-worth but of simply being part of the ongoing interpersonal flow; trust focuses on predictability, sincerity, and synchronization more than on respect or dignity; and facticity is achieved by simply sensing that each person is experiencing the situation in similar ways. Emotions are aroused when these needs are met, or go unrealized, but they will not have the same level of intensity as when self, especially core self, is highly salient. Still, failure to realize profitable exchange payoffs will generate considerable emotion, even under conditions where self is not highly salient. To a lesser extent, so will needs for group inclusion, trust, and facticity that go unfulfilled. Thus, even these "quieter" needs can set off the processes described in the principles of positive and negative emotions. Need states thus double the energy of an encounter; the more these needs are activated, the more direction to people's behavior and the greater their emotional reactions, especially when the principle of negative emotions kicks in.

In Chapter 5, I summarized the dynamics of need states in great detail, but we can ask: Is there a simple principle that we can develop that captures the contours of motivational dynamics, stripping away some of the complicating detail?

(3) *The Principle of Motivational Energy.* When individuals' needs for
     self-confirmation, positive exchange payoffs, group inclusion, trust,
     and facticity are realized, they will experience and express positive
     emotions in accordance with the principle of positive emotional
     energy; and when they are not realized, the processes specified in
     the principle of negative emotional energy will be activated.

     A. The more core-self feelings are salient, the more fulfillment of
         other transactional needs will be organized around meeting needs
         for self-verification, and the more intense the emotional reaction,
         whether positive or negative, for meeting or failing to meet needs.
     B. The less salient are core-self feelings, the more other needs will
         direct the behavioral responses of individuals, and the less intense
         will be the emotional reactions, whether positive or negative, for
         meeting or failing to meet these needs.

Normatizing Dynamics

All interaction is regulated, to some extent, by culture. As individuals enter encounters, they draw on their stocks of knowledge to discover the relevant expectations along several dimensions: categorization of self, others, and the situation; frames; forms of communication; rituals; and emotional displays. Without establishing normative expectations for the nature of the situation as work-practical, ceremonial, or social, for the frames that will specify what is to be included and excluded, for the forms of talk and body language that are to be used, for rituals to open, close, form, and repair the flow of interaction, and for the feelings that are to be expressed, it would be difficult to sustain an encounter. Without some degree of initial normatization, individuals would not know how to behave toward each other. They would expend a great deal of energy in role taking, and self-presentation, particularly with respect to problems of maintaining the focus and rhythmic flow of the interaction in the face of potential breaches.

Without normatization, all other forces driving the encounter are potentially disruptive. People's expectations are not likely to be met. They are likely to sanction negatively each other, often inadvertently. They will have trouble meeting transactional needs. They will have to work very hard to make and verify roles. They may not understand each other's status. And they will not recognize the meanings of the demography and ecology of the situation. Individuals sense this potentially disastrous outcome, and so they are highly attuned to cues, both physical and interpersonal, that give clues about how to categorize each other, how to frame the situation, how to talk and gesture, how to use rituals, and how to emote. When normatizing is incomplete or fails altogether, the processes specified in the principle of negative emotional energy become operative because people are unsure of how to behave and because all other forces driving the encounter become problematic without normative guidance. Conversely, when situations are normatized successfully, the processes summarized in the principle of positive emotional energy are put into motion.

Normatization begins with an initial categorization of self, others, and the situation, which, in turn, provides guidelines for how to frame. Once categorized and framed, just how to communicate is more readily understood; with expectations associated with categorization, frames, and talk in place, the relevant rituals and emotional displays are easier to perform. Of course, at any point in this process, these interdependent dynamics can change, as shifts in one dimension force changes in the others. Indeed, once one element is not normatized, all other dimensions of normatizing are disproportionately directed to discovering or developing expectations for this unclear normative space. When one element or dimension of normatizing is unclear, not only are the other elements questioned, but also without complete normatization along all dimensions, other forces driving the encounter become less certain for individuals.

(4) *The Principle of Normatizing.* When individuals enter encounters, they seek to establish expectations about how they are to categorize each other and the situation, what they are to include and exclude

from the situation, how they are to communicate with talk and body gestures, how they are to use rituals, and what emotions they can express; and the more they can reach consensus on these matters, the more the processes summarized in the principle of positive emotional energy will be operative. Conversely, the more individuals fail to reach consensus on these matters, the more the dynamics specified in the principle of negative emotional energy will be activated.

Role Dynamics

Human neurology is hard-wired to see patterns and gestalts, and one of the most important manifestations of this capacity is people's tendency to see the gestures of others as a syndrome of behaviors marking an underlying role. People carry in their stocks of knowledge conceptions of specific roles, combinations of roles, generalized roles that embellish a variety of more specific roles, and transsituational roles that can be enacted across many different situations. This vast stock of knowledge about roles is used in role taking and role making; when individuals can successfully make a role for themselves, take the role of the other, and verify their own and the roles of others, they are more likely to meet each other's transactional needs, thereby activating the processes in the principle of positive emotional energy and especially so when a role identity also embodies core-self feelings. Because roles are the vehicle by which individuals display their needs, particularly those for self-confirmation but others as well, people are particularly sensitive to each other's role-making efforts. They will try to find consistency in the gestures emitted by others, ignoring inconsistent information if they can, in order to impute a role to another and, then, to verify this role. Conversely, because roles are tied to transactional needs, the failure to make and verify a role will activate the processes summarized in the principle of negative emotional energy, and the more powerful are the need states that go unfulfilled, the more intense will the negative emotional energy be. People implicitly recognize this connection between roles and transactional needs; as a result, they try hard to verify each other's roles so that negative emotional energy will not be aroused and, thereby, breach the interaction.

Role making, role taking, and role verification are greatly facilitated by successful normatization of the encounter, by mutual recognition of status, and by understandings about the meaning of interpersonal demography and ecology. When people and situations can be categorized, when frames can be imposed, when forms of talk and body gesturing can be agreed on, when rituals are used appropriately, and feeling rules understood, the dynamics of roles are simplified. When people understand their position vis-à-vis each other and the larger social units in which the encounter is embedded, they are more likely to know how to make and verify each other's roles. When people understand who is present in what numbers and density and when they recognize what space, partitions, and props mean, they can more readily have success in role making and role taking. Of course, through role making and role taking much of the information about norms, status, and demography/ecology is made available, but in general, individuals already have at least a general sense of the relevant norms, status, and meanings of demography/ecology before they actively engage in role making and role taking. They may fine-tune norms, status, and meanings associated with demography and ecology as they role make, role take, and mutually verify roles; at times they can perhaps radically change the direction of these other forces. Still, most of the time, these forces circumscribe role dynamics.

(5)   *The Principle of Roles.* Individuals seek to discover the underlying role being played by others through interpreting syndromes of gestures, while at the same time, seeking to make and verify roles for themselves through the emission of syndromes of gestures; the more two individuals can successfully make and verify roles, the more likely are transactional needs to be realized, thereby activating the processes specified in the principle of positive emotional energy. Conversely, the less successful are role taking, role making, and role verification, the more likely are transactional needs to go unmet, thereby activating the dynamics specified in the principle of negative emotional energy.

Status Dynamics

In all encounters, individuals occupy positions vis-à-vis one another, even in relatively informal gatherings. Much like role taking, individuals "position take," seeking to discover the status of others relative to their own status; and on the basis of this assessment, people mutually adjust their conduct. Without understanding each other's status, interaction becomes strained and tentative because positions remove much of the burden of role taking, normatizing, and assessing need states. Positions delimit options of individuals and, thereby, allow them to understand each other's needs, emotional dispositions, and roles, while greatly facilitating the process of normatization and the assessment of what interpersonal demography and ecology mean. And so, people are highly motivated to discover each other's status since it makes interaction so much easier.

Three properties of status are particularly important at the level of the encounter. One is the clarity of people's status. With clear markers of status, the more discrete the positions occupied by people, the more likely are other forces driving interaction to be understood by all. The emotional dispositions, the need states, the roles being made, the relevant norms, and the meaning of the demography and ecology will all be easier to discern. Another property of status is networks. The more positions are connected to each other and/or structurally equivalent, the more likely are individuals to have past or similar experiences with each other, and the easier it will be for them to size up each other's emotions, needs, and roles, while normatizing the encounter. As a result, individuals will feel more comfortable with each other, and if positions carry differences in authority or prestige, these will become less salient as the encounter is iterated. A third property of status is the degree of inequality with respect to power/authority and honor/prestige. The more inequalities of status exist in an encounter, the more likely will expectation states for performance associated with each position guide the flow of interaction. Individuals will display emotions appropriate to their status; they will play roles, normatize, and meet transactional needs in accordance with their respective status; and they will pay close attention to how demography and ecology confirm and reaffirm status. While inequalities in status tend to become legitimated, iterated encounters will often reduce the salience of inequalities, unless those in superordinate positions act in ways sustaining their salience or unless conflict between high- and low-status persons has occurred.

Like all other forces driving interaction, status invokes emotions. When the positions are clear, when network properties facilitate interaction, and when performance expectations associated with status inequalities are followed and accepted, individuals will experience positive emotions, unless status inequalities are used to disrupt subordinates' ability to play roles, meet needs, and normatize the encounter. In the latter case, subordinates will experience and express emotions in accordance with the processes outlined in the principle of negative emotional energy. More generally, when positions are not clear, when networks work against mutual understandings, and when status inequalities and differences are not honored or abused, individuals will experience and express emotions in accordance with the principle of negative emotional energy. These conclusions simplify the complex argument developed in the propositions of Chapter 8, but let us simplify even more with one compact principle on status.

(6) *The Principle of Status*. Individuals seek to discover each other's respective positions in encounters, and the more individuals can use status to discern expectations for each other's behavior, the less energy they will have to expend in sanctioning, in meeting transactional needs, in role making, role taking, and role verifying, in normatizing, and in understanding demography/ecology, thereby activating the processes summarized in the principle of positive emotional energy. Conversely, the less they are able to discern expectations associated with status, the more energy they will expend and the more likely are breaches to the interaction, thereby activating the processes summarized in the principle of negative emotional energy.

   A. When positions are clear and unambiguous, when they are densely connected or equivalent, and when they are unequal, individuals are more likely to discern the expectations of each other's status.
   B. When interactions have been iterated across encounters, initial status distinctions are likely to be relaxed, creating more informal interactions, unless conflict between positions or active imposition of inequalities by superordinates has ensued.

Ecological Dynamics

All encounters are located in space, which is often partitioned and in which props are arrayed. Typically, individuals have understandings of what the organization of space means, and on the basis of these understandings, they adjust their expectations, emotions, needs, roles, and assessments of status. Coupled with knowledge about the demography of individuals in space, they can fine-tune their responses even further. Thus, the ecology of an encounter typically offers clues about other forces, suggesting the respective status and roles of individuals, circumscribing norms, constraining what needs are salient and how they are to be met, and often dictating the emotions to be expressed. People come to rely on these ecological meanings be-cause they reduce the amount of effort that must be expended, thereby re-ducing the likelihood that their expectations will go unmet. There is, then, a simple principle of ecology guiding all encounters.

(7)   *The Principle of Ecology.* Individuals carry knowledge about the meanings of space, partitions of space, and the significance of props, and the more individuals share these meanings, the less energy they will expend in establishing mutual expectations, in sanctioning, in meeting transactional needs, in normatizing, in role making, role taking, and role verifying, and in assessing status, thereby activating the processes summarized in the principle of positive emotional energy. Conversely, the less individuals share understandings about the meanings of space, partitions, and props, the more effort they will expend in establishing expectations, in sanctioning, in meeting transactions needs, in normatizing, in role making, role taking, and role verifying, and in establishing status, thereby increasing the probability that the processes described in the principle of negative emotional energy will be activated.

Demographic Dynamics

In all encounters, the number of people copresent, their diversity, and their density in space shape the flow of interaction. When there are large numbers of individuals, it is difficult to sustain a common focus of attention across all individuals; and as a result, the encounter will typically differentiate into subencounters. When there is high diversity of individuals present, people will expend more energy keeping the interpersonal flow going as they try to take cognizance of their differences in establishing expectations, in sanction-ing, in meeting their respective transactional needs, in normatizing, in role making, role taking, and role verifying, and in working out their status dif-ferences. High density of participants will force individuals to pay more at-tention to each other; and as a result, other forces driving encounters are likely to be activated when individuals are compressed in space. Moreover, as these forces are activated, sustaining the focus of attention will be somewhat easier than is the case with the same number of individuals distributed across more space. There is, then, a simple demographic force in all interactions.

(8) *The Principle of Demography.* Individuals respond to the number and diversity of individuals under conditions of varying density.

A. The more dense and diverse are individuals in an encounter, the more they will work at establishing mutual expectations, at sanctioning, at meeting transactional needs, at normatizing, at role making, role taking, and role verification, and at assessing mutual status; and depending on their degree of success in these activities, the processes summarized in the principle of positive or negative energy will be activated.

B. The larger is the number of individuals in an encounter, and the less dense is their distribution, the more likely is the encounter to differentiate into subencounters of higher density. Depending on the degree to which individuals can hold common expectations, meet each other's transactional needs, successfully normatize, role make, role take, and role verify, and understand each other's status, the more likely are the processes summarized in the principle of positive or negative emotional energy to be activated.

Embedding Dynamics

As I have emphasized, encounters are almost always embedded within corporate and categoric units that, in turn, are part of an institutional domain. Embedding increases the likelihood that the structure and culture of a particular institutional system will guide the flow of interaction via the constraints that it imposes on the culture and structure of corporate and categoric units. When the structure and culture of an institutional domain are in flux, mesostructures are also changing, with the result that individuals may be uncertain about how to behave in encounters. And yet, most of the time, embedding within encounters increases the level of certainty about what is to occur because the division of labor of a corporate unit or the evaluations and expectations associated with categoric unit membership provide clear guidelines. Even when these mesostructures are changing, they provide guidance in short-term encounters. When encounters are iterated over longer stretches of time, however, changes in mesostructures will be reflected in encounters, often creating uncertainty for those in a given encounter. If these problems persist across encounters, and if they affect large numbers of individuals in different encounters, then adjustments at the level of the encounter will further change the structure and culture of mesounits. Still, we will get more theoretical pay-off if we focus on the top-down power of embedding, although I will close the book with some speculation on how bottom-up dynamics operate to change meso- and macrostructures.

(9) *The Principle of Corporate Unit Embedding.* The more an encounter is embedded in a corporate unit within an institutional domain, and the more the division of labor in this unit is clear-cut, hierarchical, and bounded, the more likely are the structure and culture of the corporate unit and, by extension, the institutional domain to specify (a) the appropriate emotional syntax, (b) the expectations for how self is to be confirmed, for what resources are available as exchange payoffs, and for what constitutes group inclusion, trust, and facticity, (c) the roles available to make and take, and how verification is to occur, (d) the distribution of status, (e) the organization of space, partitions of space, and props as well as the meanings associated with these dimensions of ecology, and (f) the distribution of diverse individuals in space and the meanings associated with interpersonal demography; and the more these forces of encounters are circum-scribed by the culture and structure of the corporate unit, the greater is the likelihood that individuals will experience positive emotional energy and develop commitments to the corporate unit. Conversely, the less these forces are constrained by the structure and culture of the corporate unit, the more likely is negative emotional energy to be experienced and the less likely are commitments to the corporate unit to develop or be sustained.

(10) *The Principle of Categoric Unit Embedding.* The more an encounter is embedded in categoric units, and the more discrete and differentially evaluated these units, the more likely are expectations associated with these units to specify (a) the appropriate emotional syntax, (b) the expectations for how self is to be confirmed, for what resources are available as exchange payoffs, and for what constitutes group inclu-sion, trust, and facticity, (c) the roles available to make and take, and how verification is to occur, (d) the distribution of status charac-teristics, and (e) the diversity of the demographic characteristics of individuals; and the more these forces are circumscribed by categoric unit memberships, the more likely are expectations to be realistic and, hence, the more likely is positive emotional energy to ensue.

Conversely, the less categoric unit membership constrains expectations, the more likely are expectations to be unclear and, hence, the more likely are at least some of these to go unrealized, thereby activating negative emotional energy.

Embeddedness thus increases the likelihood that people will understand what is possible and what to expect, and even when expectations are low or even when they work to legitimate inequalities, the congruence between expectations and outcomes from interpersonal behavior will generally keep the encounter from activating the processes summarized in the principle of negative emotional energy. The positive energy may be minimal—low satisfaction—or it may even be neutral, but as long as it stays away from the negative side, the interaction will proceed smoothly. Still, there is ample room in embedding for things to go wrong. The division of labor and the discreteness of categoric units are rarely completely clear, leading individuals to establish markedly different expectations or creating a situation where they do not know what to expect in terms of how to meet transactional needs, to normatize, to make, take, and verify roles, to recognize status differences, to understand the meanings of interpersonal ecology, or to recognize the significance of interpersonal demography. As a result, expectations are not realized and the processes specified in the principle of negative emotional energy are activated in ways that can reduce commitments to corporate units, increase the ambiguity over categoric units, and disrupt the encounter and, potentially, the mesostructures in which the encounter is embedded. For, when things consistently go wrong at the level of encounters, pressures are placed on the structure and culture of mesostructures.

How Does Microreality Change the World?

Thus, we need to explore one last issue that has been mentioned but not addressed: the ways in which microlevel processes work to change meso- and macrolevel processes. It is difficult to develop a precise theoretical formulation of how the micro changes the meso, but we should close this theory of face-to-face interaction by suggesting how behaviors at the interpersonal level can potentially have implications for what transpires at the meso- and macrolevels of human social organization. Too much theorizing simply assumes that such is the case, and obviously at some ultimate metaphysical level, the meso and macro are constituted by iterated encounters. But simply asserting metaphysics is different than demonstrating the precise dynamics involved. In a sense, I have tried to indicate in detail the dynamics flowing down from the macro to meso to micro; let me close by reversing the causal arrow.

Most of the time, mesostructures and culture constrain what transpires in encounters, but constraint does not mean control; humans are apes, after all, and they recoil against structures that limit their options too much and that fail to activate the forces specified in the law of positive emotional energy. Still, even when individuals are unhappy with events in an encounter and, in fact, restructure the encounter, these changes will not typically alter mesostructures and culture, unless these structures are small and the culture is local. Yet, obviously, if individuals' behaviors in encounters have no effect on more inclusive systems, social change would be impossible. Since this is not the case, we need to specify some general conditions under which changes in the flow of interpersonal behavior in encounters have ramifications for alterations in the structure and culture of corporate and categoric units and, by extension, institutional systems.

One condition is the power and prestige of individuals in corporate and categoric units. The higher the power and prestige of individuals in corporate or categoric units, the more likely are their efforts at change to have effects on the more inclusive structures and cultures. Thus, high-ranking members of corporate units are more likely to change the structure of the corporate units than are low-ranking ones. Perhaps this is obvious, but it is nonetheless fundamental. Similarly, highly prominent members of categoric units will be more likely to change the culture of categoric units than low-ranking ones, especially if they begin to string encounters together to form a corporate unit, as is the case, for example, in the formation of a social movement organization. In general, the more membership in categoric units serves as a basis for creation of change-oriented corporate units, the more likely will change in encounters among members of a categoric unit have effects on changing the culture and structure of more inclusive systems.

Another condition increasing the likelihood that change at the level of the encounter can alter mesolevel systems is the centrality and density of an encounter within networks of encounters. The more other encounters are connected by joint memberships, by lines of authority, by flows of resources, by communication, or by any other force that ties members of different encounters to each other, the more change in one will have cascading effects on others. Density, per se, will have this effect because change will radiate along all ties, but centrality increases this effect when the change comes from one source and radiates out to other encounters. Moreover, even in less dense networks, changes in central networks can reach out and change other encounters that are not directly connected to each other (except by virtue of their common tie to members of the central encounter in the network).

A related condition is the degree of embeddedness of encounters in corporate and categoric units. Encounters that are an essential part of the division of labor of a corporate unit or are critical to the maintenance of categoric distinctions have more change potential than those that are more peripheral. This conclusion runs counter to the image of "revolutionaries" as coming from "outside" the system, but in fact such revolutionary change is rather rare. Much more common are changes initiated within encounters highly embedded in corporate and categoric units because it is here that the networks to other encounters will be most dense. Sometimes encounters from outside corporate and categoric units can penetrate these units and initiate a chain of events causing change, but more frequent are changes from central encounters initiated by the powerful and prestigious within corporate and categoric units.

Another condition is the nature of the institutional system in which an encounter is embedded. When a corporate or categoric unit is embedded in what Amos Hawley (1986) has called a "key function" institutional domain, the changes initiated at the level of the encounter will have a greater impact not only on the mesostructure and culture but the institutional domain as well. What, then, is a key function domain? These are the institutional systems that deal with the "external environment" and, thus, are critical to sustaining a population in its environment. Therefore, changes in the corporate units within the economy and polity will generally have more impact on the structure of a society than those devoted to more internal processes such as reproduction. For example, encounters that change market relations with other societies, shift technologies, involve plans to wage war, and other activities that deal with the external relations of a population with its biophysical and sociocultural environments will have greater effects on changing other corporate and categoric units than those involved in socialization, education, and religion (although these can have great effects *to the extent that* they are directly involved in political and/or economic activity). Changes at the level of the encounter within the corporate and categoric units of "key" institutional domains will, therefore, have potentially greater effects on meso- and macrostructures than those in other types of corporate and categoric units; and this effect will be greater when high-power or -status individuals in dense and central networks push for change.

Another condition is the extent to which change-inducing encounters are iterated. The more an encounter is iterated, while meeting the other conditions listed above, the greater is the possibility for changing corporate and categoric units as well as the institutional systems in which they are embedded. A one-shot encounter rarely changes a corporate unit or institutional system; rather, it takes repeated encounters to work longer-term and comprehensive changes on more inclusive systems.

Another condition is the number of people involved in a change-oriented encounter. The larger the number of individuals in encounters where a focus of attention can be sustained (in spite of the tendencies for loss of focus specified in the principle of demography) and the larger the number of individuals reached via networks to other encounters, the greater is the likelihood that change in this encounter will have effects on corporate and categoric units. To change more inclusive systems, then, larger numbers of individuals must be reached, and they must subsequently begin to implement changes within their own encounters. Oftentimes, individuals resist changes imposed on them from "outside," and so, more is involved than just reaching larger numbers of individuals. They must also be receptive, by virtue of the principle of negative emotional energy, to implementing changes.

Another condition is the visibility of change-oriented encounters. The more visible are those engaging in change at the level of the encounter, the more likely will they alter more inclusive structures, if other conditions enumerated above are met. For most of human history, visibility was limited to physical copresence of individuals, thereby arresting how far and fast change at the level of the encounter could radiate, but mass media have dramatically increased the potential for visibility. For this reason changes at the level of the encounter are almost always staged as "media events" in order to influence the largest number of people.

A final condition is the level of emotional energy, whether positive or negative, aroused in a change-oriented encounter and in all the other encounters that will be influenced via networks and media by emotionally charged events. Indeed, change-oriented encounters often involve use of rituals to ratchet up the level of emotional energy, and strategic combinations of positive and negative emotional energy produce the greatest effects. Positive emotional energy alone, I hypothesize, does not have as far-reaching effects as negative emotional energy. Positive energy at the level of the encounter will spread to other encounters, under the conditions discussed above, but if it only supplements the existing flow of positive energy, it is less likely to change these encounters than is the case when negative emotional energy exists in these encounters. When people are happy, they rarely push for change; when they are angry, fearful, or sad, they are generally open to alternative ways of interacting and relating to corporate and categoric units. Indeed, it is their negative energy directed at corporate and categoric units that makes people receptive to changing these units. Thus, the more negative emotional energy aroused at the level of the encounter and the more this encounter is connected to other encounters where negative emotional energy exists, the greater will be the effects of emotional arousal in one encounter on others, especially when calls for change are couched in rituals increasing positive emotions focused on alternatives to the conditions generating negative emotional energy. The key to mobilization of people's sentiments to collective action has always been to tap into the negative emotions, particularly those directed at corporate and categoric units as well as the more inclusive institutional domains in which they are embedded, and then to use highly ritualized behaviors to intensify these emotions while, at the same time, offering an alternative that can arouse positive emotional energy about the future. All charismatic leaders have understood this force, and many less charismatic holders of authority and prestige have used it to their advantage to change mesostructures.

In sum, it is clear that micro-to-meso-to-macro change occurs. Indeed, such would have to be the case since, ultimately, social structures are composed of strings of encounters. Yet, as can be seen from my effort to enumerate the conditions under which the micro can potentially change the more inclusive mesosystems, there is a certain vagueness in the formulations; and this vagueness stems from the aggregation problems addressed in Chapter 2. It takes many microencounters, iterated and chained together over time, to change larger corporate and categoric units in institutional domains; so, theorizing these effects is difficult. Much social theory proclaims that the macro is built, sustained, and changed by the micro; and this is true as a metaphysical statement, but it does not take us very far in theorizing *how* such is the case. Moreover, these kinds of microchauvinist proclamations simply ignore the aggregation problem or offer further vague pronouncements about "chains" of encounters or other imprecise metaphors to express how the micro is constitutive of the macro. However, when we get hard-nosed about actually linking the macro, meso, and micro theoretically—that is, with theoretical propositions about how they are connected—the task becomes much more difficult. As I have emphasized, we will generally learn more by examining top-down rather than bottom-up linkages among the three levels of reality.

Still, we need to address the bottom-up processes, and I have done so in several senses: First, the various propositions in each chapter about how embedding influences the dynamics of encounters almost all contain propositions having implications for the reverse relationship. When emotional reactions in encounters are positive, individuals will remain committed to corporate and categoric units and, by extension, to the institutional domains in which they are lodged; as a result, these structures and their culture will be sustained by interpersonal behaviors in encounters and remain relatively stable. Second, when emotional reactions are negative, these commitments are lowered, thereby making individuals more likely to engage in, or at least be receptive to, change initiatives at the level of the encounter. Since some negative emotional energy among some individuals is often aroused in encounters, there is a constant potential for people to seek alternatives that will produce more positive sentiments and that, in the end, will exert pressure on mesostructures and culture to change. Third, in this last section, I have sought to outline some conditions under which the potential of encounters to change more inclusive structures increases. Taken together, these three lines of discussion suggest a last principle on microembeddedness:

(11)   *The Principle of Microembedding.* All corporate and categoric units are embedded in their constituent encounters; the more encounters arouse positive emotional energy, the greater will be commitments of individuals to corporate and categoric units and the institutional domains, whereas the more encounters arouse negative emotional energy, the less will be the commitments and the more likely will individuals in encounters seek to change the encounter or be receptive to change initiated by others. The more high-status individuals initiate change across iterated encounters reaching large numbers of individuals by virtue of their visibility, their density of network ties to other encounters, or their centrality in networks to other encounters and the more embedded are these change efforts in corporate and categoric units in institutional domains engaging in external relations with the environment, the greater is the likelihood that

change at the level of the encounter will alter the structure and culture of corporate and categoric units as well as the institutional domains in which they are embedded.

Of course, the specific dynamics of these processes are covered by other theories. For example, resource mobilization theory (McCarthy and Zald 1977) fills in many of the interesting details of this highly abstract principle, but my goal at this point is not to develop a complete theory of social organization, although such a theory could be developed. In the end, this is a book about face-to-face interaction. With this as the topic of theorizing, the top-down emphasis in the many propositions at the end of the chapters on each force driving an interaction is the most appropriate for understanding the dynamics of encounters. Naturally, a more general theory of social organization will pursue what I have just touched on in these last pages. If nothing else, I hope that I have demonstrated with a simple conceptual scheme how we can develop a general theory of human organization that captures the dynamics within and between the three levels of reality in the social universe. This theory will be *real* theory in the sense it will state relationships among the forces driving the organization of the social universe.

Agusti, J., P. Andrews, M. Fortelius, and L. Rook. 1998. Hominoid evolution
and environmental change in the Neogene of Europe: A European science
foundation network. *Journal of Human Evolution* 34: 103–7.

Alexander, J. C., B. Giessen, R. Münch, and N. J. Smelser, eds. 1986. *The micro-
macro link*. Berkeley and Los Angeles: University of California Press.

Allan, K. 1998. *The meaning of culture: Moving the postmodern critique forward*.
Westport, Conn.: Praeger.

Allan, K., and J. H. Turner. 2000. A formalization of postmodern theory.
Sociological Perspectives 43: 363–85.

Anderson, P. 1998. *The origins of postmodernity*. London: Verso.

Andrews, P. 1992. Evolution and environment in the hominoidea. *Nature*
360: 641–46.

———. 1989. Palaeoecology of Laetoli. *Journal of Human Evolution* 18: 173 81.

Ankel-Simons, F., J. G. Fleagle, and P. S. Chatrath. 1998. Femoral anatomy of
Aegyptopithecus zeuxis, an early Oligocene anthropoid. *American Journal of
Physical Anthropology* 106: 413–24.

Arieti, S. 1970. Cognition and feeling. In *Feelings and emotions: The Loyola
symposium on feelings and emotions*, ed. M. B. Arnold. New York: Academic.

Baker, W. E., and R. R. Faulkner. 1991. Role as resource in the Hollywood film
industry. *American Journal of Sociology* 97: 279–309.

Baudrillard, J. 1989. The anorexic ruins. In *Looking back on the end of the world*,
ed. Christoph Wulf, 29–45. New York: Semiotext(e).

———. 1983. *Simulations*. Trans. Paul Foss, Paul Patton, and Philip Beitchman.
New York: Semiotext(e).

———. [1981] 1994. *Simulacra and simulation*. Trans. Sheila Faria Blaser. Reprint,
Ann Arbor: University of Michigan Press.

———. [1976] 1993. *Symbolic exchange and death*. Trans. Iain Hamilton. Reprint,
Newbury Park, Calif.: Sage.

———. [1973] 1975. *The mirror of production*. Trans. Mark Poster. Reprint,
St. Louis, Mo.: Telos Press.

————. [1972] 1981. *For a critique of the political economy of the sign.* Trans. Charles Leven. Reprint, St. Louis, Mo.: Telos Press.

Bauman, Z. 1992. *Intimations of postmodernity.* London and New York: Routledge.

Beard, C., L. Krishtalka, and R. Stucky. 1991. First skulls of the early Eocene primate Shoshonius Cooperi and the Anthropoid-Tarsier dichotomy. *Nature* 349: 64–67.

Berger, J. 1988. Directions in expectation states research. In *Status generalization: New theory and research,* ed. M. Webster and M. Foschi. Stanford, Calif.: Stanford University Press.

————. 1958. Relations between performance, rewards, and action-opportunities in small groups. Unpublished Ph.D. dissertation.

Berger, J., and T. L. Conner. 1969. Performance expectations and behavior in small groups. *Acta Sociologica* 12: 186–98.

Berger, J., M. H. Fisek, R. Z. Norman, and M. Zelditch Jr. 1977. *Status characteristics in social interaction: An expectation states approach.* New York: Elsevier.

Berger, J., S. J. Rosenholtz, and M. Zelditch Jr. 1980. Status organizing processes. *Annual Review of Sociology* 6: 479–508.

Berger, J., and M. Zelditch Jr. 1998. *Status, power and legitimacy: Strategies and theories.* New Brunswick, N.J.: Transaction.

————, eds. 1985. *How expectations organize behavior.* San Francisco, Calif.: Jossey-Bass.

Bertens, H. 1995. *The idea of the postmodern: A history.* London: Routledge.

Blau, P. M. 1994. *Structural context of opportunities.* Chicago: University of Chicago Press.

————. 1977. *Inequality and heterogeneity: A primitive theory of social structure.* New York: Free Press.

————. 1964. *Exchange and power in social life.* New York: Wiley.

Bourdieu, P. 1989. *Language and symbolic power.* Cambridge, Mass.: Harvard University Press.

————. 1984. *Distinction: A social critique of the judgment of taste.* Cambridge, Mass.: Harvard University Press.

Brown, R. H. 1993. Cultural representation and ideological domination. *Social Forces* 71: 657–76.

————. 1990. Rhetoric, textuality, and the postmodern turn in sociological theory. *Sociological Theory* 8: 188–97.

————. 1987. *Society as text: Essays on rhetoric, reason, and reality.* Chicago: University of Chicago Press.

Burke, P. J. 1991. Identity processes and social stress. *American Sociological Review* 56: 836–49.

Burt, R. S. 1980. Models of network structure. *Annual Review of Sociology* 6. Palo Alto: Annual Reviews, Inc.

Cahoone, L., ed. 1996. *From modernism to postmodernism: An anthology.* Cambridge, Mass.: Blackwell.

Callero, P. L. 1994. From role-playing to role-using: Understanding role as resource. *Social Psychology Quarterly* 57: 228–43.

Campbell, B. 1985. *Humankind emerging.* Boston: Little, Brown.

Cerling, T., J. Harris, B. MacFadden, M. Leakey, J. Quade, V. Eisenmann, and J. Ehleringer. 1997. Global vegetation change through the Miocene/Pliocene boundary. *Nature* 389: 153–58.

Cheney, D., R. Seyfarth, and B. Smuts. 1986. Social relationships and social cognition in non-human primates. *Science* 234: 1361–66.

Chomsky, N. 1980. *Rules and representations.* New York: Columbia University Press.

———. 1965. *Aspects of the theory of syntax.* Cambridge, Mass.: MIT Press.

Collins, R. 1993. Emotional energy and the common denominator of rational action. *Rationality and Society* 5: 203–30.

———. 1988. *Theoretical sociology.* San Diego: Harcourt Brace Jovanovich.

———. 1981. On the micro-foundations of macro-sociology. *American Journal of Sociology* 86 (Mar.): 984–1014.

———. 1975. *Conflict sociology: Toward an explanatory science.* New York: Academic Press.

Conroy, G. 1990. *Primate evolution.* New York: W. W. Norton and Company.

Cooley, C. H. 1916. *Social organization: A study of the larger mind.* New York: Scribners.

———. 1902. *Human nature and the social order.* New York: Scribners.

Cosmides, L. 1989. The logic of social exchange: Has natural selection shaped how humans reason? *Cognition* 31: 187–276.

Damasio, A. R. 1997. Towards a neuropathology of emotion and mood. *Nature* 386 (24 Apr.): 769–70.

———. 1994. *Descartes' error: Emotion, reason, and the human brain.* New York: G. P. Putnam.

Denzin, N. K. 1991. *Images of postmodern society: Social theory and contemporary cinema.* Newbury Park, Calif.: Sage.

———. 1986. Postmodern social theory. *Sociological Theory* 4: 194–204.

Dunn, R. G. 1998. *Identity crises: A social critique of postmodernity.* Minneapolis: University of Minnesota Press.

Durkheim, É. [1912] 1946. *The elementary forms of the religious life.* Reprint, New York: Macmillan.

———. [1895] 1938. *The rules of the sociological method.* Reprint, New York: Free Press.

———. [1893] 1984. *The division of labor in society.* Trans. W. D. Halls. Reprint, New York: Free Press.

Eccles, J. 1989. *Evolution of the brain: Creation of self.* London, Routledge.

Ekman, P. 1992a. Are there basic emotions? *Psychological Review* 99: 550–53.

———. 1992b. Facial expressions of emotion: New findings, new questions. *Psychological Science* 3: 34–38.

———. 1992c. An argument for basic emotions. *Cognition and Emotion* 6: 169–200.

———. 1984. Expression and nature of emotion. In *Approaches to Emotion,* ed. K. Scherer and P. Ekman. Hillsdale, N.J.: Erlbaum.

———. 1982. *Emotions in the human face.* Cambridge: Cambridge University Press.

———. 1973a. *Darwin and facial expression.* New York: Academic Press.

———. 1973b. Cross-cultural studies of facial expressions. In *Darwin and Facial Expression,* ed. P. Ekman. New York Academic Press.

Ekman, P., and W. V. Friesen. 1975. *Unmasking face.* Englewood Cliffs, N.J.: Prentice-Hall.

Ekman, P., W. V. Friesen, and P. Ellsworth. 1972. *Emotion in the human face.* New York: Pergamon Press.

Emde, R. N. 1980. Levels of meaning for infant emotions: A biosocial view. In *Development of cognition, affect, and social relations: The Minnesota symposium of child psychology,* vol. 13, ed. W. A. Collins. Hillsdale, N.J.: Erlbaum.

Epstein, S. 1984. Controversial issues in emotion theory. In *Review of personality and social psychology,* vol. 5, ed. P. Shaver. Beverly Hills, Calif.: Sage.

Fedigan, L. M. 1982. *Primate paradigms: Sex roles and social bonds.* St. Albans, Vt.: Eden Press.

Fehr, B., and J. A. Russell. 1984. Concept of emotion viewed from a prototype perspective. *Journal of Experimental Psychology* 113: 464–86.

Fiske, A. P. 1991. *Structures of social life: The four elementary forms of human relations.* New York: Free Press.

Fleagle, J. 1988. *Primate adaptation and evolution.* New York: Academic Press.

Freud, S. 1900. *The interpretation of dreams.* London: Hogarth Press.

Frommel, D. K., and C. S. O'Brien. 1982. A dimensional approach to the circular ordering of emotions. *Motivation and Emotion* 6: 337–63.

Garfinkel, H. 1967. *Studies in ethnomethodology.* Englewood Cliffs, N.J.: Prentice-Hall.

Gergen, K. J. 1991. *The saturated self.* New York: Basic Books.

Geschwind, N. 1970. The organization of language and the brain. *Science* 170: 940–44.

———. 1965a. Disconnection syndromes in animals and man, part I. *Brain* 88: 237–94.

———. 1965b. Disconnection syndromes in animals and man, part II. *Brain* 88: 585–644.

Geschwind, N., and A. Damasio. 1984. The neural basis of language. *Annual Review of Neuroscience* 7: 127–47.

Giddens, A. 1984. *The constitution of society.* Berkeley and Los Angeles: University of California Press.

Gingerich, P., and M. Uhen. 1994. Time of origin of primates. *Journal of Human Evolution* 27: 443–45.

Goffman, E. 1983. The interaction order. *American Sociological Review* 48: 1–17.

———. 1974. *Frame analysis: An essay on the organization of experience.* New York: Harper and Row.

———. 1971. *Relations in public: Micro studies of the public order.* New York: Basic Books.

———. 1967. *Interaction ritual.* Garden City, N.Y.: Anchor Books.

———. 1963. *Behavior in public places: Notes on the social organization of gatherings.* New York: Free Press.

———. 1961. *Encounters: Two studies in the sociology of interaction.* Indianapolis, Ind.: Bobbs-Merrill.

———. 1959. *The presentation of self in everyday life.* Garden City, N.Y.: Anchor Books.

Gottdiener, M. 1993. Ideology, foundationalism, and sociological theory. *Sociological Quarterly* 34: 653–71.

———. 1990. The logocentrism of the classics. *American Sociological Review* 55: 460–63.

Gray, J. A. 1982. *The neuropsychology of anxiety: An enquiry into the functions of the septo-hippocampal system.* New York: Oxford University Press.

Gregory, S. W., Jr. 1999. Navigating the sound stream of human social interaction. In *Mind, brain and society: Toward a neurosociology of emotions,* ed. D. D. Franks and T. S. Smith. Greenwich, Conn.: JAI Press.

———. 1994. Sounds of power and deference: Acoustic analysis of macro social constraints on micro interaction. *Sociological Perspectives* 37: 497–526.

Habermas, J. 1970. Toward a theory of communicative competence. *Inquiry* 13: 360–75.

Harvey, D. 1989. *The conditions of postmodernity: An inquiry into the origins of cultural change.* Oxford: Blackwell.

Hawley, A. 1986. *Human ecology: A theoretical essay.* Chicago: University of Chicago Press.

Heise, D. R. 1989. Effects of emotion displays on social identification. *Social Psychology Quarterly* 53: 10–21.

———. 1979. *Understanding events: Affect and the construction of social action.* New York: Cambridge University Press.

Heise, D. R., and L. Smith-Lovin. 1981. Impressions of goodness, powerfulness, and liveliness from discerned social events. *Social Psychology Quarterly* 44: 93–106.

Hewes, G. W. 1973. Primate communication and the gestural origin of language. *Current Anthropology* 14: 5–12.

Hill, A. 1998. Causes of perceived faunal change in the late Neogene of East Africa. *Journal of Human Evolution* 16: 583–96.

Hochschild, A. R. 1983. *The managed heart: The commercialization of human feeling.* Berkeley and Los Angeles: University of California Press.

———. 1979. Emotion work, feeling rules and social structure. *American Journal of Sociology* 85: 551–75.

Holland, P., and S. Leinhardt, eds. 1979. *Perspectives in network research.* New York: Academic Press.

Homans, G. C. 1974. *Social behavior: Its elementary forms.* Rev. ed. New York: Harcourt Brace Jovanovich.

———. 1961. *Social behavior: Its elementary forms.* New York: Harcourt Brace Jovanovich.

———. 1951. *The human group.* New York: Harcourt.

Hunt, K. 1991. Positional behavior in the Hominoidea. *International Journal of Primatology* 12: 95–118.

Isbell, L. A., and T. P. Young. 1996. The evolution of bipedalism in hominids and reduced group size in chimpanzees: Alternative responses to decreasing resource availability. *Journal of Human Evolution* 30: 389–97.

Izard, C. 1992. Basic emotions, relations among emotions, and emotion-cognition relations. *Psychological Review* 99: 561–65.

James, W. 1890. *The principles of psychology.* New York: Holt, Rinehart and Winston.

Jameson, F. 1998. *The cultural turn: Selected writings on the postmodern, 1983–1998.* London: Verso.

———. 1991. *Postmodernism, or, the cultural logic of late capitalism.* Durham, N.C.: Duke University Press.

———. 1984. Postmodernism, or the cultural logic of late capitalism. *New Left Review* 146: 52–92.

Johnson-Laird, P. N., and K. Oatley. 1992. Basic emotions, rationality and folk theory. *Cognition and Emotion* 6: 201–23.

Jolly, A. 1985. *The evolution of primate behavior.* New York: Macmillan.

Kaas, J., and T. P. Pons. 1988. The somatosensory system of primates. In *Neurosciences*, ed. H. Steklis and J. Erwin. New York: Alan Liss.

Kemper, T. D. 1987. How many emotions are there? Wedding the social and the autonomic component. *American Journal of Sociology* 93: 263–89.

———. 1978. *An interactional theory of emotions.* New York: Wiley.

Kemper, T. D., and R. Collins. 1990. Dimensions of microinteraction. *American Journal of Sociology* 96: 32–68.

Kingston, J. D., B. D. Marino, and A. Hill. 1994. Isotopic evidence for Neogene hominid paleoenvironments in the Kenya Rift valley. *Science* 264: 955–59.

Knapp, M. L., and J. A. Hall. 1992. *Nonverbal communication in human interaction*. 3d ed. Fort Worth, Tex.: Harcourt Brace.

Koffka, K. 1935. *Principles of gestalt psychology*. New York: Harcourt, Brace.

Köhler, W. 1929. *Gestalt psychology*. New York: Liveright.

Lash, S., and J. Urry. 1994. *Economies of signs and space*. Newbury Park, Calif.: Sage.

———. 1987. *The end of organized capitalism*. Madison: University of Wisconsin Press.

LeDoux, J. 1996. *The emotional brain: The mysterious underpinnings of emotional life*. New York: Simon and Schuster.

———. 1993a. Emotional networks of the brain. In *Handbook of emotions*, ed. M. Lewis and J. M. Haviland. New York: Guilford Press.

———. 1993b. Emotional memory systems in the brain. *Behavioural Brain Research* 58: 69–79.

———. 1991. Neuroscience commentary: Emotion and the brain. *Journal of NIH Research* 3: 49–51.

———. 1987. Emotion. In *Handbook of physiology*, vol. 5, ed. F. Plum. Bethesda, Md.: American Physiological Society.

Lemert, C. 1995. *Sociology after the crisis*. Boulder, Col.: Westview Press.

———. 1992. General social theory, irony, postmodernism. In *Postmodernism and social theory: The debate over general theory*, ed. Steven Seidman and David G. Wagner. Cambridge, Mass.: Blackwell.

———. 1990. The uses of French structuralism in sociology. In *Frontiers of social theory: The new syntheses*, ed. George Ritzer. New York: Columbia University Press.

Lewis, H. B. 1971. *Shame and guilt in neurosis*. New York: International Universities.

Linton, R. 1936. *The study of man*. New York: D. Appleton-Century.

Lyotard, J.-F. [1979] 1984. *The postmodern condition*. Minneapolis: University of Minnesota Press.

Malatesta, C. Z., and J. M. Haviland. 1982. Learning display rules: The socialization of emotion expression in infancy. *Child Development* 53: 991–1003.

Malone, D. 1987. Mechanisms of hominoid dispersal in Miocene East Africa. *Journal of Human Evolution* 16: 469–81.

Marsden, P., and N. Lin., eds. 1982. *Social structure and network analysis*. Newbury Park, Calif.: Sage.

Maryanski, A. R. 1997. African ape social networks: A blueprint for reconstructing early hominid social structure. In *The archaeology of human ancestry*, ed. J. Steele and S. Shennan. London: Routledge.

———. 1992. The last ancestor: An ecological-network model on the origins of human sociality. *Advances in Human Ecology* 2: 1–32.

Maryanski, A. R., and J. H. Turner. 1998. Network analysis. In *The structure of sociological theory*. Belmont, Calif.: Wadsworth.

———. 1992. *The social cage: Human nature and the evolution of society*. Stanford, Calif.: Stanford University Press.

McCall, G. P., and J. L. Simmons. 1978. *Identities and interactions*. New York: Basic Books.

McCarthy, J., and M. Zald. 1977. Resource mobilization and social movements. *American Journal of Sociology* 82: 1212–41.

McKee, J. 1996. Faunal turnover patterns in the Pliocene and Pleistocene of southern Africa. *South African Journal of Science* 92: 111–12.

McPherson, J. M., and J. Ranger-Moore. 1991. Evolution on a dancing landscape: Organizations and networks in dynamic blau-space. *Social Forces* 70: 19–42.

Mead, G. H. 1938. *The philosophy of the act*. Chicago: University of Chicago Press.

———. 1934. *Mind, self, and society*. Chicago: University of Chicago Press.

Menzel, E. W. 1971. Communication about the environment in a group of young chimpanzees. *Folia Primatologica* 15: 220–32.

Moreno, J. [1934] 1953. *Who shall survive?* New York: Beacon House.

Móya-Sóya, S., and M. Köhler. 1996. A dryopithecus skeleton and the origins of great-ape locomotion. *Nature* 379: 156–59.

Napier, J. R., and P. H. Napier. 1985. *The natural history of the primates*. Cambridge, Mass.: MIT Press.

Norman, R. Z., R. Smith, and J. Berger. 1988. The processing of inconsistent information. In *Status generalization: New theory and research*, ed. M. Webster and M. Foschi. Stanford, Calif.: Stanford University Press.

Osgood, C. E. 1966. Dimensionality of the semantic space for communication via facial expressions. *Scandinavian Journal of Psychology* 7: 1–30.

Panksepp, J. 1982. Toward a general psychobiological theory of emotions. *Behavioral and Brain Sciences* 5: 407–67.

Park, R. 1926. Behind our masks. *Survey Graphics* 56: 135–50.

Parsons, T. 1966. *Societies: Evolutionary and comparative perspectives*. Englewood Cliffs, N.J.: Prentice-Hall.

———. 1951. *The social system*. New York: Free Press.

Plutchik, R. 1980. *Emotion: A psychoevolutionary synthesis*. New York: Harper & Row.

Radinsky, L. B. 1977. Early primate brains: Facts and fiction. *Journal of Human Evolution* 6: 79–86.

————. 1975. Primate brain evolution. *American Scientist* 63: 656–63.

————. 1974. The fossil evidence of anthropoid brain evolution. *American Journal of Physical Anthropology* 41: 15–28.

Ridgeway, C. L. 2001. Inequality, status, and the construction of status beliefs. In *Handbook of sociological theory*, ed. J. H. Turner. New York: Plenum.

————. 1998. Where do status beliefs come from? In *Status, network and structure*, ed. J. Szmatka and J. Berger. Stanford, Calif.: Stanford University Press.

————. 1994. Affect. In *Group processes: Sociological analysis*, ed. M. Foschi and E. Lawler. Chicago: Nelson-Hall.

————. 1982. Status in groups: The importance of emotions. *American Sociological Review* 47: 76–88.

Ridgeway, C. L., and J. Berger. 1988. The legitimation of power and prestige orders in task groups. In *Status generalization: New theory and research*. Stanford, Calif.: Stanford University Press.

————. 1986. Expectations, legitimacy, and dominance in task groups. *American Sociological Review* 51: 603–17.

Ridgeway, C. L., and K. G. Erickson. 2000. Creating and spreading status beliefs. *American Journal of Sociology*, in press.

Ridgeway, C. L., and C. Johnson. 1990. What is the relationship between socio-emotional behavior and status in task groups? *American Journal of Sociology* 90: 1189–1212.

Ritzer, G. 1997. *Postmodern social theory*. New York: McGraw-Hill.

————. 1990. Micro-macro linkage in sociological theory: Applying a metatheoretical tool. In *Frontiers of sociology: The new synthesis*. New York: Columbia University Press.

————. 1988. The micro-macro link. *Contemporary Sociology* 17: 703–6.

Ritzer, G., and P. Gindoff. 1994. Agency-structure, micro-macro, individualism-holism-relationalism: A metatheoretical explanation of theoretical convergence between the United States and Europe. In *Agency and structure: Reorienting social theory*. London: Gordon and Breach.

Rose, K. D., and J. G. Fleagle. 1987. The second radiation—prosimians. In *Primate evolution and human origins*, ed. R. L. Ciochon and J. Fleagle. New York: Aldine de Gruyter.

Sailer, L. D. 1978. Structural equivalence. *Social Networks* 1: 73–90.

Savage-Rumbaugh, E. S., D. Rumbaugh, and K. McDonald. 1985. Language learning in two species of apes. *Neuroscience and Biobehavioral Reviews* 9: 653–65.

Savage-Rumbaugh, S., J. Murphy, R. Seveik, D. Brakke, S. Williams, and D. Rumbaugh. 1993. *Language comprehension in the ape and child*, vol. 58 (Monographs of the Society for Research in Child Development). Chicago: University of Chicago Press.

Scheff, T. J. 1990. Socialization of emotion: Pride and shame as causal agents. In *Research agendas in the sociology of emotions*, ed. T. D. Kemper. Albany: State University of New York Press.

———. 1988. Shame and conformity: The deference-emotion system. *American Sociological Review* 53: 395–406.

Schutz, A. [1932] 1967. *The phenomenology of the social world.* Evanston, Ill.: Northwestern University Press.

Shibutani, T. 1968. A cybernetic approach to motivation. In *Modern systems research for the behavioral sciences: A sourcebook*, ed. W. Buckley. Chicago: University of Chicago Press.

Smith-Lovin, L. 1990. Emotion as confirmation and disconfirmation of identity: An affect control model. In *Research agendas in the sociology of emotions*, ed. T. D. Kemper, 238–70. Albany: State University of New York Press.

Smith-Lovin, L., and D. R. Heise, eds. 1988. *Analyzing social interaction: Research advances in affect control theory.* New York: Gordon and Breach.

Smuts, B., D. Cheney, R. Seyfarth, W. Wrangham, and T. Struhsaker. 1987. *Primate societies.* Chicago: University of Chicago Press.

Sroufe, L. A. 1979. Socioemotional development. In *Handbook of infant development*, ed. J. D. Osofsky. New York: Wiley.

Stephan, H. 1983. Evolutionary trends in limbic structures. *Neuroscience and Biobehavioral Reviews* 7: 367–74.

Stephan, H., and O. J. Andy. 1977. Quantitative comparison of the amygdala in insectivores and primates. *Acta Antomica* 98: 130–53.

———. 1969. Quantitative comparative neuroanatomy of primates: An attempt at phylogenetic interpretation. *Annals of the New York Academy of Science* 167: 370–87.

Stephan, H., G. Baron, and H. Frahm. 1988. Comparative size of brains and brain components. In *Neurosciences*, vol. 5, ed. H. Steklis and J. Erwin. New York: Alan R. Liss.

Stryker, S. 1980. *Symbolic interactionism: A structural version.* Menlo Park, Calif.: Benjamin/Cummings.

Swann, W. B., Jr. 1987. Identity negotiation: Where two roads meet. *Journal of Personality and Social Psychology* 53: 1038–51.

Swann, W. B., Jr., and C. A. Hill. 1982. When our identities are mistaken: Re-affirming self-conceptions through social interaction. *Journal of Personality and Social Psychology* 43: 59–66.

Swann, W. B., Jr., B. Pelham, and D. S. Krull. 1989. Agreeable fancy or disagreeable truth? How people reconcile their self-enhancement and self-verification needs. *Journal of Personality and Social Psychology* 57: 782–91.

Swann, W. B., Jr., J. G. Hixon, A. Stein-Seroussi, and D. T. Gilbert. 1990. The fleeting gleam of praise: Cognitive processes underlying behavioral reactions to self-relevant feedback. *Journal of Personality and Social Psychology* 59: 17–26.

Swartz, S. 1989. Pendular mechanics and kinematics and energetics of brachiating locomotion. *International Journal of Primatology* 10: 387–418.

Tattersall, I., E. Delson, and J. van Couvering. 1988. *Encyclopedia of human evolution and prehistory*. New York: Garland Publishing.

Trevarthen, C. 1984. Emotions in infancy: Regulators of contact and relationship with persons. In *Approaches to emotion*, ed. K. R. Scherer and P. Ekman. Hillsdale, N.J.: Erlbaum.

Turner, J. H. 2001. Can functionalism be saved? In *The sociological theory of Talcott Parsons: Essays in socio-historical context*. New York: Rowman and Littlefield.

———. 2000a. *On the origins of human emotions: A sociological inquiry into the evolution of human affect*. Stanford, Calif.: Stanford University Press.

———. 2000b. A theory of embedded encounters. *Advances in Group Processes* 17: 283–320.

———. 1999a. Toward a general sociological theory of emotions. *Journal for the Theory of Social Behavior* 29: 109–62.

———. 1999b. The neurology of emotions: Implications for sociological theories of interpersonal behavior. In *Mind, brain, and society: Toward a neurosociology of emotion*, ed. D. D. Franks and T. S. Smith. Greenwich, Conn.: JAI Press.

———. 1998. *The structure of sociological theory*. 6th ed. Belmont, Calif.: Wadsworth.

———. 1997a. *The institutional order*. New York: Longman.

———. 1997b. The nature and dynamics of "the social" among humans. In *The mark of the social*, ed. J. D. Greenwood. New York: Rowman and Littlefield.

———. 1996a. Cognition, emotion and interaction in the big-brained primate. In *Social processes and human relations*, ed. K. M. Kwan. Greenwich, Conn.: JAI Press.

———. 1996b. The evolution of emotions in humans: A Darwinian-Durkheimian analysis. *Journal for the Theory of Social Behavior* 26: 1–34.

———. 1995. *Macrodynamics: Toward a theory on the organization of human populations*. New Brunswick, N.J.: Rutgers University Press.

———. 1994a. Roles and interaction processes: Toward a more robust theory. In *Self, collective action and society*, ed. G. Platt and C. Gordon. Greenwich, Conn.: JAI Press.

———. 1994b. A general theory of motivation and emotion in human interaction. *Osterreichische Zeitschrift fur Soziologie* 8: 20–35.

———. 1989. A note on Mead's behavioristic theory of social structure. *Journal for the Theory of Social Behavior* 18: 354–72.

————. 1988. *A theory of social interaction.* Stanford, Calif.: Stanford University Press.

————. 1987. Toward a sociological theory of motivation. *American Sociological Review* 52: 15–27.

————. 1984. Theoretical strategies for linking micro and macro processes. *Western Sociological Review* 14: 4–15.

————. 1982. A note on G. H. Mead's behavioristic theory of social structure. *Journal for the Theory of Social Behavior* 12 (July): 213–22.

————. 1981. Returning to "social physics": Illustrations for the work of George Herbert Mead. *Current Perspectives in Social Theory* 2: 153–86.

————. 1972. *Patterns of social organization: A survey of social institutions.* New York: McGraw-Hill.

Turner, J. H., and D. E. Boyns. 2001. Expectations, need-states, and emotional arousal in interaction. In *Theory, simulation and experiment,* ed. J. Szmatka, K. Wysienska, and M. Lovaglia. New York: Praeger.

————. 2002. The return of grand theory. In *Handbook of sociological theory,* ed. J. H. Turner. New York: Plenum.

Turner, R. H. 2002. Roles. In *Handbook of sociological theory,* ed. J. H. Turner, New York: Plenum.

————. 1968. *Roles: Sociological aspects.* New York: Macmillan.

————. 1962. Role-Taking: Process versus conformity. In *Human behavior and social processes,* ed. A. Rose. Boston: Houghton Mifflin.

Ungar, P. 1996. Dental microwear of European Miocene Catarrhines: Evidence for diets and tooth use. *Journal of Human Evolution* 31: 335–66.

Wagner, D. G., and J. H. Turner. 1998. Expectation state theory. In *The structure of sociological theory.* Belmont, Calif.: Wadsworth.

Wasserman, S., and K. Faust. 1994. *Social network analysis: Methods and applications.* New York: Cambridge University Press.

Weber, M. [1922] 1968. *Economy and society,* ed. and trans. Guenther Roth and Claus Wittich. Berkeley and Los Angeles: University of California Press.

Webster, M. A., and M. Foschi, eds. 1988. *Status generalization: New theory and research.* Stanford, Calif.: Stanford University Press.

Webster, M., and S. J. Hysom. 1998. Creating status characteristics. *American Sociological Review* 63: 351–78.

Wellman, B. 1983. Network analysis: Some basic principles. *Sociological Theory*: 155–200.

White, H. C., S. A. Boorman, and R. C. Breigh. 1976. Structure from multiple networks: Block models of roles and positions. *American Journal of Sociology* 8: 730–80.

Wrangham, R. 1980. An ecological model of female-bonded primate groups. *Behaviour* 74: 262–99.